MASS KILLERS

MASS KILLERS

COMPELLED TO DESTROY

BILL WALLACE

Futura

A *Futura* Book

First published by Futura in 2009

Copyright © Omnipress 2009

ISBN: 978-0-7088-0208-3

Produced by Omnipress Limited, UK

Printed in Great Britain

Futura
An imprint of
Little, Brown Book Group
100 Victoria Embankment
London EC4Y 0DY

An Hachette UK Company

Photo credits: Getty Images

CONTENTS

Introduction.. 8

PART ONE: CRIMES AGAINST HUMANITY

Vlad the Impaler 20

Nazi War Crimes.. 28

    Hermann Goering.................................... 29

    Ernst Kaltenbrunner 40

    Adolf Eichmann...................................... 48

    Dr Josef Mengele.................................... 61

The Massacre of the Acqui Division............... 72

Japanese War Crimes of World War Two 80

My Lai Massacre.. 93

The Killing Fields...................................... 104

Dr Wouter Basson and Johan Theron............... 114

Slobodan Milosevic...................................... 123

Radovan Karadzic 133

Osama bin Laden 141

Saddam Hussein 153

PART TWO: ON THE RAMPAGE – SPREE KILLERS

Bath School Disaster.................................... 164

Charles Starkweather and Caril Ann Fulgate 173

Percy Smith and Richard Hickock 185

Joseph 'Mad Dog' Taborsky 195

16th Street Baptist Church Bombing................ 203

University of Texas Massacre.......................... 210

The Neptune Murders 222

The Hungerford Massacre............................. 231

George Banks... 240

Standard Gravure Shooting 250

Ecole Polytechnique Massacre 257

Julio Gonzalez: The Happy Land Fire 266

Aramoana Massacre.................................... 275

Luby's Massacre.. 283

Timothy McVeigh and the Oklahoma

   City Bombing 289

The Dunblane School Shooting....................... 300

The Port Arthur Massacre............................. 308

Columbine High School 318

The Jonesboro Massacre............................... 326

Thurston High School Massacre 334

Virginia Tech Massacre 342

Amish School Shooting................................ 351

Northern Illinois University Shooting............... 358

Akihabara Massacre.................................... 364

PART THREE: SERIAL KILLERS

William 'The Mutilator' MacDonald 374

Richard Kuklinski: the Iceman 384

Henry Lee Lucas and Ottis Toole.................... 393
Andrei Chikatilo: Citizen X 402
Pedro Alonzo Lopez.................................... 412
The Green River Killer............................... 429
Herman Mudgett a.k.a. H. H. Holmes 431
Pee Wee Gaskins Jr.................................... 440
Gerald Eugene Stano.................................. 452
John Wayne Gacy 462
Ted Bundy... 472
Richard Trenton Chase............................... 483
Anatoly Onoprienko 493
Dr. Harold Shipman.................................... 500

INTRODUCTION

Death comes in many forms, but so, too, does murder. Shooting, burning, strangling, stabbing; there are countless ways of dispatching an object of hatred, jealousy or distrust to the next world. But there are also an almost limitless number of reasons why people feel the need to murder, feel that urge sufficiently to free themselves of the restraints of decency, break through the border between humankind and the animal kingdom and take another life. Sometimes, as in the case of white supremacist Fred Cowan, that state can be reached over the most trivial of matters – he got into a dispute at work over his refusal to move a refrigerator. The fact that he did, in fact, work for a removal company is, of course, irrelevant. He did not want to do it, was suspended and took a journey down the road to a kind of madness that resulted in the deaths of six fellow workers and his own suicide in New Rochelle in New York in 1977.

Murder such as those Fred Cowan committed, where there are multiple deaths, is classified as mass murder and mass murder can be defined as the murder of a large number of people, typically at the same time, but also over a period of time, sometimes relatively short. Some sources are very precise, suggesting, in fact, that a mass murderer is someone who has killed four or more people.

A killer such as Richard Trenton Chase, the so-called 'Vampire of Sacramento' slips easily and bloodily into the category of mass murderer, having killed six people in an insane, blood-seeking rampage across a neighbourhood in Sacramento between 29 December 1977 and 27 January 1978. He killed all of his victims in just under a month of disorganised madness and could, therefore, also conceivably be described as a spree killer.

At the other end of the scale, of course, are murderers such as the English doctor Harold Shipman, killer by injection of at least 215 people, mostly defenceless elderly ladies. No one really knows how many Shipman actually killed and some estimates put the number of deaths at his hands at closer to 1000, making him the most prolific serial killer who ever lived.

Shipman's closest rival for the unenviable title of world's greatest serial killer would be Pedro Alonzo

Lopez, serial rapist and killer of around 300 women and young girls in South America – 110 in Ecuador and 100 each in Peru and in his native Colombia in the 1970s. Meanwhile, the number of murders committed by another rival to Shipman, the American killer, Henry Lee Lucas, is hard to say because Lucas had a gift for confession. Many say that in order to clear murders off their books the police gave him information about killings and he confessed to them. In prison towards the end of his life, in a recorded interview, he smiles as he admits to confessing to around three thousand murders over the years. He was eventually convicted and sentenced to life on a mere eleven murders, although the number of people who died at his hands is undoubtedly much higher. He did claim at one point that he had killed on average once a week from his release from prison in mid-1975 until his eventual arrest in mid-1983 which would make his total around the four hundred mark and the task force assembled to deal with his extraordinary case suggests that a figure of 350 is much more credible. Unfortunately, we will never know for sure as he died of heart failure in prison in 2001. The fact that he recanted all his confessions at one point, stating, 'I am not a serial killer' demonstrates how difficult he was to pin down.

Spree killers are an entirely different phenomenon to serial killers. Their rampage of death is often extremely short – in the case of Julio Gonzalez, who fell out with his girlfriend and burned down the Happy Land social club in East Tremont, New York in March 1990, killing eighty-seven people, it took just a few minutes to make it into the mass murder hall of fame. Timothy McVeigh killed 186 people with a bomb at the Alfred P. Murrah federal building in Oklahoma City in April 1995, almost all of them, including nineteen children being looked after in a day centre, dying at the scene. Disgruntled ex-sailor George Hennard took just ten minutes to shoot dead twenty-two people at a Luby's Cafeteria in Killeen, Texas. Amongst the most gruesomely efficient of all was Thomas Hamilton who took a mere four horrific minutes to shoot dead fifteen children and a school-teacher in Dunblane Primary School in Scotland in March 1996.

As we all know, spree killings have increased in frequency in recent times for reasons about which we can only speculate. Many claim that the daily exposure to violent death in computer games, in films and on television has removed death's sting. We have become immune to it and those who commit such spree killings have often been reported to be in a trance-like state, faces expressionless, voices flat and monotone, as if they are numb to what they are doing, as if, in fact, it is happening on a screen.

There has been a shocking increase in school and workplace shootings in the last few decades. The Columbine shootings carried out by seventeen-year-old Dylan Klebold and eighteen-year-old Eric Harris in 1999 launched a wave of similar incidents to the extent that barely a week goes by without some kind of gun outrage occurring at a school or university in the United States or in other parts of the world. Often these are the work of teenage outsiders, loners who have often been bullied and who frequently suffer from mental health problems. The worst so far was the incident at Virginia Polytechnic Institute and State University – Virginia Tech – where South Korean misfit, Seung-Hui Cho, shot dead thirty-two students and teachers. Cho suffered from a plethora of social and mental problems, was bullied and mocked and worshipped the Columbine killers, even at one point threatening to repeat what they had done. He was the prototype school killer and he certainly achieved greater notoriety than his idols, with the deadliest school massacre in America to date.

Workplace shootings are another grisly modern phenomenon. It seems that some people do not just take their work-related problems to the union or a tribunal. They go out and arm themselves for a Third

World War and take their frustrations and disappointments out on their bosses and workmates. It is worth noting, however, that before they unleash their own version of hell, many already have problems and the work-related problems are really just the straw that breaks the camel's back or throws the switch in their head that turns them into killers. Joseph 'Rocky' Wesbecker was one such. He had a history of psychiatric problems that seem to have been exacerbated by medication that he was taking. Coupled with that were two failed marriages and a pair of sons with problems. None of this was helped by his bosses moving the workers' car park away from the plant and banning ink-stained printers – of whom he was one – from travelling in the lift. When his bosses stopped his disability payments, he cracked. The following day he returned to work with an arsenal of guns and shot dead seven colleagues.

Often, however, it is just a slowly deteriorating mental state that launches a spree killing. George Banks had been becoming more erratic as time passed and, obsessing about perceived racism that he claimed had blighted his entire life, began to ramble about bombs and mass murder to his terrified colleagues at work. He also told them that he was preparing his children for war and hero-worshipped such monsters as Charles Manson and Jim Jones. It was not long before he tragically took a gun to his entire family, girlfriends, children and babies alike.

Of course, mass murder can also be defined as the murder of a large number of people by an organisation, often a government or regime. This can fall into any number of categories – the murder of demonstrators or opponents, the carpet bombing of cities or the random execution of citizens, for instance.

For the purposes of this book, we have grouped together such killings and acts under the heading of 'Crimes Against Humanity', defined by the International Criminal Court in its Rome Statute to be offences that constitute a serious attack on human dignity or grave humiliation or degradation of human beings. They are part of a concerted government policy, the statute continues, or of an extensive practice of atrocities tolerated by a government or a de facto authority. The widespread murder, torture, extermination, rape and so on, represent crimes against humanity as well as war crimes.

Of course, in modern times, the notion of crimes against humanity immediately conjures up the Nazi treatment of the Jews in the Second World War. Their grim attempt to exterminate an entire race, and their horrific success in almost achieving their aim has to be one of the most heinous crimes in all history and as we know human history is already littered with grave crimes against humanity, exterminations carried out in the name of religion, conquest or just pure hatred.

Hitler's Germany of the 1930s brought to power a group of men and women who in normal times would not be tolerated, people twisted by hatred and a perverted hunger for power. They succeeded in turning their hatred into government policy, infecting an entire nation with a kind of national hysteria that was fuelled by fear and the desire to throw off what they perceived as the mistakes and betrayals of the past. Men such as Hermann Goering and Ernst Kaltenbrunner were able to indulge their hate-filled ambitions and monsters such as Josef Mengele were given free rein to vent a bloodlust never before seen, cloaking it in spurious scientific research but, in reality, just killing hundreds of thousands, perhaps even millions, in a variety of horrific ways. Mengele's treatment of children – the twins he selected for special attention, known as 'Mengele's Children' – was abhorrent beyond the bounds of human credibility. The fact that he escaped justice by fleeing to South America and dying there in 1979 aged sixty-eight, left his surviving victims with an overwhelming sense of disappointment and frustration.

The Nazis were also capable of terrible acts of war that breached the conventions governing such things. Their invasions of countries across the European continent inevitably led to brutal suppression and execution of anyone who opposed them and sometimes of people who did not oppose them in any overt way. In their invasion of Poland in 1939 – the act of unadulterated aggression that launched the Second World War – they executed Polish prisoners of war, bombed hospitals, murdered civilians, shot fleeing refugees and executed wounded soldiers. At least sixteen thousand died in this initial onslaught, but it was repeated across the occupied nations of Europe.

They carried out mass murders too of armies that had surrendered. At least five thousand Italian soldiers who had already surrendered, were executed on the Greek island of Cephalonia in 1943 in a bloody rampage of revenge that lasted for a week.

The Japanese, too, were gripped by a national hysteria, an unflinching need to obey orders and to believe that everyone who was not Japanese was a creature of a lower order. The low value they put on human life in the Second World War was criminal. Their treatment of Allied prisoners of war was a disgrace that even now many cannot forgive, especially the generation that lived through the war. Beheadings, starvation and slave labour were common and their debauched practice of forcing captured women to become prostitutes, euphemistically called 'comfort women' before being killed, represents a nadir in human behaviour towards other humans just as much as the Nazis' treatment of the Jews does.

One would imagine that mass murder would be a thing of the past, a charge to be laid at the door of a monster from centuries ago such as Vlad the Impaler. However, as Columbine, Virginia Tech and men like Ted Bundy, Gerald Stano and others in this book have reminded us in the last few decades it is still very much alive and well and being practised in workplaces, schools and shopping centres around the world.

PART ONE

CRIMES
AGAINST
HUMANITY

VLAD THE IMPALER

As the ninety thousand men of the Ottoman Sultan Mehmed's army rode towards the lands of their mortal enemy, Vlad III, their nostrils were met with a nauseating stench. The closer they came the worse it was, an indefinable smell, but rotten all the same. Suddenly, in the distance the horizon seemed to be punctuated by lines of sticks with something at the top of them. There were thousands of them stretching as far as the eye could see. Suddenly, with sickening certainty, they realised what they were looking at. It was a forest of stakes, about thirty thousand of them, hammered into the ground and on each was impaled the body of a Turkish soldier. Today, Vlad the Impaler is probably best remembered as the inspiration for Bram Stoker's famous novel, *Dracula*. In reality, though, his story is far more sordid than any vampire story.

Vlad Dracolya was the second son of the Prince of

Wallachia, Vlad Dracul. He was born in the town of Sighisoara in the principality of Wallachia in the early 1400s. They were ruthlessly violent times and as a young boy, Vlad would experience extreme brutality. His father was a member of The Order of the Dragon which was a group of Slavic rulers and warlords who swore to uphold the Christian faith. They did this by fighting off any advancing Turks of the Ottoman Empire and warfare became the way of life in Wallachia and the surrounding areas.

The first battle Vlad participated in – probably at a very young age – he was taken captive by the Turks together with his younger brother, Radu the Handsome. Being the sons of a local prince, the two boys were considered valuable hostages, and were taken to Istanbul and imprisoned by the Sultan Mehemet.

When Vlad Dracul learned of his sons imprisonment, he did everything in his power to obtain their release. However, his bargaining was seen as a form of treason by the head of The Order of the Dragon, Hunyadi, and he hired assassins to kill Dracul and his eldest son, Minhead.

Meanwhile, back in Istanbul the sultan was trying his best persuasive powers to indoctrinate Vlad and Radu into the Islam faith. By making them his allies, the sultan hoped to use their claim to the Wallachian throne to his own advantage. Radu was a pushover and quickly converted to the Islam faith, thereby obtaining his freedom. Vlad, however, was a different kettle of fish, a far more stubborn character. It is believed that his sadistic tendencies started during his period of incarceration by the sultan, brought on by constant torture and cruelty. Vlad became subdued and, for a while, the sultan believed that he was winning him over.

With Vlad on his side, or so he believed, the sultan returned to his original quest of overpowering Wallachia. After capturing its capital, he set up Vlad as the new prince. For a few months Vlad behaved regally, but he was not prepared to be a puppet ruler, and decided to flee the country, going north into Moldavia. He took refuge with his close friend and cousin, Steven.

Vlad spent every waking hour planning how to oust the Turks from Wallachia, so that he could become the true prince. Against his better judgement, Vlad knew he needed to enlist the help of Hunyadi – the very man who had murdered his father and brother. Vlad, however, was prepared to overlook this matter so long as Hunyadi would help him defeat their common enemy, the sultan.

Hunyadi was relieved to have his life saved and willingly agreed to help Vlad by giving him military back-up. Vlad's brother Radu was now reigning prince in Wallachia, placed there by the sultan after Vlad had fled. Radu was driven out by Vlad and Hunyadi who quickly took control of Wallachia. Vlad then retook the throne on his own terms, and began his second, and most infamous reign.

Vlad Dracolya was neither a good nor a kind ruler and he was soon feared and hated by his subjects. He would constantly raid certain towns within his territory and didn't think twice about killing innocent citizens. He seemed to aim his hatred at towns whose population had a largely German ancestry for some reason, and as a result much of what has been written about Vlad comes from documents printed by the Germans.

It was during this period of meaningless attacks that Vlad became infamous for his favoured method of killing – impalement. When he wanted to kill a large number of peasants he would drive them in large numbers over the side of a cliff onto a bed of spikes below. Not satisfied with just one cruel way of destroying his victims, he also employed methods such as boiling, quartering and decapitation. There are many stories of his cruelty and perhaps one of the most documented is the following:

The sultan sent two ambassadors to Vlad with a message. When they entered his throne room, Vlad asked them to remove their turbans as it was considered rude to be in the presence of a prince without removing your hat. The Turks, however, were not happy about this request, as the turban was a symbol of their religion. They refused to remove their headgear, not realising what a serious mistake it was to insult the prince. Vlad immediately ordered his guards to seize the ambassadors and said with a sickly grin on his face, that if they were not prepared to remove their turbans then they should be nailed there permanently. Vlad got great pleasure out of watching the Turks writhing and screaming as large nails were driven into their skulls.

During the period of Vlad's second reign, Wallachia had remained for the most part free of invasion. This was all to change, however, as a new sultan, Suleiman II, had come to power. The Ottoman Empire once again turned its eyes towards Wallachia.

Vlad was informed by his many spies, that an enormous Turkish army was heading his way. He knew that he did not have adequate forces to beat the Turks in open battle, nor the resources to survive a long siege. Vlad's only option was to take desperate measures. Using the cover of night, Vlad personally led a small, elite army into the Turkish camp in the hope of catching the sultan off guard and killing him. He felt that if their leader were dead, the Turkish troops would be demoralised forcing them to retreat.

Thanks to the element of surprise, and Vlad's personal knowledge of the local area, his midnight attack was mostly successful. They seriously wounded the sultan, although not fatally, and all of Vlad's men managed to escape without injury. The attack, however, did not have the desired effect of stopping the Turkish army from their original quest.

Vlad retreated to his castle in Targoviste and got ready to run. Then disaster struck. His wife, believing that escape was impossible, committed suicide by leaping of a clifftop into a river with strong currents. The river later became known as the Princess River. Then Vlad was hit by a second tragedy as he tried to escape through the forest on horseback accompanied by his servants. One of the servants carrying Vlad's infant son, accidentally dropped him, but the pursuing Turks were too close for Vlad's party to risk turning back to look for the child. They were forced to leave the infant behind, so in one foul day Vlad had lost both his home and his family.

Vlad knew he needed help, so he turned to the king of Hungary, Mathias. Unfortunately, Vlad's evil past had caught up with him, and many of his subjects had witnessed his mass killings and wanted to get their revenge. They had already spoken to the king and warned him that Vlad was an ally of the Turks and that he was coming as a spy. When Vlad arrived at the castle, he was immediately thrown into the dungeons.

The Turks didn't stay long in Targoviste, their stomachs just couldn't take it. They were greeted by rows and rows of impaled heads, the stench of which caused many of the soldiers to physically vomit. Before Vlad had fled his home, he had set fire to the city, leaving it in ruins. The Turks decided to take the city anyway and to try and rebuild what was left, but within a few weeks, the plague broke out among the soldiers and they were forced to retreat out of Wallachia.

Vlad's story was more successful though. Despite being imprisoned by the king for several months, Vlad caught the eye of the king's sister, Ilona. She was smitten and managed to talk her brother into having Vlad freed. Within a very short space of time the couple were married, and Vlad received a royal pardon so long as he stayed within the bounds of the city. He was presented with a large home, where he lived happily with his new wife and baby son.

Once Vlad had regained the king's full confidence, he was free to leave the city and he returned to Wallachia to claim the throne for the third and final time. He built a new capital, Bucharesti (now called Bucharest, the capital of modern-day Romania).

A few months after retaking the throne, a peasant called at the castle and asked to speak with Vlad. The peasant was accompanied by a young boy, who he claimed to have found wandering in the forest on the night of the Turkish attack. The boy was Vlad's lost son and the prince was so delighted that he showered the peasant with gifts as a reward.

Although it is uncertain exactly how Vlad died, it is widely believed that he died in battle when he was in his fifties. Others say that he was decapitated by the Turks who sent his head preserved in honey to Istanbul as proof of his death. When his tomb was opened many years later, his face was covered with a piece of cloth, indicating that he probably suffered the same torture as his father and elder brother. Unfortunately, this fact could not be proved, because, just moments after the tomb was opened and the corpse exposed to light, it crumbled to dust, as in all the best vampire movies.

Most people will remember Vlad the Impaler as a cruel fiend who murdered thousands of innocent victims. However, he was also a proud and fierce defender of his territory, so perhaps he should be remembered for both.

NAZI WAR CRIMES

The depravity of Adolf Hitler's regime in Germany in the 1930s has few equals in human history. Not only did the Nazis attempt to exterminate the entire Jewish race they also targeted the weak and infirm, people with disabilities or even mental health problems, embracing the science of eugenics to prove their perverted and debased theories of racial purity. Subject peoples, too, coming under the Nazi jackboot as Hitler's army, navy and air force destroyed everything in its way, became the victims of brutal repression and heartless cruelty.

Of course, the Final Solution, the extermination of the Jews, was perhaps the most heinous war crime of all, carried out by a special breed of monster that seemed to prevail in Germany at the time and to whom National Socialism became an obsession. Men such as Adolf Eichmann and especially Josef Mengele were involved in acts so horrific that they beggar belief. These were men who plumbed the deepest recesses of depravity to create a horror beyond any that Europe had ever seen.

The collective madness that was Nazism spread like a cancer into the military, and the German army, too was responsible for acts that went far beyond the normal acts of war – the Massacre of the Acqui Division, detailed below and other barbaric acts such as the massacres at Kalavryta, Marzabotto and le Paradis represent just a small sample of such incidents. At Kalavryta in Greece, in 1943, Wehrmacht troops machine-gunned the entire male population of the town – 1258 of them – and subsequently destroyed it. In 1944, at Marzabotto in the mountains near Bologna in Italy, the SS killed around 1800 civilians in reprisal for the support given to local partisan and resistance movements. In 1944, at le Paradis, a small village in northern France, ninety-seven British troops were machine-gunned by troops of the SS Division Totenkopf after they had surrendered.

The instances and people detailed below are a very few examples of the horrors for which the Nazis were responsible.

HERMANN GOERING

They had planned to hang Goering first, appropriately the first of a parade of Nazis who had been responsible for probably the most murderous few years in Europe since Roman times and maybe even since further back than that. He had outsmarted them at the last, however. The night before he was due to be hanged, he had swallowed cyanide, the source of which remains unknown to this day, although an American lieutenant, Jack Wheelis has claimed that he might have unwittingly provided Goering with the poison. The German's girlfriend persuaded him to smuggle in a vial of a liquid she claimed was medicine.

On 1 October 1946, they hanged the rest – amongst them men such as Julius Streicher, Gauleiter of Franconia, Joachim von Ribbentrop, Hitler's foreign minister, Fritz Sauchel, the Nazi boss of slave labour and Ernst Kaltenbrunner, head of the Nazi secret police. Once the last of them, Arthur Seyss-Inquart, former Gauleiter of Holland and Austria, had fallen to his death through the trapdoor, the doors to the gymnasium in Nuremberg jail swung open and American soldiers walked in carrying Goering's body on a stretcher and set it down between the first and second of the three black-painted gallows in the gym. The body of this man famous for his extravagantly designed uniforms which he had changed sometimes five times a day, was covered by a khaki-coloured US Army blanket and an arm clad in blue silk dangled over the side of the stretcher.

The blanket was removed so that witnesses could confirm that Goering was, in fact, dead, to prevent any escape stories developing from the fact that he was not hanged. He was wearing black silk pyjamas, a blue jacket shirt over them, soaking wet, probably from the efforts of the doctors to revive him so that he could face his punishment. His face was contorted with the pain of a cyanide death. They picked up the stretcher and carried him over to a curtained cubicle where the rest of them lay, their dreadful, hate-filled lives at last at an end.

Born into a bourgeois family, in 1893 in Rosenheim in Bavaria, Hermann Wilhelm Goering's father, Heinrich, a cavalry officer, had been the first Governor-General of the German Protectorate of South West Africa which today is Namibia. He also had such illustrious antecedents as the aviation pioneer, Count Ferdinand von Zeppelin, the 19th century German nationalist, Hermann Grimm, the pharmaceutical magnates, the Merck family and the Swiss diplomat and historian, Carl J. Burckhardt.

With his parents away on diplomatic postings, the young Goering spent much of his childhood with governesses and relatives. When his father retired, however, the family moved in with a friend, Hermann, Ritter von Epenstein who owned two large, run-down castles, one in Bavaria, the other near

Salzburg. The Goerings would live in these castles until 1913 and they would eventually be inherited by Hermann Goering. Ironically, given what would occur later, von Epenstein was Jewish.

Before the First World War, Goering visited England, studying English with a vicar, John Francis Richards, in Rutland. He then attended boarding school in Ansbach in Franconia before enrolling at the cadet institute at Karlsruhe and the military college at Lichterfelde in Berlin. In 1912, he was commissioned in the Prussian army's Prinz Wilhelm Regiment, stationed at Mulhouse.

In the 1914–18 war, he served with an infantry regiment in the Vosges region, spending some time in hospital as a result of rheumatism suffered due to trench warfare. He tried to obtain a transfer to the Luftstreitkräfte, the air arm of the German army but his request was turned down. Despite this he arrogantly arranged his own transfer, but was found out and confined to barracks for three weeks. Nonetheless, he got into the Luftstreitkräfte, flying as an observer for his friend, Bruno Loerzer. The pair flew reconnaissance and bombing missions and were awarded the Iron Cross. Goering eventually qualified as a pilot and shot down twenty-two enemy planes, winning a chestful of medals including Prussia's highest military honour, the *Pour La Mérite*, known as the Blue Max.

Nevertheless, the arrogant, loud and domineering Goering was never popular, which was confirmed by the fact that after the war, he was the only member of his squadron never to be invited to reunions.

Like Hitler, he took Germany's defeat in the First World War and the subsequent abdication of the Kaiser personally. He felt betrayed by the politicians and at the conclusion of hostilities ensured that all the planes in his squadron were wrecked rather than handed over to the Allies. Following the war, he remained in flying and was also a Generalmajor in Germany's peacetime army.

He met Adolf Hitler and joined the Nazi Party in 1922, his connections with the German aristocracy and conservative industrialist proving invaluable to the new party trying to raise funds as well as support. He was appointed leader of the Brown Shirts, the *Sturmabteilung* (Stormtroopers) and utilised his organisational skills in drilling some order into its eleven thousand members. He was by Hitler's side when he made his unsuccessful bid for power in the Beer Hall Putsh in Munich in 1923 but was seriously wounded in the groin when the police broke up the march. He managed to avoid arrest, escaping to Austria, while Hitler was sentenced to five years, although he only served six months. During an operation on his wound in Innsbruck, Goering was dosed with morphine to ease the great pain he was in.

It would be the beginning of a life-long addiction to the drug.

By now, he and his wife had little money and, unable to return to Germany where he would undoubtedly be arrested, they survived on funds provided by Nazi sympathisers, moving to Venice followed by Rome – where he had a meeting with Mussolini – and then on to Florence and Siena. They then journeyed to Sweden.

By now, however, Goering's morphine addiction was taking its toll. He had become violent and his body was ravaged by the drug. When he met his wife's family in Sweden they were shocked by his appearance. Eventually, exasperated by his behaviour, his wife and doctors handed him over to the police who certified him a dangerous drug addict and sent him to a clinic where he had to be restrained by wearing a straitjacket.

In August 1927, he returned finally to Germany following an amnesty for all involved in the Beer Hall Putsch declared by President Paul von Hindenberg. He began working with Hitler again, using his connections with the German upper classes to obtain funding and support for the Nazi cause. In 1928, he was elected to the Reichstag, the German parliament. In 1932 he was elected President of the Reichstag and would retain that position until the end of the war.

Hitler became Chancellor of Germany on 30 January 1933, Goering one of only two other Nazis in the coalition cabinet, in the role of minister without portfolio, although it was understood that he would be made Aviation Minister just as soon as Germany's air force had been built up. He was also appointed Interior Minister of Prussia which gave him overall command of the largest police force in Germany. His job was to instill Nazism into them and to use them against Hitler's enemies, political parties such as the Social Democrats and the Communists. He forced the police authorities to recruit from within the Nazi militia and to turn a blind eye to the violent acts that the Sturmabteilung were committing on the streets of Germany. Critically, he formed a secret police force – the Gestapo (Geheime Staatspolizei) – from the intelligence and political wings of the Prussian police force. It became especially useful during the elections of March 1933 when Goering's men were used to harrass and suppress the opposition parties.

Following the burning of the Reichstag, an act the Nazis blamed the Communists for, but which many believed Goering to have been responsible for, Civil liberties in Germany were suspended, giving Goering the opportunity to order the suppression of the Communist Party. In Prussia he ordered the arrest of twenty-five thousand Communists and many anti-

Nazis were rounded up at the same time. They were incarcerated in the first concentration camps – created by Goering. He gave the police free rein, informing them that '. . . all other restraints on police action imposed by Reich and state law are abolished . . .'

Following his victory in the election, Hitler adopted dictatorial powers with the passing of the Enabling Act. Goering, for his part, refused to commute the death sentences passed on four Communists who had been convicted of the murder of two Stormtroopers and sixteen others in a riot that had broken out during a Nazi march in July 1932. These were the first executions of the Third Reich.

In 1934, Goering lost control of the Gestapo when Hitler transferred it to be part of Heinrich Himmler's SS. He retained the Special Police Battalion, however, which he converted to a paramilitary group called Landespolizeigruppe General Goering and which played a major role in the 'Night of the Long Knives' when Hitler eliminated all of his rivals within the Nazi Party.

In 1938, Goering took on the role of War Minister and became instrumental in Germany's invasion of Austria, the action known as the Anschluss.

Goering was the highest-ranking member of Hitler's government to actually issue written orders for the extermination of the Jews in the Final

Solution. On 12 November 1938, he warned of a 'final reckoning' with the Jews should Germany go to war and he announced their elimination from the German economy, the 'Aryanisation' of their property and businesses and their exclusion from schools, resorts, parks and almost everything else. He wrote a memo to Heydrich about its practical details and this communication resulted in the Wannsee Conference attended by senior Nazis at which they made arrangements for the Holocaust. It was announced that Heydrich was to be responsible for the Final Solution. Goering had written to him, 'submit to me as soon as possible a general plan of the administrative material and financial measures necessary for carrying out the desired final solution of the Jewish question.' At Wannsee, Heydrich laid out a plan for the deportation of the Jewish population of Europe to German-occupied Eastern Europe where they would be put to work on road-building and other such projects. Those who survived were to be exterminated after the completion of the work.

As the war progressed and the other nations of Europe fell to the Nazis, Goering extended the Reich's anti-Jewish laws to them. The decrees were signed by him even if their execution was left to Himmler.

Meanwhile, he zealously pursued the Jewish

question. He had been made Minister and Supreme Commander of the Luftwaffe – the German air force – in 1935 when Hitler repudiated the Treaty of Versailles, and then in 1938 he was given the unique rank of Generalfeldmarschall of the Luftwaffe, making him the highest ranking officer in Germany. His air force became the most advanced in the world and he got the opportunity to try it out when he was asked in 1936 by Hitler to send several hundred planes to Spain to fight on General Franco's side in the Spanish Civil War. He had so much confidence in the air force that he had built that he boasted that in the event of war not a single bomb would be dropped on the Ruhr, Germany's great industrial area. The Luftwaffe also possessed its own infantry troops and these became Goering's very own private army.

In promoting Goering, Hitler also named him as his heir apparent and he became even more extravagant in his tastes, living in ostentatious luxury in a palace in Berlin and a magnificent hunting lodge that he named after his first wife. It was located fifty miles from Berlin and a monument to his gargantuan ego. There he staged feasts, state hunts and showed off the art treasures he had stolen from the Jews he had sent to the death camps. It formed a collection that was later valued at £60 million.

The Luftwaffe started the war well, but then the

invasion of Britain stalled when it failed to defeat the RAF and bring the British to their knees in the Battle of Britain. He authorised the bombing of civilian targets that both angered and horrified the entire world. His planes also failed at Stalingrad and by 1943 he was out of favour with his Führer, Himmler, Speer and Goebbels supplanting him in Hitler's inner circle. Ignored and shunned, he lived virtually in retirement for the final two years of the war, hunting, collecting more art and designing ever more extravagant uniforms and decorations.

As the Russians closed in on Berlin, Goering sent a telegram to Berlin in which he proposed that he should assume the leadership of the Reich as the man Hitler had designated to succeed him. Hitler was furious and considered the proposal to be treason. He placed Goering under arrest, dismissed him from all his political offices and expelled him from the Nazi Party. Two days before he killed himself, Hitler sent orders for the SS to execute Goering and his wife and young daughter. Fortunately for Goering, at this point Germany and Hitler's authority had disintegrated to such an extent the order was ignored.

He surrendered to the Allies on 9 May 1945 and was tried at Nuremberg, the third-highest Nazi to be tried, behind Admiral Karl Dönitz and erstwhile Deputy Führer, Rudolf Hess. He defended himself with some vigour, having endured cold turkey in prison to wean himself off the drugs to which he had long been addicted. He did it fairly well, joking with the audience and, on occasion, outwitting the Prosecutor. Nonetheless, he was convicted on all four charges – conspiracy to wage war, crimes against peace, war crimes and crimes against humanity.

Sentenced to death, he offered to accept his punishment if shot like a soldier. The court refused, telling him he would hang. Arrogant to the end, he decided he would die as he chose. His ashes were scattered in a ditch in Bavaria.

ERNST KALTENBRUNNER

He was an imposing figure, at just over six feet seven inches tall and with deep scars on his face that he had gained from dueling in his student days . . . or, actually, were they? Some sceptical sources claim that his scars were not the result of dueling, but that he really got them in a car accident when he was driving while under the influence of alcohol.

Born in 1903 in Ried im Innkreis in Austria, 60 kilometres north of Salzburg, Kaltenbrunner was the son of a lawyer and after attending Graz University, where he gained a law degree, he also became a lawyer, working first at Salzburg and from 1928 at Linz.

In 1932 he joined the Nazi Party in Austria, becoming the Gauredner (district speaker) and Rechtsberater (legal consultant) of Division VIII of the SS, the Nazi paramilitary force. In 1933 he was appointed Führer of Regiment 37 and later of SS Division VIII.

In January 1934, Kaltenbrunner was jailed in the Kaisersteinbruch concentration camp along with other Nazis by the government of Austrian Chancellor, Englebert Dolfuss. All 490 national Socialist prisoners were released from the camp after Kaltenbrunner started and led a hunger strike. The next year, he was arrested again and accused of high treason, involvement in the assassination of Dolfuss who had been shot by eight Austrian SS men as he was entering the Chancellery building. The shooting was part of an attempted coup d'état that was thwarted by the Austrian army as well as by a threat by Mussolini to Hitler that if he invaded Austria Germany would face war with Italy. However, Kaltenbrunner's high treason charge was reduced to one of conspiracy and he was jailed for six months. By now his right to practice law had been suspended due to his Nazi beliefs and activities.

In spring 1935, he was appointed head of the Austrian SS and he played a major role in the 11 March 1938 Nazi invasion of Austria, an action known as the Anschluss that resulted in Austria being incorporated into the German Reich. Germany had pressured Austria for a number of years to merge and in the meantime had provided support for the Austrian Nationalist Socialist party. Austria, ruled by the Austrofascist Party, headed by Kurt Schuschnigg, was determined to remain independent of the Nazis. Kaltenbrunner tried to hold a referendum to find out directly from the Austrian people whether they wished to remain independent or whether they wanted the merger. But the referendum was cancelled when the Austrian Nazi party staged a coup d'état in Vienna, seizing control of the state institutions. Kaltenbrunner personally led five hundred Austrian SS troops in surrounding the Chancellery and a special detachment under his adjutant's command entered the building while Nazi official Arthur Seyss-Inquart was negotiating with President Miklas. As a result of the actions of the Austrian Nazis, which had been ordered by Hitler's deputy, Herman Goering, German troops entered Austria. Hitler permitted a plebiscite to allow the people to vote on what had already happened and the Nazis inevitably won with 99.73 per cent of the vote.

Hitler promoted Kaltenbrunner to Brigadenführer on the day that the Anschluss was effected. The following September he was made Gruppenführer and was by then also a member of the Reichstag in Berlin. In April 1941, he became Major General of the Police.

On 30 January 1943, Ernst Kaltenbrunner was appointed Chief of the Security Police and the Sicherheitsdienst (SD) and the RSHA or Reichssicherheitshauptamt – the Reich Main Security Office, replacing Richard Heydrich at the RSHA following his assassination in 1942. Kaltenbrunner had become a very powerful man in Nazi Germany, running an organisation that boasted the main offices of the Gestapo, the SD and the Criminal Police. He had the power to order that people be taken into protective custody and also to order the release of individuals from concentration camps.

There is little doubt that he was fully aware of the conditions in the camps, having visited Mauthausen camp – ironically situated just 20 kilometres from Linz where he had practiced law – and witnessed various types of execution. Prisoners were hanged, shot in the back and gassed in front of him in a grim demonstration of the variety of methods of extermination that could be used. In fact he was responsible for overseeing both executions and execution orders from the office of Heinrich Himmler, head of the SS.

At the end of the war, Kaltenbrunner arranged for the evacuation of the concentration camps and the rapid extermination of thousands of inmates to prevent their liberation by the advancing Allied armies.

As head of the RSHA, Kaltenbrunner was also responsible for the mistreatment and murder of prisoners of war. He was in charge of the Einsatz-kommandos, who were responsible for systematically killing Jews and Soviet political activists during Operation Barbarossa, Hitler's invasion of the Soviet Union. He introduced the 'Bullet Decree' under which certain prisoners of war who escaped and were recaptured were taken to Mauthausen and shot. Furthermore, an order for the execution of any Allied commando troops captured was extended to include paratroops. In December 1944, he personally participated in the execution of a French general who was being held as a prisoner of war.

It was not just POWs and ethnic groups that Kaltenbrunner's men targeted, of course. The Gestapo and SD were deeply involved in the mistreatment and murder of civilian populations in Nazi-occupied territories. Torture and incarceration in concentration camps were used as punishments and Kaltenbrunner's name was on every order.

He also established a series of slave labour camps to deal with people subject to forced labour by the Nazis. The RSHA was one of the leading players in the execution of the Final Solution, the extermination of the Jews with a special section of the organisation devoted purely to this matter. Six million Jews were murdered in a programme of horrific extermination that was managed with ruthless efficiency. Two million of that number were murdered by Einsatzgruppen and other elements of the Security Police under Kaltenbrunner's command. Special units of the RSHA scoured the occupied territories and the Axis satellite countries to arrange the deportation of Jews to the camps; in one letter that he wrote on 30 June 1944, he talked about the shipment of twelve thousand Jews to Vienna, directing that all who were unable to work should be subject to 'special action', by which, of course, he meant extermination.

Towards the end of the war, Kaltenbrunner's power grew to such an extent that even Heinrich Himmler feared him, especially when he began to have direct access to Hitler. Following the assassination attempt on Hitler in July 1944, he called stridently for all involved to be executed.

In 1943, Kaltenbrunner masterminded an assassination attempt on the Allied leaders, Stalin, Churchill and Roosevelt who were to hold a conference in Teheran. German intelligence had broken a United States Navy code and had learned of the time and the location of the conference. Kaltenbrunner chose Otto Skorzeny, an Obersturmbahnführer in the SS and the man who had liberated Italian dictator Benito Mussolini who had been deposed and imprisoned earlier that year. Soviet and British intelligence learned about the attempt, however, and German radio transmissions were intercepted. Once the Germans realised this, the plot was abandoned.

In 1944, as the war began to turn in the Allies' favour, Hitler granted all SS General officers military rank so that if they were captured by the enemy, they would be treated as military personnel rather than police officials, so Kaltenbrunner became Ober-gruppenführer und General der Polizei und Waffen-SS.

On 18 April 1945, as the war drew to a close with the Allies closing in on Hitler in Berlin, Ernst Kaltenbrunner was promoted to Commander in Chief of the remaining German forces in southern Europe. He reorganised his intelligence agencies so that they would remain as an underground force even after defeat and ensured that there were agents in all the southern European capitals. In late April, he re-located from Berlin to Alt-Aussee in Austria where on 12 May he was captured by a United States Army patrol.

Kaltenbrunner was charged at the Nuremberg Trials with conspiracy to commit crimes against peace, war crimes and crimes against humanity. The most prominent witness at his trial was none other than Rudolph Hess, the camp commander at the

Auschwitz death camp. He was accused of the mass murder of civilians of occupied countries by Einsatzgruppen; screening of prisoner of war camps and executing radical and political undesirables; the taking of recaptured prisoners of war to concentration camps, where in some cases they were executed; establishing concentration camps and committing racial and political undesirables to concentration and annihilation camps for slave labour and mass murder; deportation of citizens of occupied countries for forced labour and disciplining of forced labour; the execution of captured commandos and paratroopers and protection of civilians who lynched Allied fliers; the taking of civilians of occupied countries to Germany for secret trial and punishment; punishment of citizens of occupied territories under special criminal procedure and by summary methods; the execution and confinement of people in concentration camps for crimes allegedly committed by their relatives; seizure and spoliation of public and private property; murder of prisoners in SIPO and SD prisons; persecution of Jews and persecution of the churches.

His trial did not go well and he asked his guards to thank the prosecution for providing him with such a stupid attorney. He denied signing his name so often that he became known as 'Der Mann ohne Unterschrift', 'the man without a signature'. It was no surprise when this fervent Nazi was found guilty and sentenced to death.

On 16 October 1946 he was hanged at 1.40 in the morning. His last words were, 'I have loved my German people and my fatherland with a warm heart. I have done my duty by the laws of my people and I am sorry this time my people were led by men who were not soldiers and that crimes were committed of which I had no knowledge. Germany, good luck.'

ADOLF EICHMANN

On 11 May 1960, following intense surveillance of their target's every move, four agents of the Israeli secret service agency, Mossad, waited for him to return home from his latest job, as a foremen in a Mercedes Benz factory near Buenos Aires in Argentina. One waited for the bus he would be travelling on, while another two pretended to repair a broken down car near the bus stop. The fourth agent was on the bus with their target.

Arriving at his destination, the man climbed down from the bus, setting out in the direction of his house. As he passed the car, one of the agents nonchalantly asked him if he had a cigarette. The man reached into his pocket, but as he did so, was jumped by the other two, one of them, a black belt in karate, dealing him a sharp blow to the back of the neck, rendering him unconscious. Quickly bundling him into the car, they drove him to a safe house.

Here, he was stripped naked and examined. They found what they were looking for. Under his armpit was the absolute proof that he was an SS man – a partially-removed tattoo. All members of the SS were tattooed as a form of identification. When they asked him for his name, he replied, 'Ich bin Adolf Eichmann!'

He was a thin man with bow-legs and an all-too-predictable liking for the compositions of Richard Wagner. To his mind, back in the 1930s he had merely been pursuing a career, something he had had problems with during his civilian life, moving from job to job without making much of an impression. It was a career that would lead to the gallows, a career in which he would be responsible for the deaths of millions, and as a result of which he would be remembered as one of the greatest mass murderers of all time.

Otto Adolf Eichmann was born in Solingen in Germany in March 1906, to an industrialist, Adolf Karl Eichmann, and his wife, Maria. In spite of his five brothers, as a child he was withdrawn and solitary. When he was eight years old, his family moved to Linz, in Austria, but there he still remained something of a difficult child. Ironically, around this time his dark complexion and distinctive facial features led his schoolmates to taunt him with the nickname, 'der kleine Jude' – the little Jew – and, neglected by his parents and doing badly in his school work, he became even more difficult and moody.

His lack of academic achievement forced him to leave school early and he decided to train to be a mechanic. It did not work out, however, and, aged just seventeen, he went into his father's business, a mining company, as a sales clerk. He left that job two years later and worked for a couple of years for the Oberösterreichische Elektrobau, before becoming a district agent for an oil company.

Like many young men in Germany and Austria, Eichmann was seduced by Adolf Hitler's notion of a Third Reich. In 1932, despite having no real interest in politics, he became a member of the National Socialist Party and the SS in Austria, on the advice of a friend, Ernst Kaltenbrunner, who was a senior official in the organisation. For Eichmann it was an opportunity. He had limited prospects and the Nazi party offered him a chance to be somebody, which he desired more than anything. At last, after stopping and starting so many times in his life, he would have a proper career.

He was accepted as a full member of the SS in November 1932, based in Salzburg. In 1933, Hitler became Chancellor of Germany and Eichmann applied for active duty in the SS in Germany. In November, 1933, he was promoted to the rank of Scharführer and was assigned to the administrative staff of Dachau concentration camp, responsible for cataloguing items taken from Jewish prisoners. He began to learn the basic principles of Nazism, that the state was more important than life itself and, as he said at a later date, 'If they had told me that my own father was a traitor and I had to kill him, I'd have done it!'

A year later, he applied for a position with the Sicherheitspolizei, by this time a powerful force in Hitler's Germany. His application was successful and he went to work in the organisation's Berlin headquarters. In 1934, he was promoted to the rank of Hauptscharführer and later that year, having ascertained that she was of the proscribed racial purity – mandatory for wives of SS members – he married Veronika Liebl.

In 1937, now an SS-Untersturmführer, Eichmann was sent on an important mission with his superior, Herbert Hagen, to the British Mandate of Palestine. They were assessing the possibility of German Jews being forcibly made to migrate to Palestine. However, the British authorities refused them entry into Palestine, and their mission was fruitless.

Eichmann returned to Austria in 1938, following the

Anschluss, the annexation of Austria by Germany. His role was to organise the SS in Vienna, work which earned him another promotion, to SS-Obersturmführer. This role also led to his being selected to create the Central Office for Jewish Emigration, the department with responsibility for forcibly deporting and expelling Jews from Austria. Eichmann threw himself into his work enthusiastically, reportedly becoming a student of Judaism, even trying to learn Hebrew. His assiduousness earned him a reputation as the Nazi who understood the Jewish people.

In his first eight months in the job, having first stripped them of all lands and possessions, he forced forty-five thousand Jews out of Austria and by the end of the year, one hundred and fifty thousand Jews had disappeared. His superiors were impressed and he estimated that by the time he ended his assignment, he had removed almost quarter of a million people, many being sent to the extermination camps and others fleeing the country with nothing more than the clothes they stood up in.

He held the rank of SS-Hauptsturmführer – equivalent to captain – at the start of the Second World War, when he returned to Berlin as head of the notorious Section IV B4 of the Gestapo, the department that, with cruel efficiency, would organise the extermination of millions of people in the next few years. Eichmann now wielded real power and he used it ruthlessly. By 1941 he had risen to the rank of Obersturmbahnführer.

The Wannsee Conference, held in 1942, formulated Germany's anti-Semitic measures into an official policy of genocide of the Jews – the 'Final Solution to the Jewish Question'. Richard Heydrich, chief of the Reich Security Main Office which included the Gestapo, Sicherheitsdienst and Kripo Nazi police agencies, invited Eichmann to the conference as recording secretary and he was also given a key role in the genocide process – Transportation Administrator. He would control all the trains that would be employed to carry Jews to the concentration camps in occupied Poland.

The death factories of Auschwitz, Dachau, Treblinka and Buchenwald were killed twenty-four hours a day, seven days a week. Some of them were capable of killing as many as ten thousand people a day. And like ordinary factories, they were expected to turn a profit. The victims were robbed of all possessions, no matter how small. Human hair was removed to be used in commercial products and tons of gold were ripped from the teeth of the dead to be melted down and re-used.

Eichmann delivered to these camps the raw materials – millions of innocent and terrified Jews and

Gypsies from Austria, Holland, the Baltic countries, France and Yugoslavia. They were 'resettled' in Poland, the Warsaw ghetto becoming a particularly ferocious killing ground with tens of thousands starving to death and others being shot, or gassed in mobile gas chambers. 316,322 Jews were killed in that city alone. Eichmann, by now a stranger to reality, wrote later, 'Jewry was grateful for the chance I gave it to learn community life at the ghetto. It made an excellent school for the future in Israel – basically most Jews feel well and happy in their ghetto life.'

The demands on his logistical skills were increasing. He was responsible for delivering people to no fewer than one hundred and sixty-four camps in Eastern Europe. He improved efficiency, making the death trains larger, to accommodate more people. They travelled often huge distances without food or water and thousands died on the trains even before arriving at their destinations.

Eichmann also used his organisational skills to improve the efficiency of the killing. Vast, windowless rooms, disguised as shower rooms served as gas chambers. He considered the carbon monoxide gas used not cost-effective and advocated the use of the cyanide-based insecticide, Zyklon B. An incident in France in 1942 shows Eichmann's cold efficiency, his absolute abandonment of humanity. He had ordered a round-up of Jews in Paris which yielded a total of seven thousand people, 4,051 of them children, planning to transport them all to the camps in the east. However, the city powers objected and days of negotiation took place while the Jews were held in a cycling stadium, without food or water. After six days of talks, he won the day. The adults were taken to Eichmann's trains and shipped to the east. Several days later, the children, too, were put on trains and transported to Auschwitz and the gas chambers. Eichmann's response when questioned about the incident later was to deny responsibility. 'Once a shipment was delivered to the designated stations,' he told the Israeli police, '. . . my powers ceased.'

In 1944, fearful of a Russian invasion, Germany invaded Hungary and Eichmann was sent there to organise the deportation of Hungarian Jews. He sent 400,000 to their deaths in the gas chambers.

It was obvious to many in the German leadership by 1945 that the war was lost and they hastily began to cover their tracks. Heinrich Himmler, head of the SS, put a stop to the extermination of the Jews and hastily ordered all traces of the Final Solution to be destroyed. Eichmann was appalled by Himmler's orders, deciding arbitrarily to carry on as before, sending tens of thousands of Jews to the camps. He was also terrified that he would be assigned to the last-ditch fighting that was taking place. In 1944, he had been commissioned as a Reserve Untersturm-führer in the Waffen-SS which made him eligible for combat duty.

In 1945, the Russians entered Hungary and, finally, Eichmann fled, returning to Austria and trying to solicit help from his old friend, Ernst Kaltenbrunner. Kaltenbrunner, now a major figure in the Nazi party was trying to save his own skin and would have nothing to do with Eichmann. His work in the camps had made him a dangerous man to be associated with.

The US Army captured Eichmann around this time, but he gave a false name and escaped from custody in 1946. He went into hiding in Germany, moving from place to place and, although he actually obtained a landing permit for Argentina in 1948, he chose not to use it until later. Instead, he travelled to Italy, in 1950. Alois Hudal, a Roman Catholic bishop who had praised Hitler before the war and who helped many Nazi war criminals escape, helped Eichmann to obtain a humanitarian passport from the International Committee of the Red Cross and an Argentinean visa made out to 'Riccardo Klement, technician'. He finally sailed for Argentina on 14 July 1950.

Once established in his new country, he brought his family over and for ten years his career followed a similar trajectory to the earlier years of his life. He worked in a number of jobs in the Buenos Aires area, amongst which were factory foreman, water engineer and even rabbit farmer.

Meanwhile, the authorities were fully aware of his presence. The CIA knew that he was living in Argentina, they thought under the name 'Clemens', but took no action as his arrest would represent an embarrassment to both America and Germany by focusing attention on the former Nazis they had recruited at the conclusion of the war, not least of which was Hans Globke, German President Konrad Adenauer's national security advisor. Globke had worked directly with Eichmann on Jewish affairs and, in 1935, had helped draft the Nuremberg Laws, justifying racial discrimination against German Jews. Globke's name was even deleted from Eichmann's memoirs which had been sold to *Life* magazine by the Eichmann family.

Meanwhile, not even the Israelis could find Eichmann, but many other Holocaust victims refused to give up searching for him. Famous Jewish Nazi-hunter, Simon Wiesenthal, suspected that he was in Argentina, a suspicion confirmed by a postcard from a friend who had moved to the Argentinean capital: 'Ich sah jenes Schmutzige Schwein, Eichmann,' (I saw that dirty pig, Eichmann) he wrote, adding that he was living near Buenos Aires and working for a water company. Wiesenthal and the Israelis used this and other information to build a picture of Eichmann's life in exile.

Lothar Hermann, a German of Jewish descent, had been an inmate of Dachau at the time that Eichmann was an administrator at the camp. Fleeing to Argentina at the end of the war, he had established a new family there. Coincidentally, his daughter, Sylvia, became involved with one of Eichmann's sons, Klaus. Klaus foolishly boasted to Sylvia about his father's past, crediting him with responsibility for the Final Solution and when Sylvia informed her horrified father about this, he realised he was onto something.

He wrote to Fritz Bauer, Chief Prosecutor of the German state of Hesse and also contacted Israeli officials. For several years they worked on a plan to capture Eichmann. Finally, in 1960, the Israeli government approved the plan to kidnap him and bring him to Israel where he could be tried as a war criminal.

On 21 May, heavily sedated, Eichmann was smuggled out of Argentina as part of a delegation of Jewish trade union members on a commercial flight to Israel. A few days later, when Israeli prime minister, David Ben Gurion, announced to the Knesset, the Israeli parliament, that Eichmann had been captured, he received a standing ovation.

Eichmann's capture created an international incident between Argentina and Israel. At the United Nations Security Council, the Argentineans insisted that Eichmann's abduction was a 'violation of the sovereign rights of the Argentine Republic'. Israel retorted that Eichmann had been captured not by Israeli agents, but by private citizens. The Security Council accepted the Argentinean allegation and ordered Israel to make 'appropriate reparation'. However, it also noted that its decision in no way condoned the crimes with which Eichmann was charged.

His trial began on 11 April 1961 in the newly built Beth Ha'am (House of the People) where he was indicted on fifteen charges. These included crimes against humanity, consisting of the murder of millions of innocents in the death camps; the introduction of the poison gas, Zyklon B; the creation of plans that murdered 80,000 in Lithuania, 30,000 in Latvia, 45,000 in Byelorussia, 75,000 in the Ukraine and 33,000 in the city of Kiev. He was further accused of issuing the orders to send hundreds of thousands to Auschwitz, causing the suffering and death inside the Warsaw ghetto in 1939 and 1940, the slaughter of 500,000 Hungarian Jews in just eight months in 1944, enslaving millions across eastern Europe in forced labour camps, performing forced abortions on pregnant women, forced sterilisation of thousands of

Jewish men in Germany and, finally, of being the person in command of the entire Nazi bureaucratic structure that brought starvation, ruin and death to millions of people before and during the Second World War.

The trial, broadcast live around the world, included testimonies from many Holocaust survivors. One vital witness, American judge, Michael A. Musmanno who had questioned the defendants at the Nuremberg trials said that Hermann Goering, Hitler's second-in-command, had 'made it very clear that Eichmann was the man to determine in what order, in what countries, the Jews were to die.'

Eichmann did not dispute the facts of the Holocaust. His defence was the same as many other Nazi war criminals – he was merely obeying orders. 'I never did anything, great or small,' he claimed, 'without obtaining in advance express instructions from Adolf Hitler or any of my superiors.'

After fourteen weeks, as anticipated, he was convicted on all counts and sentenced to death by hanging. He appealed unsuccessfully and than had a plea for mercy turned down by Israeli president Yitzhak Ben-Zvi on 29 May 1962.

In the only execution ever to be carried out in Israel, Adolf Eichmann was hanged just after midnight on 1 June 1962 at Ramla prison. His body was cremated and the ashes were scattered in international waters in the Mediterranean.

On the gallows, he had refused to don the customary black hood. He went to his death declaring: 'Long live Germany. Long live Austria. Long live Argentina. These are the countries with which I have been most closely associated and I shall not forget them. I had to obey the rules of war and my flag. I am ready.'

DR JOSEF MENGELE

It was the white cotton dress gloves that distinguished him and that they would all remember, those who lived, that is, the ones who weren't sent to the gas chambers and then fed into the crematoria whose furnaces spewed forth smoke that stank of human flesh and burning hair twenty-four hours a day at the camp known as Auschwitz.

He had begun wearing the gloves when he was a young man. They went with the hand-tailored suits and shirts that he liked to wear. He was a good-looking young man, a favourite of the young women in the Bavarian village of Gunzburg where he was born in 1911 to Karl Mengele, owner of a factory that manufactured farming equipment. His mother Walburga was an immense, unforgiving woman, hated by the workers in her husband's factory whom she would berate for laziness, and unloving in her personal relationships. She ruled her home with an iron discipline, ensuring that her three sons adhered to the tenets of the church about which she was fanatical.

However, although his home life was lacking in affection and warmth, Josef Mengele, or Beppo as he was popularly known, was a bright, happy boy who did well at school.

Naturally, Karl Mengele saw his sons' future lying in the family business and he had Josef marked down to be an accountant. Josef had other ideas, however, harbouring ambitions to leave Gunzburg to study anthropology. He was accepted by the University of Munich, enrolling there in October 1930.

It was an exciting time to be in Munich, the city at the centre of the growing National Socialist movement, led by Adolf Hitler. Like countless others, the nineteen-year-old Mengele was swept away by the talk of a German super-race and a new German Empire. He was a conservative, anyway, firmly anti-Bolshevik, and Hitler's philosophy dovetailed perfectly with his own. He decided that Nazism would be the means by which he would advance his career and in 1931 joined the Stahlhelm (Steel Helmets) an organisation not yet a part of the Nazi Party, but which shared the same extreme views.

He was studying anthropology, paleontology and

medicine at the time, but the main focus of his attention was eugenics, the study of improving the human species by means such as discouraging reproduction by people with genetic defects while encouraging reproduction by people with desirable traits. It was perfect for the Nazis – the means of producing the master race they so desired and a number of German scientists were researching in this area, putting forward the belief that some lives were just not worth living. Mengele threw himself into this work, determined to distinguish himself. There was still nothing about him, however, to suggest that he would become a monster within a few years.

He certainly had some fine examples to follow, however. His teacher was Dr Ernst Rudin who not only espoused the theory that there were lives that were not living; he also believed that doctors had a responsibility to eradicate such life. He helped compose the 1933 Nazi Law for Protection of Hereditary health that led to the sterilisation of people with mental health problems.

Mengele became a member of the SA (Sturmabteilung), also known as Brownshirts, the Nazi paramilitary group that had helped Hitler to seize power, in 1934. He was forced to resign, however, when he fell ill with a kidney ailment. Nonetheless, he was awarded a Ph.D. in 1935 after writing a thesis entitled 'Racial Morphological Research on the Lower Jaw Section of Four Racial Groups' in which he claimed that racial groups could be determined from the shape of the jaw. In 1936, he became a doctor and began practising at the university medical clinic.

The critical moment in his career arrived in 1937 when he obtained a position as a research assistant at the Third Reich Institute for Hereditary, Biological and Racial Purity at the University of Frankfurt, working under Professor Otmar Freiherr von Verschuer. Von Verschuer, an ardent supporter of Hitler, became Mengele's mentor and something of the father figure he had missed as a child. That year he became a member of the Nazi Party and the following year he was accepted into the SS (Schutzstaffel), the most rabid and brutal of all the bodies that Hitler created to ensure racial purity and strict adherence to Nazi ideology. He received military training with the German Army and dreamed of fighting for the Fatherland. In June 1940, he reached the pinnacle of Nazi achievement when he was accepted into the Waffen SS, the elite combat branch of the organisation whose members were Hitler's most ardent fans.

His dream of fighting for Germany came true and he won the Iron Cross 2nd Class for fighting on the Ukrainian Front in 1941. In 1942, he pulled two German soldiers out of a burning tank and was awarded the Iron Cross 1st Class. He was wounded, however, and unable to return to the front.

Instead, they promoted him to captain and sent him to the Race and Resettlement Office in Berlin. In May 1943, Mengele was given a new assignment – he was sent to the Nazi Concentration camp at Auschwitz in Poland.

Auschwitz had been established in 1940, at an old Polish army barracks. Initially used to intern Polish intellectuals and members of the resistance, Soviet prisoners of war were added. German criminals, homosexuals and eventually Jews were sent there. The complex consisted of three camps. Auschwitz I held twenty thousand inmates, Auschwitz II (Birkenau) was the extermination camp, mostly Jews passing through it – more than a million dying there – and Auschwitz III was a work camp with approximately forty thousand slave labourers working there or nearby.

Mengele's job at Auschwitz was to research human genetics, funded by a grant that von Verschuer had obtained for him. He stood out in the camp as the only doctor with military decorations and he sported them at all times on his immaculate SS uniform. He also distinguished himself with his callous and ruthless commitment to his work, to the extent that even his fellow SS officers feared him.

He began as he meant to carry on. When a typhus epidemic broke out in the camp, he ordered the extermination in the gas chambers of a thousand Gypsies who had been infected.

Where he really held sway over life and death was in the selection process. Mengele liked nothing better than to stand by the trains bringing Jewish deportees to Auschwitz and indicate with the riding crop he always carried which direction people should go in. Those directed to the left with the one word, 'Links!' – only around 10-30 per cent of new arrivals were spared and put to work while those directed to the right – 'Rechts!' – were on a path that led directly to the gas chambers. Families were separated, unaware that this was the last time they would see each other.

While others loathed and were disgusted by the work – getting drunk just so they could carry it out – Mengele loved it, even volunteering to do it when it had been assigned to another colleague. He would whistle happily as he chillingly sent thousands of people to a horrific death. He often displayed the charming side of his personality, the one that had delighted the young women of Gunzburg, as he spoke soothingly to exhausted women and children on the ramp leading from the trains, but a moment later he would be consigning them to the gas chambers. He used this aspect of his personality to chilling effect in his dealings with prisoners and colleagues alike and it became one of the most terrifying things about this terrifying man.

His 'scientific' experiments were debased in the extreme. He dissected live children and castrated boys and men without anaesthetic. Women were subjected to high-voltage shocks to ostensibly test how much they could take. If they died in the process, it did not matter; there were plenty more where they came from. He sterilised a group of Polish nuns on one occasion using an X-ray machine. They were horrifically burned.

He sexually degraded prisoners as well, parading naked Jewish women prisoners in front of him and asking them intimate questions about their sex lives. It is hard to dismiss the thought that he did in fact harbour a deep-seated secret longing for these woman whom he, nonetheless, described as 'dirty whores'.

He never failed to display extreme cruelty. Once when the crematoria were full and working to capacity, he had trenches dug, filled with burning petrol and then ordered that men, women and children be thrown into them alive. On another occasion when a camp Kapo, a Jewish inmate with the responsibility for herding inmates into the gas chamber was discovered trying to smuggle a few into the labour line, Mengele pulled his pistol and shot the man on the spot.

Mengele's mentor, von Verschuer was particularly interested in the subject of twins and saw an opportunity for his protégé, Mengele, to work in vivo, with living twins. Mengele, anxious to please his mentor, ordered the guards to search for twins in the lines of arriving Jews. He reserved a special barracks for them, as he did for dwarves, cripples and others with specific qualities that interested him. The barracks came to be known as 'The Zoo' and its inhabitants received special treatment, were fed better than other inmates and allowed to keep their hair and their own clothes. They were even lavished with affection and comfort and the guards were not permitted to mistreat them. When they learned of the fate of their parents in the gas chambers, Mengele became a complex figure in their minds – the man who had killed their parents but spared them, almost a kind of perverse father-figure. He would walk with them to the gas chambers, making the walks a game he called 'on the way to the chimney'.

Hundreds of his twins – 'Mengele's Children', as they have become known – died during his experiments. He took daily blood samples from them and sent them to von Verschuer's institute in Berlin. He injected blood from one twin into another and analysed what happened. They invariably became ill with a fever. To investigate if eye colour could be genetically altered, he injected dye into their eyes which was always followed by a painful reaction and, often, blindness. Twins who died in this way had their eyes harvested and pinned to the walls of his office. They were castrated and sterilised, injected with contagious diseases and had limbs amputated and organs removed, all without anaesthetic.

It had little to do with scientific research and everything to do with Mengele's fanatical obsession with the Nazi obsession with Aryan purity.

On 17 January, Mengele fled from Auschwitz in the face of the Soviet advance towards Berlin. For a few years he hid on a farm close to his home town of Gunzburg, working, under a fake identity, as a farm-hand. Initially and naively believing that he could resume his work as a research scientist, he quickly came to realise that the Allies were not going to let people get away with the horrific crimes they had committed during the war. He decided, in that case, to escape to Argentina, arriving there in 1949. Soon, he had established a new identity for himself and had begun a new life.

For the next thirty years he remained a fugitive with the help of the neo-Nazi network in Argentina, Paraguay and Brazil as well as the right-wing governments in those countries. The lack of commitment to his capture displayed by the West

German Government and the United States Justice department also helped in no little way. The Israelis made strenuous efforts, almost capturing him on a number of occasions in the early 1960s but their kidnapping of another Nazi war criminal, Adolf Eichmann, in Argentina in 1960 caused an uproar and coupled with their wars with the Arabs, efforts to capture Mengele were put to one side. Mengele vanished for a number of years.

In 1985, however, thanks to the efforts of Auschwitz survivors who tried Josef Mengele in absentia in a globally televised broadcast, his case was re-opened by the Israelis and the Americans. It all came to an end in May 1985 when it was discovered that Mengele had drowned in Brazil in 1979, aged sixty-eight. The families who had harboured him led the Brazilian authorities to his grave and the remains were confirmed as being Josef Mengele's following forensic tests.

The life of one of the most perverted human beings ever to walk the earth was over, but during his life he was a living example of the insanity that Adolf Hitler brought to Germany. Who could have predicted that the handsome, debonair and popular young man, 'Beppo' Mengele would develop into the monster known as the 'Angel of Death', a man who perpetrated horrors that go beyond description and certainly beyond belief.

In 1981, the office of the West German Prosecutor drew up seventy-eight separate indictments against Josef Mengele. Amongst the heinous crimes with which he was charged were: 'Having actively and decisively taken part in selections in the prisoners' sick blocks, of such prisoners who through hunger, deprivations, exhaustion, sickness, disease, abuse or other reasons were unfit for work in the camp and whose speedy recovery was not envisaged . . . Those selected were killed either through injections or firing squads or by painful suffocation to death through prussic acid in the gas chambers in order to make room in the camp for the 'fit' prisoners, selected by him or other SS doctors . . . The injections that killed were made with phenol, petrol, Evipal, chloroform, or air into the circulation, especially into the heart chamber, either with his own hands or he ordered the SS sanitary worker to do it while he watched.'

THE MASSACRE OF THE ACQUI DIVISION

The Massacre of the Acqui Division, also known as the Cephalonia Massacre, began on 21 September 1943 and continued through seven days of callous murder and brutal lack of respect for human life. It was one of the largest massacres of prisoners of war during the Second World War and one of the worst atrocities to be carried out by troops of the Wehrmacht, the German army. It has become known in recent years as the backdrop to the bestselling novel by Louis de Bernieres, *Captain Corelli's Mandolin.*

Commanded by fifty-two-year-old General Antonio Gandin, the 11,500 soldiers and 525 officers of the Acqui Division had arrived on the Greek island of Cephalonia in May of that year. Gandin was a decorated hero of the Russian front during which action he was awarded the top German medal, the Iron Cross.

Italy surrendered to the Allies in September 1943 with Mussolini being arrested and General Pietro

Badoglio assuming power. This left General Gandin with a problem. He could either surrender to the Germans or fight them. He awaited orders from Italy and in the meantime opened negotiations with the German commander in the area, Colonel Johannes Barge, who had arrived with two thousand men of the 966th Fortress Grenadier Regiment, along with self-propelled guns and nine tanks.

The day after the Italian surrender, the commander of Italian troops in Greece, General Carlo Vecchiarelli instructed Gandin that if his men were not attacked by the Germans, he should not attack them. Additionally, the Italian forces were not to cooperate with Greek partisans or the Allies in the event of an Allied invasion of Cephalonia. The order, however, was not entirely clear in its wording, implying that the Italians should attack if they had to. A further order later that day removed Gandin's only means of escape when his naval and merchant vessels were ordered back to port in Brindisi.

Technically, however, Gandin and Barge were under German command as Badoglio had agreed to the merging of the Italian and the German armies to placate the Germans after the fall of Mussolini. Italians disobeying German orders could, therefore, conceivably be treated as mutineers.

Gandin and Barge met on 9 September and

decided to await orders as to how they should proceed in what was an unusual and complicated situation.

On 11 September, the order arrived from Italian High Command that Gandin should treat the Germans as hostile. Furthermore, if the Germans tried to disarm Italian troops they were to be met with force. At the same time, Barge sent a note to the Italian general giving him three options – he could fight on the side of the Germans; he could fight against the Germans or he could disarm.

Gandin convened a meeting of his senior officers and chaplains. They agreed that he should comply with German demands, but Gandin could not do so as to do that would directly contradict Badoglio's instructions. However, he was reluctant also to enter into a conflict with these men alongside whom he and his men had fought. He chose to play for time by prolonging the negotiations.

On 12 September, he agreed to hand over his weapons to Barge but was now under pressure from his junior officers who threatened to mutiny if he made an agreement with Barge. This was supported by news from the Acqui regiment on Corfu who had already refused to comply with German demands. The Germans had promised repatriation to soldiers who surrendered, but Gandin discovered that they were actually being deported rather than repatriated. He decided to ask for the opinion of his men, giving them the three stark choices that had been given to him. They overwhelmingly elected to resist the Germans. Consequently, he sent an ultimatum to Colonel Barge, demanding that he and his troops vacate the island by 9 am the next morning.

The Germans presented their own ultimatum that ran out at two o'clock on the afternoon of 15 September and when it had expired they began dive-bombing Italian positions. The battle began well for the Italians and they took four hundred German prisoners. The Germans responded by sending in more crack troops. The Italians needed help but had effectively been abandoned. The Allies refused to let three hundred planes based within reach of Cephalonia become involved as they feared that they would defect to the German side and no word came from the Italian Ministry of War in Brindisi. After several days of fierce fighting, the Italians proved no match for the battle-hardened Germans and Gandin ordered his men to surrender. One thousand three hundred Italians troops and three hundred German troops had died.

Following Gandin's surrender, Adolf Hitler issued a decree stating that all Italian officers who had committed treason could be summarily executed.

This was followed on 18 September by an order from German High Command that 'because of the perfidious and treacherous behaviour [of the Italians] on Cephalonia, no prisoners are to be taken.'

The executions began almost at once, Italian soldiers being machine-gunned in groups of four to ten. Some German soldiers baulked at the idea and were themselves threatened with execution unless they followed orders. After these initial executions the Italians still alive were marched to San Teodoro town hall where they were executed by detachments of eight men.

Gandin and 137 Italian officers were court martialled on 24 September and sentenced to death for treason, their bodies being disposed of at sea. Before Gandin was shot, however, he angrily threw his Iron Cross on the dirt in front of the firing squad.

The Germans were ruthlessly efficient. On one occasion, some of them went around shouting loudly that they would provide treatment for any Italians lying on the ground who had been wounded and not killed by the firing squad. When a number of men began to crawl forward, they opened up with a machine gun and put them beyond help.

Officers handed personal belongings over to German troops and asked that they be delivered back to their families in Italy. The items never arrived, mainly because they were never sent; the Germans kept them.

Officers from Trieste and Trentino were spared because on 8 September these two provinces had been annexed by the Germans, but one of the regiment's chaplains, Father Formato took the opportunity to beg for the lives of all the officers. The commanding officer relented and thirty-seven officers were saved. However, when twenty Italian sailors were ordered to load the bodies of dead Italian officers onto rafts and dispose of them at sea, the Germans blew the rafts up, killing the sailors on board.

One Italian, well-known on the island for singing opera in the taverns, was forced to sing while his comrades were being executed. No one knows what became if the singer but his fate is likely to have been the same as the men he sang to as they died.

There were mountains of bodies and the German soldiers began to plunder them, taking boots and other items of clothing. They got rid of the bodies in huge cremations, the island air becoming thick with dark smoke and the stench of burning flesh. Or they took them out to sea and dumped them. Some were executed in front of Greek islanders and their bodies were left to rot. Back streets of villages were littered with corpses.

Five thousand were killed and few survived, those

that did very often being helped by the local population. Three thousand survivors drowned when the ships – the Sinfra and the Ardena – in which they were being transported to prisoner of war camps, were blown up by mines in the Adriatic.

The massacre on Cephalonia was not unique. On Corfu all two hundred and eighty officers of the Acqui's 18th regiment were executed within two days of their surrender to the Germans. Following the Battle of Kos, the Italian commander and ninety of his officers were shot.

Of the officers responsible for the Massacre of the Acqui Division, Major Harald von Hirschfeld was not prosecuted, having been killed in Poland in 1945; his superior, General Hubert Lanz was tried at Nuremberg and sentenced to twelve years in prison even though his men had committed other atrocities in Greece such as the Massacre of Kommeno the month before the Cephalonia Massacre. His sentence was light because the authorities did not initially believe that the massacre took place. Consequently, Lanz was only charged with the murder of Gandin and his officers and his lies saying that he refused to follow Hitler's orders to kill all the prisoners were believed. He further claimed that his report that five thousand had been executed was a trick to make German High Command believe that he had followed orders. His version said that only around a dozen officers were actually shot and that the remainder of the troops were transported to Piraeus. Other high-ranking Germans supported his story. He was also helped by the fact that the Italians, stung by their punishment after the war refused to cooperate with the Nuremberg process and did not, therefore, provide any evidence to support the view that a massacre had actually taken place. The court, therefore accepted Lanz's version and he escaped with his comparatively light sentence.

There have been several attempts to re-open the case but none have come to anything and the three hundred German survivors who took part in the massacre are now well into their old age. It seems unlikely that they will be prosecuted.

In the 1950s, the remains of three thousand Italian soldiers and one hundred and eighty-nine officers were exhumed on Cephalonia and returned to Italy where they were buried in an Italian War Cemetery in Bari. It is not known if General Antonio Gandin was amongst them.

JAPANESE WAR CRIMES OF WORLD WAR TWO

War crimes are defined by the Nuremberg Charter as 'violations of the laws or customs of war' and take in crimes against both enemy civilians as well as enemy combatants. Japanese military personnel have been accused of committing such crimes from the end of the 19th century until the middle of the 20th century, perpetrating a series of human rights abuses against civilians and prisoners of war in East Asia and the Western pacific. Such instances were common during the Sino-Japanese War of 1937 to 1945 but especially in the Asian and Pacific campaigns against the Allies during the Second World War.

The Empire of Japan never signed the Geneva Conventions – the four treaties that set the standards for international law regarding humanitarian matters, dealing especially with the treatment of non-combatants in war as well as with the way in which prisoners of war should be treated. However, an Imperial Proclamation in 1894 had stipulated that soldiers of the Empire should make every effort to win the war – the Sino-Japanese War, at that time – without violating international law. Furthermore, many of the crimes committed in the Second World War were still in violation of Japanese military law and should have been punished on that basis. They had signed the Hague Conventions of 1899 and 1907 that banned such things as the use of chemical weapons and provided protection for POWs and their personnel should thereafter have been subject to the terms of those treaties.

The Japanese had come to believe, with the rise of Shinto as the state religion and the increasing jingoism that they, like most countries, experienced towards the end of the 19th century, that the Emperor was divine and he and his representatives should be obeyed unquestioningly. Japan also became a military power around this time, defeating the Chinese in the First Sino-Japanese war that was fought between 1894 and 1895. Prisoners were treated properly then, with 1790 Chinese prisoners being released unharmed and more than seventy-nine thousand were released after the Russo-Japanese War of 1904–5. The Russians were even paid for the work they performed in captivity, as stipulated by the Hague Convention. In fact, some German POWs in the First World War enjoyed their enforced stay in Japan so much that they elected to remain there afterwards.

It was a rise in militarism, similar to that of Nazi Germany that resulted in a callous approach to prisoners and non-combatants in war. The paranoia of such regimes inevitably produces brutality, hatred and fear and in Japan the Nazi Gestapo was mirrored by a similar secret police force, the Kempeitai. Disrespect towards the Emperor brought harsh punishment and cruelty was commonplace in the military with officers callously beating lower ranks. This became endemic as each rank passed this cruelty down the line to those beneath them. Eventually, it would be used against the enemy.

While the Nazis were responsible for the deaths of at least six million Jews and twenty million Soviet citizens, the Japanese were probably culpable for the deaths of thirty million Filipinos, Malays, Vietnamese, Cambodians, Indonesians and Burmese. Like the Nazis, the Japanese looted the nations they conquered but the Japanese did it for longer than the Germans. Both countries enslaved millions in forced labour and the Japanese enslaved women as prostitutes for front-line troops. The death rate for Allied prisoners of war held in Nazi POW camps was four per cent; Allied troops in a Japanese camp faced a thirty per cent chance of dying. The survival rate of Chinese prisoners was negligible and only fifty-six Chinese prisoners were released by the Japanese after the surrender.

The Chinese suffered especially badly. The Nanking Massacre of December 1937 followed the capture by Japanese forces of Nanking, then capital of the Republic of China. Over a six-week period Japanese troops committed atrocities such as rape, arson and looting. Civilians and prisoners of war were executed. Two Japanese officers are reported to have entered into a killing contest and, astonishingly, the contest was covered like a sporting event in several Japanese newspapers, the score being updated in each new edition. In another incident, around fifty thousand people were shot dead as they tried to escape from the Japanese advance by swimming across the Yangtze River.

It is estimated that eighty thousand women were raped in Nanking and its environs. Many were raped multiple times and were then killed afterwards. This was often done through mutilation – cutting off breasts or stabbing in the vagina with bamboo, knives, bayonets or other objects. Families were forced to commit incest, sons forced to rape their mothers, fathers their daughters. Celibate monks were forced to rape women.

Emperor Hirohito personally removed the constraints on Japanese troops to observe international law where Chinese prisoners were concerned. In one incident, known as the Straw String Gorge Massacre, Japanese troops shot dead an estimated 57,500 Chinese prisoners of war. They also blew up or burned to death countless other Chinese POWs while around twelve thousand Chinese civilians were mass-executed and buried in a trench. Horrifically, live victims were used as bayonet practice for young Japanese soldiers.

Allied Service personnel were the victims of a number of massacres. The Battle of Ambon took place when the Japanese invaded the island of Ambon in the Dutch East Indies, held by Dutch and Australian forces, in January and February of 1942. Following the surrender of the Allied forces on the island, personnel of the Imperial Japanese Navy randomly selected three hundred prisoners at regular intervals for the next fortnight and executed them, revenge, it has been suggested, for the sinking of a Japanese minesweeper. The men taken prisoner on Ambon suffered terribly in captivity for the next three years, initially on Ambon and then on the Chinese island of Hainan. Seventy-five per cent of the 582 Australians captured did not live to see the end of the war, killed by starvation, overwork and untreated disease as well as often being beaten to death. It resulted in one of the largest of the post-war Japanese war crimes trials, with ninety-three Japanese personnel being tried and Commander Kunito Hatakeyama being hanged.

On 16 February 1942, Japanese soldiers machine-gunned twenty-two Australian nurses, all but one dying in the attack. They had been travelling on a merchant ship that had left Singapore just before it was taken by the Japanese. After it was sunk by shelling, the nurses made it to shore on Japanese-occupied Banka Island with a number of troops, some wounded. They were confronted by ten Japanese soldiers who ordered all the wounded who were mobile to walk round a headland. Once there, they were shot and bayoneted to death. Returning, the soldiers ordered the twenty-two nurses to walk out into the surf. A machine gun was set up on the beach and when the women were waist-deep in the water, the soldiers opened fire. Sister Lieutenant Vivian Bullwinkel was left for dead, but was only unconscious. She avoided capture for ten days on the island before being taken prisoner and surviving to give evidence at a war crimes trial in Tokyo in 1947.

On 14 December 1944, Japanese troops on the Philippine island of Palawan, were reluctant to allow their American POWs to be liberated by the advancing

Allied forces. They herded all one hundred and fifty of them into three covered trenches which then had barrels of petrol poured into them before being set alight. Any prisoner attempting to escape the flames was shot. Those who got out by climbing over a cliff running alongside one of the trenches were hunted and killed. Only eleven escaped this horrific death.

The SS *Tjisalak* was a Dutch freighter that also had accommodation for passengers. Used during the war to transport supplies across the Indian Ocean, she was sunk by a torpedo from the Japanese submarine I-8 while carrying a cargo of flour and naval mail between Melbourne and Colombo in Ceylon without an escort. As the ship began to list badly, the captain ordered its Chinese and English eighty-man crew, five passengers – including American Red Cross nurse, Verna Gorden-Britten – and twenty-two Indian sailors whose ship had been sunk, to abandon ship. 105 people were collected from boats and rafts by the Japanese and landed on the submarine's deck as a conference was held on the vessel's conning tower. They were then tied together in pairs and each pair was walked around the back of the conning tower where Japanese submariners attacked them with a variety of weapons and blunt instruments. Five men leapt from the submarine, surviving the massacre and succeeding in making it to safety. When there were twenty people left, the Japanese roped them together, pushed them overboard and then submerged.

The I-8 was also responsible for similar atrocities towards the SS *Jean Nicolet* and, it is surmised, probably others. Its captain committed suicide when Japan surrendered but at least three of its crew were prosecuted, although their prison terms were later commuted by the Japanese government.

The cruelty of the Japanese towards prisoners of war has been depicted in numerous films and books since the end of the Second World War. Intelligence was extracted from Allied prisoners using torture and tortured prisoners were then executed. In the Philippines, electric shocks from a car battery were the preferred method, administered to the nose and the testicles. Waterboarding, known then as 'Water Cure', for which the American government has recently been condemned in interrogating terror suspects, was in use back then. A prisoner in the Dutch East Indies recalled a form of this torture that he underwent, describing how a towel was fixed under his chin and over his face. Then the Japanese poured buckets of water into the towel so that the water began to rise, gradually reaching his mouth and then his nostrils. He described becoming unconscious at that point, as if he was being drowned. The procedure was repeated half a dozen times.

Emperor Hirohito himself issued the directive that removed all constraints on the violation of international law regarding the treatment of prisoners and even banned the use of the term 'prisoner of war'. Many died – both civilians and POWs, as a result of the Japanese use of forced labour during the Second World War. The Koa-in – Japanese Development Board – is said to have mobilised more than ten million Chinese civilians for this purpose.

One of the most costly war crimes committed by Japan during the Second World War was the construction of the Burma-Siam Railway during which more than 180,000 civilians and 60,000 POWs died. Living and working conditions were horrific. Labourers were overworked and malnourished and were ravaged by diseases such as cholera, malaria and dysentery. In another case, around 270,000 Javanese labourers were sent to work in other parts of Japanese-occupied South East Asia. Only 52,000 ever returned to Java – a chilling death rate of eighty per cent.

One of the most horrific of all abuses of people by the Japanese between 1939 and 1945 was the practice of enslaving women, either by force or deception, to be what were termed 'comfort women' (jugun ianfu) – in other words, sex slaves. Around 200,000 women are believed to have been used in this way, the majority coming from China, Korea and Japan, itself, although women from other Japanese-occupied territories such as Dutch East Indies, the Philippines, Thailand, Vietnam, Malaysia, Taiwan and Indonesia were also used. 'Comfort Stations' as the military brothels were euphemistically called, were situated throughout the occupied territories.

Women were abducted from their homes or sometimes attracted by offers to carry out military work. The creation of these stations was ostensibly to prevent rape by Japanese military personnel in occupied areas and thereby reducing the hostility felt by the local population towards the occupying force. It was also thought that they would serve as protection against the spread of venereal disease amongst troops. Interestingly, it has also been suggested that they helped to prevent revolt amongst unhappy soldiers.

Providing 'comfort' for soldiers was not a new practice in Japan. The first such facility was provided in the Japanese concession in Shanghai in 1932 and before that, Japanese prostitutes had always volunteered to provide such a service. The truth was that by the time of the outbreak of the war, there simply were not enough Japanese volunteers to service the needs of the now huge Japanese army and new sources had to be found from the local populations. The authorities also believed that it damaged the image of the Japanese Empire to have its women working in such a way. They turned, therefore, to subject peoples, announcing the need to recruit factory workers or nurses. Women volunteered in droves only to discover that they were actually going to be forced to work as prostitutes.

Comfort women were treated appallingly and it is estimated that only twenty-five per cent survived the war, most of these rendered unable to have children due to the multiple rapes they endured – sometimes servicing twenty-five to thirty men a day – and the beatings to which they were subjected on a daily basis or the diseases to which they fell victim.

There are numerous reports and testimonies to the effect that Japanese military personnel in the Asia and Pacific theatres of war indulged in cannibalism. It resulted from the effectiveness of Allied forces in interrupting supply lines and the subsequent starvation suffered by Japanese soldiers. Some suggest, however, that it was done systematically under the supervision of officers, individuals being murdered solely for the purpose of being eaten. There are eye-witness accounts of human flesh being sliced off and fried and even instances where flesh was witnessed being cut off living bodies. An Indian POW described how in New Guinea the Japanese selected one prisoner each day who was taken away and eaten by guards. He reported how flesh was cut from their bodies while still alive and that they were later tossed into a ditch where they were left to die.

Lieutenant General Yoshio Tachibana and eleven other Japanese soldiers were convicted after the war for beheading US airmen and eating at least one of them. International law did not provide for cannibalism – they were tried for murder and 'prevention of honourable burial'. Tachibana was sentenced to death.

The Japanese military engaged in theft and looting on a grand scale during the war, plundering money and valuables from banks, depositories, temples and other religious sites, commercial premises, museums and private houses. A great deal of this loot was stashed in the Philippines and the organisation of the stealing partly involved yakuza gangsters and officials working for the Emperor whose objective was to channel as much of it as possible towards the government. There was even a secret government organisation for this purpose – the Kin no yuri, or Golden Lily, headed by Prince Chichibu, Hirohito's brother.

Following the defeat of the Japanese in August 1945, the International Military Tribunal for the Far East (IMTFE), also known as the Tokyo Trial, the Tokyo War Crimes Tribunal was established and sat from 3 May 1946 until 12 November 1948. The Allies indicted twenty-five people as Class A War Criminals and into the Class B and C categories were placed 5,700. Nine hundred and eighty-four were initially condemned to death and 920 were actually executed. 475 received terms of life imprisonment, the remainder, of whom 1018 were acquitted, went to prison for shorter terms.

Emperor Hirohito and other members of the Japanese royal family, such as Prince Chichibu, Prince Asaka, Prince Takeda and Prince Higashikuni were exonerated by US General MacArthur and the civilian criminal suspects all coordinated their stories in such a way that the Emperor was presented as innocent of any wrongdoing.

MY LAI MASSACRE

By 1968 Quang Ngai Province was the biggest hotbed of Viet Cong activity in all of South Vietnam. The Vietnam War had by that time been going on for a number of years, starting out in the 1950s with a few American advisers being sent in to help the South Vietnamese resist their communist northern neighbours who were supported by their communist allies. As the years passed, however, the number of American troops and the quantity of American hardware being used increased until by the middle of 1968, there were more than half a million US combat troops in Vietnam.

The year 1968 would be an important one in the war. In January, the North Vietnamese had launched the Tet Offensive, a campaign designed to strike at military and civilian command centres in South Vietnam and to create an uprising that would bring down the South Vietnamese government and bring the war to an end.

However, 1968 was also important because it was the year that United States troops participated in a horrific mass murder in the South Vietnamese village of My Lai, killing around five hundred innocent civilians, many of them women and children, in just under two hours of madness on 16 March. Victims were murdered, sexually abused, beaten, tortured and maimed by twenty-six American soldiers of Charlie Company of the 23rd Infantry Division. Worse still, senior army officers engaged in a wholesale cover-up of the massacre, the truth emerging only thanks to the efforts of one twenty-two-year-old ex-serviceman from Phoenix, Arizona, Ronald Ridenhour, who made it his job the following year to inform people in authority about the events of that grim March day.

In 1967, Quang Ngai had been declared a 'free-fire' zone which, in military terms, meant that weapons could be fired in the area without additional coordination with headquarters. Planes flew frequent bombing missions over the region and it was subject to missile attacks. Tens of thousands of villages were wiped out in those attacks and close to 150,000 people were left homeless as a result. Needless to say, the Americans became even more unpopular than they had been before and the relationship between the indigenous population and the GIs was at an all-time low. Furthermore, this bad feeling was not helped by the fact that senior military men liked nothing better than a high number of kills to report back to their political masters in Washington. A high body count came to indicate progress in the war and GIs began to joke that, 'anything that's dead and isn't white is a VC (Viet Cong)'.

C Company, known as 'Charlie', had arrived in Vietnam in December 1967 and moved into Quang Ngai Province in January 1968, its mission to suppress the North Vietnamese in an area known as 'Pinkville'. In charge of Charlie Company was a tough thirty-three-year-old Mexican-American, Captain Ernest Medina, an able officer who was liked by the men under his command. One of his junior officers, platoon leader, twenty-four-year-old Lieutenant William Calley, was less able, however, disliked intensely by his men, one of whom dismissed him as 'a kid trying to play at war' while another called him a 'glory-hunter'. Captain Medina had little respect for him, addressing him as 'Lieutenant Shithead' in front of his own men. Calley's lack of respect for the Vietnamese they encountered was evident to all and if his men treated civilians badly he made no effort to reprimand them.

By the time Charlie Company had spent a few months in the front line, violence had become commonplace, as had, according to some sources, murder of civilians. It was everyday practice to burn down entire villages and pour poison into wells providing drinking water. Even rape seemed to be tolerated.

On 14 March, some members of C Company were surprised by a booby trap. A sergeant, who had been well-liked, died as a result, one GI was blinded and a few others were wounded. The remaining soldiers were angry, calling for revenge for their fallen comrades. On the night of 15 March, following a service in memory of the dead man, Captain Medina briefed his seventy-five men on the action they would undertake the following morning. The mission was to make an assault on a village called My Lai 4 near an area in which the Viet Cong's 48th Battalion had been reported to be operating. My Lai, he told them, was a village of about seven hundred people and was bordered to the east by a drainage ditch while to the southern edge of the settlement there was a large plaza-type area that was used for village meetings. Dense vegetation made up the north and western perimeters of the village.

Medina informed the men that there would be no villagers in My Lai and that the only people they would be likely to encounter would be Viet Cong. Their orders were to blow up houses made of brick, set fire to those made of straw, kill livestock, poison wells and destroy the enemy.

The men left at 7.22 the next morning on board nine helicopters and by the time Charlie Company put down in a paddy field about 150 yards south of My Lai 4, helicopters had softened up the area with small arms fire. It seems likely that by the time they leapt from the helicopter, whatever Viet Cong had been in the vicinity of the village were long gone.

The plan was for Calley to lead his platoon into the village, followed by a second platoon led by Lieutenant Stephen Brooks. Medina, meanwhile, held another platoon back in reserve, ready to move in when the area had been secured. Overhead, two helicopters circled observing the action below, one containing Lieutenant Colonel Frank Barker, the other, Colonel Oran Henderson.

Calley's men had crossed the plaza area by eight o'clock and entered the village passing families boiling rice in front of their houses. The normal procedure was launched. People were dragged out of their homes and interrogated and houses were searched for signs of the Viet Cong. The violence began when one villager was bayoneted in the back. Then, a middle-aged man was thrown down a well and a grenade was tossed in after him. Around twenty elderly women kneeling on the ground in front of their temple were killed with bullets to the back of the head. Another eighty villagers were herded together in the plaza area, shouting desperately all the while, 'No VC! No VC!' with soldier Paul Meadlo guarding them. Calley said to Meadlo as he walked off to another part of the village, 'You know what I want you to do with them.' Ten minutes later, when Calley returnèd, he was furious. 'Haven't you got rid off them yet? I want them dead. Waste them!' Meadlo was a young farm boy who feared that he would be shot if he failed to obey orders and Calley had previously kicked him when he had disobeyed him. He opened fire on the villagers from a distance of between ten and fifteen feet, with Calley shooting beside him. Meadlo cried hysterically as he fired, desperately urging other soldiers to join in, eager to spread the blame and the guilt for something he knew was very wrong.

Captain Medina, meanwhile, was running back and forward amidst the chaos of the village, some said, although Medina claimed that he did not enter the village until the shooting had stopped, at around 10 am. He said he did not see anyone being killed. Others said he was right there in the midst of it at 9 am.

US Army photographer Ronald Haeberle had been sent along on the mission to photograph what was anticipated to be a significant encounter with a crack Viet Cong battalion. What he saw would horrify him at the time and later on would sicken the American public. 'Guys were about to shoot these people,' he said later. 'I yelled, "hold it", and shot my picture. As I walked away, I heard M16s open up. From the corner of my eye I saw bodies falling, but I didn't turn to look.' He also described seeing 'a little boy walking toward us in a daze. He'd been shot in the arm and leg. A GI fired three shots into the child.' He recalled seeing about thirty GIs kill around one hundred civilians and recounted how several GIs became angry at him when he attempted to photograph them fondling the breasts of a girl aged about fifteen.

Helicopter pilot Chief Warrant Officer Hugh Thompson alighted from his helicopter at around 9 am and was horrified by the bodies he saw lying around and the events still taking place around him, including children being shot at point-blank range.

Calley, meanwhile, was still on the rampage. About eighty people – old men, women and children – were gathered next to the drainage ditch. He ordered his men to push them into the ditch and then ordered them to open fire on them. Some obeyed him but a number refused. When a two-year-old child managed to get out of the ditch and start running back to the village, Calley grabbed him, threw him back into the ditch and shot him.

Thompson was beside himself with anger at what he was witnessing. He told Calley to hold his men there while he evacuated the survivors, ordering the men in the helicopters to fire on Calley and his men if they opened fire on the civilians. Placing himself between the civilians and the GIs, he waited until a helicopter landed and helped the nine survivors, including five children, onto the aircraft. He later plucked a baby from the arms of its dead mother and took it to safety.

By 11 am, the operation was complete. My Lai and its occupants had been wiped off the face of the map. That night the Viet Cong returned to the village and buried around five hundred villagers in three mass graves. The official reports of the action described it as a great success – 128 enemy dead and only one US casualty; a GI who had deliberately shot himself in the foot. Chief warrant Officer Thompson, however, had filed a complaint, alleging that war crimes had been committed. An investigation was undertaken, but the commander in charge of it, General Samuel Koster proclaimed himself satisfied after listening to testimony from a number of the GIs who had been present at My Lai. His report stated that only twenty civilians had been killed.

While in Vietnam, GI Ronald Ridenhour had heard eye-witness accounts of My Lai from other soldiers and decided to carry out his own investigation when he was discharged from the army in December 1968. He wrote to a number of people, including President Richard Nixon, the Joint Chiefs of Staff and a number of Congressmen, telling them what he had learned and asking for an official investigation.

In June 1969, William Calley was flown back from Vietnam and in September a number of charges were made against him, including six of premeditated murder.

The massacre became public knowledge in November when it was a cover story in both *Time* and *Newsweek* magazines. CBS also featured an interview with Paul Meadlo.

Meadlo had been discharged after losing a foot in a mine explosion a few days after My Lai. Charlie Company were on the side of a hill that Calley ordered them to climb although there was nothing to be gained from doing so. Most disobeyed the order and Meadlo was the only man to accompany him, acting as a mine-sweeper. Seeing that no one was following him, Calley went back down, ordering Meadlo to follow him but not to bother sweeping for mines as it would take too long. Almost immediately Meadlo stepped on a mine and his foot was blown off. Calley was struck in the face by a piece of shrapnel. As he was evacuated by helicopter, Meadlo screamed down at Calley, 'You'll get yours! God will punish you!' Ironically, both Meadlo and Calley were awarded with the Purple Heart medal for this incident.

Ultimately, only a few men would be court-martialled for what happened at My Lai and only one would actually be convicted – William Calley.

Medina was charged with the murder of 102 civilians, based on the theory of command responsibility – he was reckoned to be responsible for the actions of his men. Famous defence attorney, F. Lee Bailey, who would later defend O. J. Simpson, got him acquitted of all charges.

The evidence against Calley, however, was overwhelming. Paul Meadlo testified against him in a chillingly emotionless voice. Calley, called to the witness stand, blamed Medina, saying that at one point the captain had asked him why he hadn't wasted the civilians yet? Medina contradicted him, saying when he was asked at the 15 March briefing if women and children were to be killed he had answered, 'No, you do not kill women and children … Use common sense.'

The time it took the jury to reach a verdict – thirteen days – was the longest deliberation of any jury in the history of American court-martials but it delivered a guilty verdict – Calley was guilty of premeditated murder. He was sentenced 'to be confined at hard labour for the rest of your natural life; to be dismissed from the service; to forfeit all pay and allowances.'

It was not over, however. There was huge public disapproval of the verdict and President Nixon responded by removing Calley from the army prison after just one weekend's incarceration and placing him under house arrest. Nixon announced he was reviewing the sentence.

In 1974, William Calley was paroled.

THE KILLING FIELDS

The history of twentieth-century Cambodia can only be described as a major tragedy. At the height of this disastrous era, lies one particular period, mid 1975 to early 1979, the years when the Khmer Rouge ruled. Why were they called the 'Killing Fields'? It was the name given to a number of sites where the Khmer Rouge took people to execute them during their bloody reign. They killed at least 200,000 people in these killing fields, but their policies killed many more. It is believed that anything from 1.4 to 2.2 million people died as a direct result of policies of class war, extermination and ethnic cleansing, all of which created starvation and disease.

The architect of this collective national psychopathy that gripped Cambodia during this time was the leader of the Khmer Rouge – Pol Pot – the man who styled himself as 'Brother Number One'. He is estimated to have been responsible for the deaths of as many as twenty-six per cent of the entire population of his country.

Born on 19 May 1925 in Prek Sbauv in Kampong Thum province, Pol Pot was the son of a prosperous farmer. His family also had connections to the Cambodian royal family. Ironically, Pol Pot tried to impose an agrarian and social revolution on Cambodia, of which the peasant class was the heart, conveniently forgetting his own peasant connections.

The name Khmer Rouge (*red Khmer* – Khmer denoting somebody from Cambodia) was the label given to communist tendencies by Prince Norodom Sihanouk, who ruled Cambodia for sixteen years. Unhappy with French colonial rule, as in Vietnam, Sihanouk and his followers sparked indigenous political action.

We need to go back to 1930 to understand the background behind the mass killings that took place in Cambodia. Ho Chi Minh founded the Indochinese Communist Party (ICP) in an attempt to dispel the growing revolutionary ideas throughout Indochina. The fact the ICP was mainly a Vietnamese initiative, under the guidance of the USSR, would eventually become a significant issue. Cambodia and Laos sought to establish their own identity, rather than take orders from their Vietnamese comrades.

After the devastation of the Second World War, the ICP and Cambodian nationalists found common ground in trying to free Cambodia from French colonialism, but their efforts failed. By 1945, Ho Chi Minh had declared an independent Vietnam, which started the long road towards a self-governing communist state. Although the revolution was not so advanced in Cambodia, it was still a crucial period in the formation of Cambodian communism. Anti-French groups started to rebel against colonial rule and many of the future leaders of the Khmer Rouge, including Pol Pot, were involved at this time.

In 1951, the first Cambodian communist party, the Khmer People's Revolutionary Party (KPRP), formed in secret. Keen to maintain control of communism in Indochina, the Vietnamese did not consider the KPRP as a legitimate party. It wasn't long before communism in Cambodia was undermined under the terms of the 1954 Geneva conference, which forced Vietnam to agree to end their anti-colonial struggle.

The Cambodian king, Norodom Sihanouk, took advantage of the situation and began playing the different parties off against each other, suppressing with force any groups that he believed to be extremist. Buoyed by his successful crusade for independence, Sihanouk staged a *coup d'état* and formed his own political movement, the Sangkum. Sihanouk's attempts at repressing communist activities were not helped by high levels of communist defections to the Cambodian government.

By 1960, communism in Cambodia needed a new approach and in September the First Party Congress was held in Phnom Penh. Tou Samouth was elected their leader, with Pol Pot in the third most powerful position, of the party now called the Workers' Party of Kampuchea (WPK).

In 1962, Samouth mysteriously disappeared and was immediately replaced by Pol Pot. The following year, large offshoots of the WPK had moved out of the cities and into the jungle. It was here, under the guidance of Vietnam, that the party slowly but surely began to expand. It was at this time that Pol Pot started to feel resentment about the way the Vietnamese treated their 'inferior' comrades. Some left-wing elements of the WPK remained in Phnom Penh and became absorbed into Sinahouk's government. Sinahouk did not want them as part of his set up and turned on them, forcing them to flee Phnom Penh.

In 1967, following a revolt by peasants against an increased tax on rice, offshoots of the WPK, now called the Khmer Rouge, instigated a series of armed operations against the government. This escalated to such an extent that, for the next five years, Cambodia experienced a bloody and rather confusing civil war. As the war progressed, the Khmer Rouge army expanded, increasing their territory at the same time. The corrupt and ineffective Cambodian army were no match for the well-trained communist guerilla fighters, and the Khmer Rouge emerged victorious on 17 April 1975.

The success of the Khmer Rouge was not good news for Cambodia. Pol Pot's rule was both brutal and radical and Cambodia was turned into an autocratic nightmare. The country was completely sealed off from the outside world and then divided into two separate zones. All the major cities were evacuated and the inhabitants forced to move to the countryside and learn the peasant's way of life. Religion was effectively banned, money became worthless overnight, and all the citizens were required to obey the orders of the organisation (Angkar).

The Khmer Rouge were so confident that they believed they could create communism in one giant leap. In the next three years, thousands of people were exterminated in an attempt to purify the revolution, while many more died from malnutrition and famine. The first significant killings took place in the Northern zone, Northwestern zone and finally the Eastern zone.

The fields in which these vast number of people had to work became known as the 'Killing Fields'. The peasants effectively became slaves to the Khmer Rouge and if they didn't die from overwork or malnutrition, disease finished the job. They had to survive on as little as 180 grams of rice each day. Work started at four o'clock in the morning and ended at ten at night. They were constantly watched by armed guards, who were ready to fire at the slightest provocation.

To the Khmer Rouge, life was cheap. They estimated they would need around two million people to build their new agrarian communist utopia, and the rest of the population were superfluous. Hundreds of thousands of people were forced to dig their own graves while shackled, and then beaten to death with iron bars or their own farm implements, as the soldiers had been told not to waste their precious ammunition.

Before Pol Pot came to rule, he had actually compiled a list of people to be killed following the Khmer Rouge victory. Originally it only contained seven names, but then expanded to twenty-three incorporating all senior government leaders and the leaders of the army and police. Then the list expanded to include anyone who was wealthy or educated. Buddhist monks, teachers, doctors, laywers and government officials were killed, and even their families were not exempt from the Pol Pot paranoia. The crippled and disabled were considered to be worthless, and Pol Pot even stooped as low as having many of his own colleagues either axed or shot to death.

Like any organisation, there were elements of the Khmer Rouge that did not totally support Pol Pot. Needless to say many of these objectors were simply wiped out, and the majority of party members who died were in fact loyal to the revolution but had fallen victim to Pol Pot's own paranoia.

Over twenty thousand victims were sent to an old school in a suburb of Phnom Penh, called Tuol Sleng, which was where the Khmer Rouge had their main prison camp. To be held in a detention centre meant almost certain death, and to be 'accused' meant they had already been found 'guilty'. The prisoners were subjected to ritual torture and then forced to sign false confessions, admitting to their betrayal of the revolution. Then they were led away blindfolded, told to turn around leaving them standing on the edge of a pit, and then killed by a blow to the head with a spade.

By 1978, the ever-increasing clashes between the Khmer Rouge and their Vietnamese comrades, escalated into a full scale war. In December, Vietnam invaded Cambodia and just two months later they were victorious. They forced what remained of the Khmer Rouge, including their leader Pol Pot, to flee to the Thai-Cambodia border. Pol Pot remained in Thailand for the next six years, where be spent his time trying to regroup his flailing organisation. He eventually resigned from the party in 1985, due to ill health, but remained de factor leader of the Khmer Rouge.

The Khmer Rouge continued to fight government forces in the mountainous jungle near the Thai border, but in 1966 almost half of the guerillas broke away from their ruthless leadership and made a deal with the Phnom Penh government. Pol Pot had passed the day-to-day running of the remaining Khmer Rouge to Son Sen, whom he had hand picked for the job. However, when Son Sen tried to make a settlement with the government in 1997, Pol Pot slipped back into his old habits and had him executed. He also ordered the killing of eleven members of his family.

Later the same year, a group led by General Ta Mok, known as 'the butcher', came close to negotiating a similar deal with the government. The now ageing Pol Pot got wind of the deal, and started a bloody purge of the Khmer Rouge ranks. This last action ended up with Pol Pot being put 'on trial' in what the Khmer Rouge described as a people's tribunal. He was sentenced to house arrest and three of his close associates were executed. When pictures appeared on a television network of the trial, it was the first time the outside world had got a glimpse of Pol Pot in years.

Just as the news broke that Pol Pot was to be handed over to an international tribunal for trial on charges of genocide, the man pulled the final trump card. He was found dead the following morning. Although it was reported that he died of heart failure, there were rumours that he had either committed suicide or been poisoned. No one will ever really know as his body was cremated within days of his death before anyone got a chance to inspect it.

Many Khmer Rouge defectors said that without Pol Pot there would be no Khmer Rouge. It is certainly true that the guerilla organisation started to collapse as a result of internal factionalism, frustration at poverty and ideological decay. In fact the group ended up fighting itself.

Even today, the Khmer Rouge's legacy of death, starvation and suffering can still be witnessed across much of Cambodia. It is most visible in the piles of skulls and bones littered across the country, but it can also be seen in the countless numbers of unexploded landmines. Many Cambodians still suffer from psychological problems because they simply cannot forget what they saw. New human remains turn up around the exhumed mass graves of the Killing Fields on a daily basis. These are continuous, if silent, reminders of the tragedy. Bones and teeth are ceremoniously placed into makeshift shrines in tree hollows or cement planters.

You only have to look around Cambodia to realise that the population is suspiciously young – as many as fifty per cent are under the age of fifteen. The economy is in shambles, which is partially due to the

Khmer Rouge's execution of the upper and educated classes.

During their three year and eight month reign of Cambodia, the Khmer Rouge committed some of the most heinous crimes in modern history. An estimated two million people lost their lives during this period and it is still hard to comprehend the motivations behind such an atrocity.

DR WOUTER BASSON AND JOHAN THERON

To the outside world, Dr Wouter Basson was nothing more than an eminent South African cardiologist and military surgeon. If you were a member of the ANC, struggling against the South African government's apartheid regime in the 1970s and 1980s, however, he was Doctor Death, the embodiment of evil, perverting his medical knowledge on behalf of a top-secret government initiative that he headed, known as Project Coast.

South Africa had been involved in the development of chemical weapons since the First World War. However, the 1925 Geneva Convention banned such weapons and the threat from other countries to which the South African government was responding, diminished. The programme continued, regardless, and during the Second World War, the government ignored the Geneva Convention and its programme was stepped up to counter the threat of the Nazis. After the war, it focused on producing tear gas, CX powder and mustard gas. As the threat of the Communist take-over of neighbouring Angola and Mozambique increased, the South African government felt a need to develop chemical weapons.

In 1981, Dr Wouter Basson was hired to visit other countries to examine similar programmes and report back. His recommendation was that South Africa should increase its work in this area and Project Coast was initiated with him as head.

Project Coast covered a multitude of sins. In the late 1970s, South Africa was deeply involved in the Angolan civil war, taking action against Soviet-backed troops from the South West Africa People's Organisation, Cuba and Angola itself. The Soviets also sponsored the African National Congress and were keen to get an interest in southern Africa's mineral wealth – diamonds, titanium and zirconium oxide. In the face of a perceived threat that their enemy had access to chemical and biological weapons, the South African government Project Coast became an important initiative.

It had other uses, too. The government was keen to devise a better way of dealing with its internal problems and Project Coast was tasked with coming up with chemical means of crowd control and the dispersal of rioters. Gradually, the emphasis moved from defensive capability to offensive.

It was to remain secret and in order to maintain its covert status, Basson formed four front companies – Delta G Scientific Company, responsible for the research, development and production of the materials; Roodeplaat Research Laboratories, a testing facility; Protechnik, a large and highly secretive nuclear, biological and chemical warfare plant; and Infladel, dealing mainly with the financial and administrative aspects of the companies. These were created for a number of reasons. Firstly, to maintain a distance between Project Coast and the South African military. Secondly, to obtain chemical and biological substances; the military would not have been allowed to purchase such materials. The front companies were also valuable in their use for channelling funds secretly from defence accounts to research facilities. Basson controlled all aspects of the initiative, recruiting around two hundred medical and scientific researchers from around the world, many of whom had little idea that they were involved in the development and use of chemical and biological weapons. He also controlled the $10 million budget provided for the project and was left to operate virtually unsupervised due to the lack of scientific or medical knowledge of his superiors.

Amongst the lethal offensive agents that were created were anthrax, botulinum, cholera, plague, ricin, E. coli, Ebola and Marburg virus. Research was also carried out to find out whether there were agents that would work only on non-white people. As the Soviet Union had done, everyday objects were created that actually contained the lethal toxins and these were to be used in assassinations. Umbrellas and walking sticks were made that fired poison pellets, syringes were disguised as screwdrivers and cans of beer and envelopes were also made lethal by the addition of poisons.

Although a number of projected assassination attempts failed to come to pass, such as giving Nelson Mandela an agent that would develop cancer in him before he could be released from prison, many did. Basson is thought to have eliminated hundreds of enemies of the government using deadly toxins. In 1987, a South African Airways plane, Flight 295, suffered a catastrophic fire, crashing into the sea off Mauritius. The investigation into Basson's activities found a receipt showing that 300 grams of a highly volatile, carbon-based substance had been placed on the aircraft before take-off, possibly by representatives of Project Coast.

During Basson's trial, testimony was provided by a former information officer in South Africa's Special Forces whose superior was Dr Basson. Fifty-seven-year-old Johan Theron told the court that he had

117

personally caused or supervised the murder of more than two hundred anti-apartheid political prisoners between 1979 and 1987. The deaths were a solution to the increasing overcrowding of South Africa's prisons due to the number of anti-apartheid activists being arrested. He disposed of these men by strangling, burning, beating, poisoning and strangulation. He did it all on the orders of Dr Wouter Basson.

He explained how in northern Kwazulu-Natal in 1983, he was ordered by Basson to tie three prisoners to a tree and smear their bodies with lethal toxins that were in a jelly-like form. He was ordered to leave them overnight to see if the men were killed by the substance. Next day, when he was disappointed to find them still alive, he loaded them onto a small plane and flew out over the ocean, injecting them with muscle relaxants en route before throwing them out of the craft into the sea about 100 miles from land. He disposed of many people in this way, he testified.

Poisoning was his favourite method of dispatch, however, and he injected his victims with fatal cocktails of drugs, often directly into the heart. The drugs were supplied by Basson and, on occasion, the doctor was also involved in personally administering them.

Retired French Foreign Legionnaire, Chris Pessarra, recalled seeing Basson injecting poison into the stomachs of political prisoners – five guerrillas of the Zimbabwe African National Liberation Army – before they were thrown from a plane. Before they were thrown out, however, they were dressed in camouflage uniforms, had rifles strung around their shoulders and had false papers stuffed into their pockets. They were also sprayed with a powdery substance, an unknown chemical agent that was intended to infect other enemy soldiers who might find them. It is estimated that around twenty-four such flights were undertaken.

In the late 1980s, Basson was hired by the Civil Cooperation Bureau (CCB), a covert, Special Forces organisation, run by South African Defence Minister, General Magnus Malan, founded to prevent popular black military leaders from taking over the government. He is thought to have supplied the CCB with chemical weapons and has been linked to several assassination attempts.

The clothes of the Reverend Frank Chikane, an anti-apartheid activist and General Secretary of the South African Council of Churches, were soaked with a lethal nerve agent that had been produced, it is believed at one of Basson's companies. There is little doubt, as claimed by South Africa's Truth and Reconciliation Commission, that Basson was behind that attempted assassination, as well as the failed attempt to kill ANC government Justice Minister, Dullah Omar.

In the 1980s Basson continued to travel the world making contacts and researching other countries' development of chemical weapons. On his travels, it is thought that he set up numerous companies through which he and colleagues could launder millions of dollars skimmed off activities relating to Project Coast.

When Nelson Mandela was released from prison in 1990 and the prospect of a black majority government looked ever more likely, the future of Project Coast became threatened. The South African Defence Force and Basson began producing huge quantities of non-lethal drugs – Ecstasy, the sedative Mandrax or Quaaludes, CR, a powerful and irritating riot control agent and BZ, a psychoactive incapacitant. Some of these were never accounted for, presumably exported for a huge profit. In 1991 Basson asked for $2.4 million to import five hundred kilos of ecstasy into South Africa. It is believed there may have been two reasons for the importing and production of the drug. It may have been to temporarily incapacitate rioters by incorporating it in tear gas and it may also have been planned to distribute it in black townships to increase drug dependency.

The drug BZ was apparently used by South African forces in Mozambique in 1992 when it is thought to have been released from a plane flying over several hundred Mozambique government troops. Within half an hour of the plane passing overhead, many of the soldiers had become sick. Four died and large numbers of them were hospitalised.

This incident alerted the British and American governments to the dangers of Project Coast and they began to put pressure on the South African government to end it. Finally, in 1993, the programme was cut. Basson was given early retirement but concerns remained that he would sell his secrets to the highest bidder. There is still concern that Basson did not destroy all chemical weapons agents, as ordered by President de Klerk, and, instead, he simply moved them to another location to be sold to another country. Certainly, hundreds of kilos of materials are unaccounted for.

In 1995, Basson was re-employed by Nelson Mandela's new South African government as a defence force surgeon. It is likely that they felt they could exercise more control over his activities if he was working for them.

When the Truth and Reconciliation Commission brought many of Basson's activities to people's attention for the first time, he decided to flee the country, but the CIA tipped off the South African government. He was arrested later that month in Pretoria in a sting operation and in his possession they found one thousand ecstasy tablets and a huge number of documents relating to Project Coast. They also found a menu of items produced by his companies such as cigarettes impregnated with anthrax, botulinum-laced milk and poisoned whisky and chocolates. It appeared that he was selling his knowledge to countries such as Iraq and Libya.

After an appearance at the Truth and Reconciliation Commission, Basson was put on trial in October 1999. He faced sixty-seven charges which included murder, fraud, theft and drug possession. A week into the trial, however, the judge controversially dismissed six of the charges including two charges of murder and four of conspiracy to murder because, he said, he could not rule on crimes committed in other countries. They were vital because they were the only charges that actually placed him directly at the heart of a crime. Eighteen months after the trial had started, the number of charges against him was dropped to forty-six and then on 11 April 2002, all the remaining charges were dropped. Many thought that the South African justice system had let down the people.

Basson now spends his time lecturing on cardiology, biological warfare and stress management.

SLOBODAN MILOSEVIC

Slobodan Milosevic was the first European head of state to be prosecuted for genocide and war crimes. As Europe rang out in 1989 with the promise of the revolutions in the east, he hovered like a dark cloud on the horizon of European hope, the most dangerous person to emerge on the continent since the Second World War.

For eight years, from 1991 to 1999, Milosevic perpetrated mass murder and hellish chaos in southeastern Europe, the leader of a gang of callous villains who set little value on human life, especially if you were not a Serbian. The roll-call of places where Milosevic carried out his evil deeds will long be remembered – Srebrenica, Vukovar, Sarajevo, Dubrovnik, Banja Luka and Pristina.

Milosevic ultimately betrayed just about everyone who had ever worked with him or served him, including his general, Ratko Mladic and the Bosnian

Serb leader, Radovan Karadzic. He abandoned the Serbs of Croatia, Bosnia and Kosovo when they were no longer of any use to him. He was also responsible for the deaths of a number of his friends and opponents. Some such as Ivan Stambolic had been friends and supporters and arguably it was Stambolic who enabled him to rise to power. In late August 2000, Stambolic mysteriously disappeared while Milosevic was still President of Yugoslavia. His body was found on a mountain, Fruska Gora, in March 2003. In 2005, eight Special Operations Unit officers were convicted of his abduction and murder. It was revealed that the order for his death had come directly from Slobodan Milosevic. Other political murders that can be ascribed to him are those of senior police official, Radovan Stojijic Badza, Defence Minister Pavle Bulatovic, and the head of the Yugoslav national airline.

His legacy was two hundred thousand people dead in Bosnia and two million homeless, and he introduced the world to the practice of ethnic cleansing, evicting more than eight hundred thousand Albanians from their homes in Kosovo.

Milosevic was born in 1941 in Pozarevac in Serbia to parents who separated not long after the war and who would both later commit suicide, his father in 1962 and his mother, a Yugoslav Communist Party activist, in 1974. He was a serious child who worked hard at school and preferred the company of older children but his constant companion was Mirjana Markovic whose father and uncle were prominent members of Tito's partisans during the war and important people in his postwar regime. Her aunt was Tito's secretary and was also said be his lover. Milosevic and Mirjana would later marry.

At the University of Belgrade, where he studied law, he became involved in the Yugoslav Communist League's student branch and became friends with Ivan Stambolic, five years his senior, whose uncle Petar Stambolic had been President of the Serbian Executive Council – effectively prime minister. This was a vital connection for Milosevic as Stambolic was instrumental in his rise through the Communist League's ranks. Following university, he worked as an economic adviser to the Mayor of Belgrade and in 1968 took a job with Technogas, succeeding Stambolic as head of the company, following him to Beobanka, one of Yugoslavia's biggest banks, where he also succeeded Stambolic at the top.

Meanwhile, he had progressed steadily through the Yugoslav Communist machine, still enjoying the sponsorship of Ivan Stambolic; when Stambolic became head of the Serbian Communist Party in 1984, Milosevic replaced him as head of the Belgrade party.

Milosevic was nothing, however, if not ruthless and loyalty and friendship meant little to him. In September 1987, he obtained the support of the Yugoslav army and the party apparatus in conducting a purge of all Stambolic supporters in the Serbian party, installing his own men in their place. Stambolic was ousted from his position and retired from politics a few months later, a Milosevic puppet replacing him as Serbian President. Milosevic would seize the office of president for himself in 1990 and occupy it until 1997 when he became President of Yugoslavia.

President Tito had held together the Yugoslav federation since the Second World War, but when he died in 1980, the numerous disparate states and ethnicities that made up the federation began to come apart. Tito had put a great deal of effort into maintaining the country's ethnic balance and especially into ensuring that the largest ethnic group, the Serbs, did not dominate the federation. To help achieve this, he had made two provinces within Serbia – Vojvodina and Kosovo – autonomous.

He had also grabbed control of Belgrade television and the old Belgrade newspaper, *Politika*. He was keenly aware of the power of the media and he added it to the other instruments of his growing power – the party machine, the security services, the army and the leaders of industry. Now, he needed the support of the people and it would be Nationalism, not Communism, that would provide that.

In the 1980s, antagonism between the Serbs and Kosovan Albanians deepened. Milosevic was sent to deliver a speech in the town of Kosovo Polje on 24 April 1987 but while he was holding meetings inside the town hall, a crowd of Serb and Montenegrin demonstrators fought outside with the local police force, made up mainly of Kosovan Albanians. When the crowd began to hurl stones at the police, the authorities responded in kind, drawing their batons and beating demonstrators with them.

Milosevic went out to try to calm the situation and famously told the demonstrators, who explained that they had been attacked by the police, 'You will not be beaten'. This became a significant statement and some suggest that from that moment on, the end of Yugoslavia was inevitable.

A couple of years later, he was back in Kosovo to mark the 600th anniversary of the battle in which the Ottoman Empire conquered Serbia, leading to five hundred years of rule by the Turks. A million Serbs turned up to hear him speak and he did not let them down – he told them to prepare for war.

He launched the so-called Anti-bureaucratic Revolution in Vojvodina and Montenegro, a series of demonstrations and rallies staged between July 1988 and March 1989 that led to the fall of the governments of those two autonomous republics and their replacement by governments filled with Milosevic supporters.

Milosevic used the media to demonise the non-Serbian states of the federation who were now agitating for separation from it. He presented the Croats as genocidal fascists, the Bosnian Muslims as Islamic fundamentalists and the Kosovan Albanians as rapists and terrorists. The Slovenes were secessionist puppets of Germany; the Germans and Austrians, according to him, were aiming to destroy Serbia and incorporate it in a Fourth Reich. The rest of the world did not escape his paranoid ranting – the Americans were, of course, imperialists, the Turks were nostalgic for the days when they ruled the region and the Iranians were fomenting Islamic terrorism in the Balkans.

In January 1987, he also gained the support for his Nationalist stance from the intellectuals of the Serbian Academy who issued a memorandum demanding the extension of Serbia into the other Yugoslav republics – Croatia and Bosnia, in particular – to incorporate the 2 million Serbs living in them. In other words they were pushing for a Greater Serbia. The memorandum detailed the numerous grievances that Serbs felt as a part of Yugoslavia – Yugoslavia taking industry out of

Serbia; Albanians committing genocide against Serbians; Serbia sacrificed 2,500,000 people in the Second World War and was now a victim of the state and so on.

Milosevic adopted it as his programme and his desire to create a Greater Serbia became the basis of the war crimes charges of which he was accused at the Hague. He planned to do this, the indictment states, by creating a centralised Serbian state that incorporated Serb-dominated parts of Bosnia, Croatia and Serbia after non-Serbs had been ethnically cleansed. He was alleged to have committed atrocities in trying to create an ethnically pure Serbia.

Following the collapse of communism in Yugoslavia in 1990, multiparty elections were held in each of the six republics that made up the country. Milosevic's Socialist Party easily retained power in Serbia but in almost all the other republics secessionist governments were brought to power. The Federation began to come apart at the seams.

Fighting began in April 1992 and critics blame his incitement of Serbian Nationalism and religious and ethnic hatred as the reasons for the years of bloody fighting that followed.

No records have been discovered containing direct orders from Milosevic to his military leaders to commit atrocities. But it is clear and damning that he made no effort to punish those responsible. These included such men as Ratko Mladic who was accused of atrocities against Croats in Vukovar. Serb militias overran the city in November 1991 and massacred 264 people, aged between sixteen and seventy-seven, all non-Serbs, some of whom were civilians and others prisoners of war. Instead of being punished, Mladic was sent to lead the Bosnian Serb Army.

At Srebrenica, in Bosnia and Herzegovina, he would be responsible for one of the war's bloodiest atrocities when his paramilitary group, the Scorpions, participated in the massacre of eight thousand Bosnian men and boys, the largest mass murder in Europe since the Second World War. Milosevic refused to believe that Mladic was responsible for these crimes and some have claimed that they occurred without his knowledge or were beyond his control. Nonetheless, the indifference he showed towards them was culpable.

By late 1995, sanctions imposed by the United Nations were destroying the Serbian economy – unemployment was at forty per cent and the quality of life in Serbia was terrible. Milosevic was forced to agree a peace plan in talks at Dayton in the United States. In an attempt to improve his image, he began speaking of tolerance amongst ethnic groups and projected himself, incredibly, as a peacemaker.

In 1997, his second and final term was coming to an end but he manipulated the constitution to ensure another term of office, renaming himself President of the Yugoslav Federation instead of President of Serbia. In 1999 he refused to withdraw troops he had sent into Kosovo to stop an independence movement. As a result, NATO planes bombed Serbia for two and a half months.

In July 2000, Yugoslavia's federal parliament passed changes to the constitution that would enable Milosevic to serve two further four-year terms as president. By now, however, there was a growing popular revolt against his leadership and he had little option but to resign. Six months later, he was arrested after he had threatened to kill himself, his wife and his daughter.

In late 2001, he was sent to The Hague to face crimes against humanity brought by the International Criminal Tribunal for the Former Yugoslavia. Amongst the charges against him, he was accused of violating the laws or customs of war, serious breaches of the Geneva Conventions and genocide in Bosnia. He defended himself while refusing to recognise the legality of the court in which he was being tried.

As the trial proceeded, Milosevic became increasingly ill with high blood pressure and flu which caused delays. On 11 March 2006, he was found dead in his cell at the war crimes tribunal's detention centre in Scheveningen in The Hague. He had died of a heart attack. Some were surprised that he even had a heart!

RADOVAN KARADZIC

In July 2008, when they finally found him he was no longer the swaggering, fatigue-wearing, war-mongering leader of the Bosnian Serbs, the 'Butcher of Bosnia'. His hair was no longer wild and windswept and the jaw seemed less jutting. Instead, he looked more like Professor Dumbledore from the *Harry Potter* books – he wore large spectacles, an enormous bushy white beard and very long, shoulder-length hair, tied in a pony-tail with a strange little black tuft on the top of his head. He was a practitioner of alternative medicine working in a clinic in Belgrade under the name of Dragon Drabic. It was a strange place for this alleged mass murderer to turn up. He is allegedly responsible for the deaths of some 200,000 Muslim opponents and the displacement of around a million people and had been wanted for crimes against humanity. For a number of years, he had been lecturing on alternative medicine at local community centres and had led an open life.

Anyone who had met Karadzic and worked with him were shocked, describing the man as friendly and open. They found it hard to believe he could be the same man responsible for the notorious Srebrenica massacre, one of Post-war Europe's most shameful episodes, in which more than eight thousand Muslim men of fighting age were massacred.

Despite being one of the most wanted men in the world, Karadzic's disguise was so effective, it took almost thirteen years for the authorities to bring him to justice. Ironically though, the architect of Serbian cleansing, was not even born in Bosnia or Serbia, but in Savnik, Montenegro, in June 1945. He was raised in a remote mountain village and was influenced by his father's political status from a young age. His father, Vuko Karadzic, was a member of the Chetniks, a Serbian nationalist/royalist paramilitary organisation, formed during the Second World War to oppose the Nazi regime. Vuko spent most of his son's young life in prison.

Karadzic left home when he was fifteen years old, travelling to Sarajevo to study medicine. He eventually qualified as a psychiatrist and was also attached to Sarajevo's football team. While studying in Sarajevo, Karadzic met his wife Ljiljana, who was also studying medicine. After qualifying Karadzic obtained a job as a psychiatrist in the city's hospital.

Karadzic also demonstrated an artistic side, painting, composing folk music and writing poetry. In fact four volumes of his mordant verses were published, gloomy harbingers of the massacres to come. However, despite his literary pretensions, Karadzic was not accepted by Sarajevo's cultural elite. They looked down on the man who came from the mountainous region of Montenegro, and treated him as a lower-class citizen. For this Karadzic would eventually wreak a terrible revenge.

While in his 'poetic' phase, Karadzic fell under the influence of the Serb nationalist writer Dobrica Cosic, who encouraged him to go into politics. Many years later, after briefly working for the Green Party, Karadzic helped to set up the Serbian Democratic Party (SDS), which was formed in 1990 in response to the rise of nationalist and Croat parties in Bosnia. Its ultimate goal was the creation of a 'greater' Serbia.

Almost two years later, Bosnia Hercegovina gained recognition as an independent state. Karadzic declared the creation of the independent Serbian Republic of Bosnia and Hercegovina with its capital in Pale, and put himself as head of state. Karadzic saw himself as a statesman who would literally reshape Balkan history in his own dark and brutal way. Just like his mentor, the Serbian leader Slobodan Milosevic, Karadzic loved all the attention he received in his new elevated position. He drew up maps of Sarajevo, and foresaw the city being partitioned into Serb and Muslim sections which would be divided by a modern-day Berlin wall, where checkpoints would control access. Unlike Milosevic, who exploited Serbian nationalism, Karadzic did actually believe in the Greater Serbia project. He aimed to unite the Serbs of Serbia with their brethren in neighbouring Bosnia and Croatia.

Supported by Milosevic, Karadzic organised Serbs to fight against the Bosniaks and Croats in Bosnia – a vicious war ensued.

SREBRENICA MASSACRE

The events that took place at Srebrenica marked the climax of the war, and became the most vicious and genocidal battlefront in the Balkans conflict. One of the largest massacres in the conflict took place at a gymnasium in the village of Bratunac in April 1992. It is estimated that three hundred and fifty Bosnian Muslims were tortured to death by Serb paramilitaries and special police. Bratunac lay just outside Srebrenica and, although the Serbs were able to seize Bratunac they were not able to control Srebrenica itself. The city was defended by a Rambo-like figure called Naser Oric, whose troops and associated vigilante squads, inflicted a number of smaller atrocities in villages around Srebrenica. In April 1993, Serb forces closed in for their final assault on the town and they made no secret of the fact that they held a special grudge against the menfolk of Srebrenica.

As the soldiers approached Srebrenica, panic took hold among the local civilians, tens of thousands of whom had already taken refuge from earlier Serb offensives. The refugees were under the protection of about six hundred lightly-armed Dutch infantry soldiers. However, fuel was running seriously low and they had had no fresh food for many months.

As the Serb forces started shelling Srebrenica, many of the Bosnian Muslim men asked for the return of weapons they had surrendered to the peace-keepers, but their request was refused. As the Serbs stepped up their attack, thousands of refugees fled the town but many more found their escape routes blocked. By evening around four thousand refugees were left in the town and panic was growing. Large crowds gathered around the places where the Dutch were defending their posts. By midday the following day, more than twenty thousand refugees had managed to reach the Dutch base at Potocari.

As the Serb commander, Ratko Mladic, entered Srebrenica, he issued an ultimatum that all Muslims must hand over their weapons to save their lives. The Serbs sent buses to collect the women and children, while all men were singled out aged between twelve and seventy-seven for what the Serbs called 'interrogation for suspected war crimes'.

Within the next thirty hours it is estimated that as many as twenty-three thousand women and children were deported from Srebrenica, while hundreds of men were held prisoners in trucks and warehouses. Around fifteen thousand Bosnian Muslim fighters attempted to escape, but they were shelled as they fled through the mountains.

The first mass killings of unarmed Muslims took place in a warehouse in a nearby village, Kravica. The Dutch made a deal with the Serbs by handing over five thousand refugees in return for the release of fourteen Dutch peacekeepers. Rumours started to spread of mass killings as the first survivors of the long march from Srebrenica began to arrive in Muslim-held territory. In the five days that Bosnian forces held Srebrenica, it is believed that more than eight thousand Muslim men were killed.

Some of these mass killings were carried out at night under arc lights, and industrial bulldozers then pushed the bodies into mass graves. Some of the victims were still alive when they were buried. Serb forces killed and tortured refugees at will and streets were littered with their corpses. The panic was so great many people committed suicide to avoid having their noses, lips and ears chopped off, while others were forced to watch as the soldiers cold-bloodedly killed their children.

The events at Srebrenica marked the climax of the war in Bosnia-Herzegovina. The signing of the 1995 Dayton peace accords not only brought peace to Bosnia, but it also marked the end of Karadzic's role in the whole heinous affair. By 1995, his power had begun to waver and he was finally indicted, along with the Bosnian Serb leader Ratko Mladic, by the United Nations' Internal Criminal Tribunal on charges of genocide. Karadzic was obliged to step down as president of the SDS in 1996 and he went into hiding. To the Bosnian Serbs, he was a hero, and no more guilty of war crimes than any other military leader during a time of war.

While Karadzic was a fugitive, he managed to get a book published in October 2004, entitled *Miraculous Chronicles of the Night.* It was set in Yugoslavia in the 1980s and told a story of a man jailed by mistake after the death of former Yugoslav leader Josip Broz Tito. He managed to live underground for years, surrounded by his bodyguards, mocking the west's efforts to capture him. Added to his book, he also wrote a stage play called *Situation,* about the west's feeble efforts to capture him, which was staged in Belgrade.

During his years in secure hide-outs, Karadzic could look back on the war years with satisfaction, showing no remorse whatsoever for all the innocent lives that were lost, describing them as 'his greatest triumphs'. In Bosnian cities such as Banja Luka, which was the epicentre to the ethnic cleansing, he is still regarded with both awe and reverence. Stallholders make a good living out of selling T-shirts and key-rings emblazoned with his image.

In July 2005, Karadzic's son, Aleksandar, was arrested, but was released ten days later. Later the same month his wife, Ljiljana called upon her husband to give himself up, following what she described as 'enormous pressure' being put on her. Despite her pleas, Karadzic was not arrested until 21 July 2008.

When the news of his arrest reached Sarajevo, thousands of people took to the streets carrying the Bosnian flag that had been used during the period from 1992 to 1998. Although Karadzic is no longer with his loyal supporters, Mladic still remains at large. Only when he too is captured, can Serbia truly close their doors on one of the darkest chapters in their modern history.

OSAMA BIN LADEN

The first major international terrorist attack on American soil occurred on 26 February 1993, when a huge truck bomb exploded in the underground garage of the World Trade Center in New York. Six people died in the attack and over a thousand were injured. Four men were arrested by the FBI within a matter of weeks and charged with the bombings. They were all militant Muslims, most of them had fought against the Soviet Union in Afghanistan and all of them had one critical thing in common – Osama bin Laden, the head of the loosely organised terrorist network, al Qaeda.

Al Qaeda was founded in 1988 by Osama bin Laden in an effort to consolidate the international network he had established during the Afghan war. The organisation's goals were not only to advance Islamic revolutions throughout the Muslim world but also to repel any foreign intervention in the Middle East.

Bin Laden had been behind other attacks. His al Qaeda was involved in the bombing of two hotels in

Aden, Yemen, which targeted American troops en route to Somalia on a humanitarian and peace-keeping mission. It also gave considerable assistance to Somali militias, whose efforts brought the eventual withdrawal of US forces in 1994. Bin Laden was also directly involved in an assassination attempt against Egyptian president Hosni Musbarak in Ethiopia in June 1995. Two major terrorist attacks followed against the US military in Saudia Arabia, one in November 1995 which was an attack in Riyadh. The second in June 1996 when the Khobar Towers were bombed.

Not long after the Khobar Towers attack, bin Laden issued a twelve-page document that was an effective declaration of war on the United States. In it, he wrote:

> 'Muslims burn with anger at America. For its own good, America should leave [Saudi Arabia] . . . There is no more important duty than pushing the American enemy out of the holy land . . . The presence of the USA Crusader military forces on land, sea and air of the states of the Islamic Gulf is the greatest danger threatening the largest oil reserve in the world.'

Bin Laden was the son of a billionaire Saudi business-man, Muhammed bin Laden, and his tenth wife. By building up his construction business in the 1930s, his father had made his family the richest non-royal household in the kingdom. Muhammed became known as the royal builder after King Faisal issued a royal decree that awarded all future construction projects to his company. The company went from strength to strength until it was worth in excess of $5 billion. Tragedy struck the family in 1968, when bin Laden's father died in a plane crash, leaving his sons in charge of the family business. They followed in their father's footsteps and expanded the business into Egypt, eventually employing some forty thousand people.

Bin Laden was affected deeply by the death of his father and had to adjust to life with his mother and new stepfather. He was raised in the Sunni Muslim faith and attended a school for the sons of wealthy Saudis. He continued his education at King Abdulaziz University where he developed a keen interest in religion.

He was married for the first time at the age of seventeen to Najwa Ghanem, and he is believed to have had four wives by the time he was forty-five. Bin Laden was a strong believer in Sharia Law and considers that the time when the Taliban ruled in Afghanistan was 'the only Islamic country in the world'. 'Jihad', or holy war, is, in his mind, the only way to achieve goals and any enemies of the Jihad should be wiped off the face of the earth.

With these beliefs strong in his mind, bin Laden left University in 1979 and travelled to Afghanistan. Here he joined the Mujahadeen of Abdullah Azzam, a Palestinian Muslim Brotherhood leader. Together they ran one of seven main militias set up to fight the Soviet invasion. They established military training bases in Afghanistan and founded Maktab Al Khidamat, or Services Office, which was a support network that provided both recruits and money through worldwide centres, including the USA.

However, bin Laden and Azzam had different visions for their network. Bin Laden formed Al Qaeda, based on personal affiliations created during the fighting in Afghanistan, his own international network, his powerful reputation and also his access to vast sums of money. It was during this time that bin Laden met Ayman al-Zawahiri who would become his collaborator in al Qaeda in the years ahead.

The following year his associate Azzam was assassinated. When the war came to an end, the Afghan-Arabs either returned to their own countries or joined conflicts taking place in Somalia, the Balkans and Chechnya. This benefited al Qaeda's global connections and also helped to cultivate the second and third generations of al Qaeda terrorists.

Bin Laden returned to Saudi Arabia in 1990, and was greeted as a hero for his victory over the Soviets. It was around this time that Saddam Hussein's Iraqi forces invaded Kuwait and bin Laden offered to defend Saudi Arabia against the threat of invasion. Saudi, however, rejected his offer which caused bin Laden to speak openly about his disapproval of their dependence on the United States, forcing Saudi to make moves to silence him.

Feeling insecure, bin Laden decided to resettle in Khartoum in Sudan, where he established a new Mujahideen base. Bin Laden's constant criticism of King Fahd of Saudi Arabia led the Saudis to withdraw his passport, revoke his citizenship and also stopped his family allowance of approximately seven million dollars a year. Added to this, the Saudis were also keen to get rid of bin Laden due to constant pressure from other countries. Bin Laden got wind of his unwanted presence in Sudan and, having survived one assassination attempt, decided to return to Afghanistan in May 1996. Although his organisation was considerably weakened, he was welcomed by the Taliban leader Mullah Mohammed Omar, and bin Laden concentrated on rebuilding his resources. Back in Afghanistan he worked closely with the Egyptian Islamic Jihad (EIJ), and it was this organisation that would form the basis for his al Qaeda.

Between 1991 and 1996, bin Laden's al Qaeda took part in several major terror attacks as mentioned in the opening paragraphs. Also, after moving to Afghanistan, bin Laden concentrated his efforts on his anti-American rhetoric. When interviewed in July 1996, bin Laden openly praised the Riyadh and Dhahram attacks on US forces in Saudi Arabia, stating that it marked 'the beginning of war between Muslims and the United States'.

On 23 August 1996, bin Laden issued al Qaeda's first 'declaration of war' against America. He advised all militants to choose war against negotiation, as that was the only way they would achieve goals. Bin Laden's al Qaeda fought on a wide front, helping jihads being fought in Algeria, Egypt and Afghanistan. He assisted Algerian militants with $40,000, which turned out to be a blow to his reputation as over 200,000 Algerians were killed in the subsequent conflict. The Islamic extremists lost and were forced to surrender to the government.

Bin Laden suffered another failure and loss of face when sixty-two people were massacred at Luxor in November 1997. Egypt was appalled by the massacre and, instead of favouring Islamic extremism, they actually turned against it.

The summer of 1997 saw bin Laden on the move once again. The Northern Alliance looked as though it was going to overrun Jalalabad and he was forced to take his operation to Tarnak farms in the south of Afghanistan. Working closely with the Taliban, several hundred of bin Laden's men joined forces to attack the city of Mazar-e-Sharif, killing six thousand inhabitants.

In 1998, bin Laden and his collaborator, Ayman al-Zawahiri, issued a *fatwa* in the name of the World Islamic Front for Jihad against Jews and Crusaders. The *fatwa* claimed that it was the duty of every individual Muslim to kill North Americans and their allies. It also demanded the liberation of the al-Aqsa Mosque in Jerusalem and the holy mosque in Mecca.

In August 1998 al Qaeda reportedly conducted a number of bombings of US embassies in Nairobi, Kenya and Dar es Salaam, Tanzania. In these attacks 301 people were killed and more than 5,000 were injured.

On 21 October 2000, the American destroyer USS *Cole* was attacked in the port of Aden in Yemen, after a small boat was allowed to draw up alongside. How two men in such a small boat could wreak so much damage on an enormous guided-missile destroyer equipped with all the latest defensive systems, is still mystifying. The blast, which tore a hole in the side of the vessel, killed seventeen sailors and injured a further thirty-nine, with an estimated cost of repairs standing at $240 million. It turned out the attack had been carried out by a terrorist cell that had been trained and financed by al Qaeda.

Shortly after the attack on USS *Cole*, al Qaeda issued a chillingly prophetic statement claiming that North Americans are 'very easy targets . . . you will see the results of this in a very short time'. After the attacks on the embassies, US President Bill Clinton froze assets that could possibly be linked to bin Laden. He also signed an executive order which authorised the arrest or assassination of the wanted terrorist. What was bin Laden's response to this? To instigate the biggest terror attack of them all.

The morning of 11 September 2001 will be engraved on the memories of all US citizens and probably the rest of the world as well. It started when four commercial airliners were hijacked by nineteen Islamic terrorists. One of these planes crashed into the Pentagon in Washington, another was forced to crash in the countryside near Shanksville, Pennsylvania, while the third and fourth caused horrific casualty numbers when they crashed into the side of the twin towers of the World Trade Center in New York. The world was left stunned as the media produced images of the planes flying straight into the side of the buildings. In the attack 2,063 people died in New York, 125 people were injured at The

Pentagon and, excluding the hijackers, a further 264 passengers died on the planes themselves.

The plot had been the brainchild of Khalid Sheikh Mohammed who had presented it to bin Laden as early as 1996. Mohammed was not given permission to proceed with his plan until early 1999. Although Mohammed was in control of the operation, it was financed and oversaw by bin Laden, who selected educated men with a good knowledge of English to perpetrate the attacks. Although it is impossible to prove without doubt that bin Laden was directly behind the 9/11 attacks, it looks very likely that he used his formidable skills of organisation and leadership to assist in the plan. He has personally claimed credit for the attacks on several occasions, despite the fact that he initially denied any involvement. Then the US forces discovered a tape in Jalalabad in November 2001, on which bin Laden can be heard discussing the attacks with Khaled al-Harbi.

In 2004 bin Laden released a video – four days before the American presidential election. In the video he stated that he had personally directed the 9/11 hijackers. In 2006, more tapes were aired on the Arab news channel, Al Jazeera, which stated:

'I am the one in charge of the nineteen brothers . . .' he said. 'I as responsible for entrusting the nineteen brothers . . . with the raids.'

The film shows bin Laden with Ramzi Binalshibh, a key al Qaeda member who also helped in planning the September 11 attacks, and two of the 9/11 hijackers, Hamza al-Ghamdi and Wail al-Shehri.

Bin Laden became one of the most wanted terrorists in the world with many countries trying to lure him out of hiding. In 1998, Libya issued the first Interpol arrest warrant against him for killing two German citizens – one of them a German counter-intelligence officer – in Libya in 1994. A few months later, following his bombing of a US-run Saudi Arabian National Guard training centre in Riyadh that killed five Americans and two Indians, the United States accused him of 'conspiracy to attack defence utilities of the United States'. He was also accused of being the leader of al Qaeda and of funding Islamic terrorist actions across the world. In November 1998, he was indicted by a Grand Jury for the murder of US nationals outside the United States and for attacks on a federal facility resulting in death after his bombings in Kenya and Tanzania.

President Clinton obtained sanctions against Afghanistan from the United Nations, in an effort to persuade the Taliban to hand him over, but they remained loyal to him. Although the Taliban nearly gave in to the request when the United States began bombing Afghanistan, but unfortunately they never reached a satisfactory agreement.

President Bush announced that bin Laden would now be included on America's new list of the Most Wanted Terrorists, the only man to appear on both the FBI fugitive list and the terrorist version. The United States almost succeeded in capturing him during the Battle of Tora Bora in Afghanistan in late 2001. Apparently he was hiding in a complex of caves along the eastern border of Afghanistan. However, US troops were not deployed quickly enough and he was given time to escape.

Osama bin Laden still remains a fugitive and there is much speculation as to whether he is still alive. In 2005, there was a report, which many people believed to be authentic, that he and al Qaeda were based in Waziristan in Pakistan. But yet again, there have been numerous reports that he is dead. In April 2005, he was said to have died of organ failure, while in August 2006, a French Secret Service report said that he had died of typhoid in Pakistan. Saudi intelligence services also reported his death on 4 September 2006. All of these reports, however, still remain to be confirmed.

The long silence has fuelled rumours that bin Laden is either in poor health, or dead. The United States, however, still fears that the al Qaeda network is rebuilding itself in Pakistani tribal lands, and that it has forged ties with affiliates in Europe, North Africa and the Middle East.

It is estimated that bin Laden's network today could command as many as eighteen thousand men, of which around one thousand are currently inside Iraq. They are believed to still be active in the smuggling of explosives, high-tech weapons and millions of dollars in cash for a resurgent terror campaign.

Dead or alive, bin Laden is still revered by many as the symbolic leader of a global jihad against the United States. Until the body of the man responsible for one of the worst instances of mass murder in history is found, no one can be sure that he is not out there somewhere still planning further revenge.

SADDAM HUSSEIN

The night before the execution, he met his two half-brothers, Sabawi and Wathban Ibrahim Hassan al-Tikriti in his cell, passing messages and instructions to them to give to his family. He requested no other visitors, not even his wife, mother of his five children. US soldiers had already removed the radio from his cell so that he would be unable to hear reports about his death sentence which had been confirmed by the courts following an appeal.

Just after six in the morning of 30 December 2006, wearing a black coat, he was escorted into the room at the 5th Division Intelligence headquarters in Qadhimiya by three masked guards. Those present said that by that time he was a broken man, that there was fear in his eyes and that he seemed 'strangely submissive during the entire process. He refused, nonetheless, to have a hood placed over his head. He had been carrying a copy of the Quran which he handed to Iraq's National Security Adviser, Mowaffak al-Rubaie, asking that it be given to someone; al-Rubaie has not revealed who that person was. A moment later, the noose was placed over his head and tightened. Shortly after, Saddam Hussein, former leader of one of the world's most ruthless regimes was dead, principally for his role in the 1982 Dujail Massacre in which 148 Iraqis died in retaliation for a failed assassination attempt on him. Saddam's crimes, however, amounted to a great deal more than just that single incident.

His life had begun in 1937 in northern Iraq where he was born into a peasant family in the town of Al-Awja, not far from the larger town of Tikrit. His family were shepherds but he never knew his father who disappeared six months before his birth. When his mother re-married, he gained three half-brothers but he failed to get on with his stepfather and ran away, aged ten, to live in Baghdad with his uncle Kharaillah Tulfah, a devout Sunni Muslim who had fought against the British on the Iraqi nationalist side in 1941. Tulfah schooled the young and impression-able Saddam in his hatred for a whole range of races and nationalities – Jews, Iranians, Shiite Muslims, Kuwaitis and Westerners.

Saddam attended a nationalistic school in the capital before enrolling at an Iraqi law school where he studied for three years before dropping out in 1957.

Working as a school teacher to support himself, he joined the revolutionary pan-Arab Ba'ath Party which aimed to unite all Arab countries against western colonial rule, still prevalent at that time. Revolutions had taken place across the Arab world, inspired by the Gamal Abdel Nasser in Egypt and in 1958, General Abdul Karim Qassim led a military coup in Iraq that overthrew the monarchy of King Faisal II. The Ba'ath Party opposed Qassim and Saddam became involved in a plot, backed by the United States, to assassinate Qassim.

Qassim's government was eventually overthrown in 1963 by Ba'athist army elements and Saddam who had been forced to flee the country after the failed assassination attempt, was able to return to Iraq. In 1964, however, when the new president of the country, Abdul Salem Arif began to take action against the Ba'ath Party, Saddam, by this time party secretary, was thrown in prison. He escaped in 1967 and became a leading member of the party, playing a major role in the bloodless overthrow of Arif's government in 1968, following which Ahmad Hassan al-Bakr became president with Saddam as his deputy. By 1969, he was effectively the guiding force of the presidency. He tried to strengthen and unify the Ba'ath Party and dealt with many of the country's serious problems. He encouraged the modernisation of the Iraqi economy and created a strong security force in order to prevent coups and rebellions against the government. He oversaw the seizure of international oil interests in Iraq and then benefited the following year from the escalating price of oil.

Under his supervision, Iraq became one of the most progressive countries in the Middle East with expanding social services and a campaign to banish illiteracy. There was free education up to university level, new roads, free hospitals and subsidies for hard-pressed farmers.

In 1976, Saddam was promoted to General in the Iraqi armed forces and became increasingly involved in running the country as President al-Bakr became too frail to perform his duties. He took control of foreign policy and was, effectively, leader before actually taking over in 1979.

The catalyst for Saddam's seizure of power was a plan to unite Syria and Iraq, a move that would consign him to the sidelines. He forced the resignation of al-Bakr on 16 July 1979 and assumed power.

His first act was to convene a meeting of the Ba'ath Party at which he read out the names of sixty-eight people that he claimed were disloyal. Each of these men was removed from the room and taken into custody. Twenty-two of them would subsequently be executed for treason.

To the annoyance of conservative Muslims, Saddam appointed women to posts in industry and government; he also changed the legal system, making it more western and moving it away from the traditional Islamic law.

He had plenty of enemies apart from the traditionalists. The Shia majority opposed him as did the Kurds of northern Iraq. He sometimes attempted to placate them with government positions but was also often repressive towards these elements, his security operatives becoming feared because of their use of torture and assassination. One of his half-brothers was in command of them.

Gradually, a personality cult built up around him, portraits appearing in shops, offices and homes and statues of him being erected across the country. He appeared in tableaux dressed in the many costumes of his country in order to appeal to all its disparate elements – Bedouin dress, Kurdish costume, Muslim headdress, the traditional garb of the Iraqi peasant and, of course, the western business suit.

In 1980, war broke out between Iraq and Iran, led by Saddam's sworn enemy, the Shi'ite Ayatollah Khomeinei, after Saddam ordered an invasion of Iran. He presented himself as defending the Arab world against revolutionary Iran and had the support of the United States, Europe and the Soviet Union. A blind eye was turned to his use of chemical weapons against the Kurds and his blatant violations of international law were ignored and he received military and economic support from the West and from the Gulf States, eager to see Iran incapacitated.

By 1982 the war was going badly for Saddam and he convened a meeting of his ministers to decide what they should do next. One of them, Health Minister, Riyadh Ibrahim suggested that Saddam remove himself from office on a temporary basis so that peace talks could be held. The next day, his dismembered body was delivered to his wife.

It became a long and bloody war of attrition, ending eventually in stalemate in August 1988 with an estimated one million deaths. Saddam had used chemical weapons, supplied mainly by West German companies and in March of the last year of the war had deployed them, in the form of a mixture of mustard gas and nerve agents, in the Kurdish town of Halabja. Five thousand men, women and children were killed while ten thousand more were injured. The attack was intended to terrify the Kurdish population of northern Iraq into submission, although at the time the blame was placed on Iranian forces, an accusation upheld by the United States until a few years later.

As Saddam felt that he had fought the economically disastrous war for the benefit of the

Gulf States as well as for Iraq, he asked Kuwait to forego the debt – a sum of around $30 billion – that Iraq had built up with it during the conflict. The Kuwaitis refused, just as they refused his request to cut back on oil production in order to raise prices. There was also the historical issue of the border between Iraq and Kuwait, believed by Iraqi nationalists to be wrong since it had been created by the British in 1922. He sent his troops, still well-drilled after the war with Iran, to the border.

Saddam gambled on the United States not becoming involved in his conflict with Kuwait. Iraq was, after all, the third biggest recipient of American foreign aid and the USA had been trying to create good relations with Iraq for forty years. He invaded and annexed Kuwait on 2 August 1990, creating one of the gravest international crises since the Second World War.

Saddam's gamble failed when the United States led a United Nations coalition of forces that drove his troops out of Kuwait in February 1991. 175,000 Iraqi troops were taken prisoner and there were more than 85,000 casualties. The peace terms ordered Iraq to do away with all chemical weapons and permit UN observers to inspect the sites to ensure that they had complied with the agreement. In the meantime, trade sanctions were applied against Saddam who, naturally, claimed victory.

His government of Iraq became less secure after the war, with uprisings by the Kurds in the north and the Shi'ites in the south and centre of the country. No other country was interested in becoming involved, however, and he had soon suppressed the revolts and stabilised his regime. Relations between Iraq and the United States, however, remained tense.

Sanctions created terrible hardship in Iraq and the prevention of its oil exports seriously damaged its economy. Very soon there was a humanitarian crisis only partially alleviated by humanitarian aid and smuggling. In 1996, Saddam was allowed to sell limited quantities of oil in order to buy food and medicine in the UN Oil for Food Programme.

Accusations were constantly levelled at him that he was constructing weapons of mass destruction and violating 'no-fly' zones. There were sporadic air strikes by US and British jets and an ongoing crisis about the access of UN inspectors to weapons sites. However, the September 11 attacks on New York in 2001 changed everything. President George W. Bush described an 'Axis of Evil' that included Iraq, North Korea and Iran and announced that he might attack Iraq to bring down Saddam Hussein.

Saddam's regime collapsed three weeks after the eventual US-led invasion on 20 March 2003. Targeted air strikes had failed to kill him but by the beginning of April, the entire country was occupied. At the fall of Baghdad on 9 April, Saddam seemed to have vanished without a trace.

In July, his two sons, Uday and Qusay and fourteen-year-old grandson, Mustapha, were killed in a three hour gunfight with US forces and then, on 14 December, a heavily bearded, unkempt and exhausted-looking Saddam was captured at a farmhouse near Tikrit and taken into custody.

In prison, he was known as 'Vic' to his guards and was permitted to plant a garden close to his cell. Then, on 30 June 2004, he was handed over to the interim Iraqi government along with eleven other senior members of the Ba'ath Party. Saddam was charged with crimes against humanity, specifically the Dujail Massacre.

Dujail was a stronghold of the Shi'ite Dawa Party, a group opposed to Saddam Hussein and his war with Iran. Saddam was paying a visit to the village on 8 July 1982 to deliver a speech in praise of those who had served for Iraq against Iran. As his motorcade proceeded through the village it was attacked by gunfire from a number of Dawa members. A three-hour gunfight followed during which Saddam was unharmed.

Furious with the assassination attempt, Saddam ordered his security forces to take revenge on the town. Some 148 men, many just boys as young as thirteen, were executed and 1500 people were imprisoned and tortured, while others, many of them women and children were sent to desert camps. The town was razed to the ground by Saddam's men but was later re-built. Farmland was destroyed and no one was allowed to re-plant the area until ten years later.

On 5 November 2006, Saddam was found guilty and sentenced to death by hanging.

PART TWO

ON THE RAMPAGE: SPREE KILLERS

BATH SCHOOL DISASTER

Afterwards, they tried to find a reason for the explosions and the murder of dozens of people, most of them children. But, of course, there was none, at least none that was acceptable. On the Saturday following that dreadful day in May 1927, eighteen funerals were held in the little town of Bath, situated about ten miles northeast of Lansing in Michigan. The remainder were buried the next day, thousands thronging the streets to bid farewell to the young lives that had been destroyed by the insanity of one man – Andrew Kehoe, the perpetrator of the deadliest act of mass murder in a United States school.

He was born in 1872, in Tecumseh, Michigan, one of thirteen children of a couple who had moved to Michigan from New York state. Unfortunately, the children's mother died when Andrew was still very young and his father later re-married, to a woman with whom Andrew did not see eye to eye and, as was later proved, it did not pay to upset Andrew Kehoe. He was capable of carrying a grudge for a while and then acting on it, as his stepmother discovered one day while she was lighting an oil stove in the kitchen of the Kehoe home. The stove suddenly exploded, engulfing her in flames. Fourteen-year-old Andrew was in the house at the time but stood at the kitchen door watching the women burn for several minutes before filling a bucket of water and pouring it over her to douse the flames. His delay was decisive and she later died in hospital from multiple burns. Neighbours whispered amongst themselves that Andrew had probably tampered with the stove but nothing was ever proved.

Educated at the local high school, he went on to enroll at Michigan State College in nearby East Lansing. There he met Nellie Price who would become his wife but before marrying her, he moved out west, living in Missouri for a few years. While there, Kehoe is reported to have suffered a serious head injury as a result of a fall in 1911 while attending a school where he was learning to be an electrician. For two months he lay in a coma in hospital and it is often speculated that his irrational behaviour may have started as a result of his injury. He recovered and returned home to Tecumseh where he and Nellie were married. They bought a 185-acre farm situated just outside the town of Bath.

Kehoe seemed to most people who knew him to be a little odd. He was helpful and generous, but subject to moods when he failed to get his own way and was intolerant of anyone who disagreed with him about anything. He was also obsessively neat. More often that not, he would change into a fresh shirt in the middle of the day and as soon as he got the smallest speck of dirt on his clothing, he had to go and change.

What he was good at, however, was machinery. He liked nothing better than to tinker with his farm machinery and had a particular liking for electrical work. He was always trying to find new and innovative ways to perform his chores on the farm. Neighbours later accused him of being cruel to the animals on his farm, however. Once, they said, he beat a horse to death in a savage display of anger and cruelty.

In 1926 his reputation for being careful with money led to him being appointed to the school board in Bath as treasurer. Education in Michigan at that time was run on the basis of the one-room school of which there were many scattered across the state. Different grades were accommodated and taught in the same classroom in the belief that if they were able to attend just one school in a single location their education would be better. In Bath they had decided, after years of arguing, to invest in a new school, the Bath Consolidated School. Of course, the project had to be funded somehow and taxes were raised in order to raise enough money. Kehoe, already suffering serious financial difficulties because of the fact that his wife suffered from tuberculosis, was furious at having to fork out for the school.

He complained bitterly to anyone who would listen about the taxes and brought it up constantly at school board meetings, describing it as illegal and unfair. He blamed one man for the whole thing – school board president, Emory E. Huyck – but when his mortgage lender began foreclosure proceedings on his property, he quietly began to go mad.

Kehoe's skill with tools and machinery led to his appointment by the board as the handyman for the school. This meant that he was allowed complete access to any part of it. However, what they could not know was that his fixation with what he saw as ruinous taxation, had led him to devise an appalling plan.

For some months he had been buying Pyrotol, a high explosive. Farmers used it to excavate on their farms or to blow up tree stumps and it was, therefore, not considered unusual that he was buying it. What people would have found strange was the sheer quantity of the stuff that he was purchasing. In order to allay any suspicions, he shopped for it in different locations in Lansing, purchasing a small quantity at each. In November 1926, he bought a couple of boxes of dynamite at a sports shop. It became routine to hear explosions emanating from his farm. The neighbours thought nothing of them.

On every trip into the school to make repairs he smuggled a little Pyrotol. He had launched a re-wiring programme, but it was re-wiring that connected various explosive charges that he had secreted beneath the floor all over the school as well as in the roof. He ran thousands of feet of wire behind the walls and under the floorboards. Under the floors of the classrooms he set a lethal one thousand pounds of dynamite. By early May, he had completed his work. The charges were set and ready to go.

Back at his farm, he had done the same thing, setting charges in all the various buildings and outhouses hooked up to firebombs – tanks of gasoline – connected to a car battery to give them the charge needed to ignite them. There was a firebomb in every building.

On the afternoon of 17 May, he used a blunt instrument to bludgeon his sick wife Nellie to death before dumping her body in a wheel barrow and pushing it behind the hen house.

The next day he got up and drove to the post office in Bath to post a large package. Inside was the financial records of the school board. Characteristically, the package also contained a long and highly detailed account of a twenty-two cent discrepancy in the books. It was typical of him to exercise himself about such an insignificant matter, but it was strange that he spent so much time on it when he had the murder of a great number of people on his mind.

Meanwhile, at eight o'clock at Bath Consolidated School, the day was beginning, the children arriving for lessons and the teachers calling them to order in the school's play area. Brothers and sisters went to their separate classes, sometimes three or four members of the same family attending the school.

Kehoe had returned home to put the finishing touches to the imminent mayhem. He went into his stables and tied the legs of his five horses together with wire and hitched them to posts in their stalls using the same wire. He began making a pile of old rubbish and branches in the barn where the animals were stabled.

He then drove his pickup over to the barn and loaded it with metal junk, old engine parts, nuts, bolts and pieces of rusty machinery.

At exactly 8.45, Kehoe detonated the firebombs at his home, blowing the entire complex to pieces, debris being thrown into the air and then showering to the ground, some falling on the neighbouring farm. Neighbours ran out of their houses to find out what was going on and some ran towards his farm to give assistance. His farm became an inferno as the gasoline went up in flames, but Kehoe climbed behind the wheel of the pickup he earlier loaded. He drove out as more neighbours arrived. However, just as he was leaving, the ground shook as the rumble of an even bigger explosion was heard in the distance. The school, filled with children just beginning another busy day, had also been blown up. The people stopped in utter confusion, wondering if they were perhaps experiencing the end of the world. Realising that the sound had come from the school, where many of them had children who were pupils, they turned and ran in the direction of town, some jumping into cars.

At the school, it was like a scene from hell. The north wing had collapsed, walls had fallen and the edge of the roof had been blown off and landed on the ground. Under the roof lay many children and arms, legs and heads jutted out of the rubble, covered in dust and blood, some screaming for help, others beyond help. They were unable to move the roof and one man volunteered to go to his farm to get a rope that they could use to drag it off. As he drove away from the carnage, he passed Andrew Kehoe driving in the opposite direction. 'He grinned and waved his hand,' the man later said, 'when he grinned, I could see both rows of his teeth.'

People were running to the school from every direction and pulling at the debris with their bare hands. Mothers collapsed as they saw the bodies of their children stretched out on the ground away from the wreckage.

Kehoe arrived around thirty minutes after the explosion had rocked the school. As he pulled up, he saw the man on whom he placed the blame for all his troubles, Superintendent Huyck. He called Huyck over but as he approached the vehicle, Kehoe picked up his rifle lying on the seat beside him, turned and fired it into the area behind the driver's seat. The dynamite he had placed there exploded, killing him and Huyck and shooting out in all directions the metal debris with which he had loaded in the pickup.

The explosion also killed the town postmaster, Glenn Smith and his retired father-in-law, Nelson McFarren, but the shrapnel flying out of the vehicle also did some damage, a piece of it hitting eight-year-old Cleo Claton and killing her. Many others were injured.

The scene was horrific. Bodies lay everywhere and mothers cuddled their dead children. One woman was seen sitting on a bank, her two dead daughters lying on either side of her and her seriously injured son in her arms. The boy would die later in hospital.

The dead were taken to the town hall that had been turned into a temporary morgue and ambulances had begun to flood into the town to take the injured to hospital, or the dead to the undertakers. Fire fighters and police officers arrived from nearby towns. They and ordinary people from the town and surrounding areas worked all day freeing trapped children and teachers.

As they searched they made a disturbing discovery. Kehoe had set another huge bomb – containing approximately 500 pounds of explosive – to go off at 9.45. It had failed to detonate, however, possibly short-circuited by the first explosion. It was a small consolation that the disaster and the death toll could have been very much worse.

A total of forty-five people – thirty-eight pupils aged from seven to fourteen and seven adults – died at Bath Consolidated School that day and sixty-one were seriously injured. The quiet little town of Bath and the seriously deranged Andrew Kehoe made the front pages of the world's newspapers alongside the news that aviator Charles Lindbergh had completed the historic first non-stop flight between New York and Paris.

CHARLES STARKWEATHER AND CARIL ANN FULGATE

On the eve of his execution Charles Starkweather was asked if he would like to donate his eyes to medical research. The young spree killer people refused, snarling, 'Why should I? Nobody ever gave me anything.'

He was a red-haired, slow-witted, bow-legged killer who slew eleven people during a road trip through Nebraska and Wyoming in 1958 with his girlfriend, Caril Ann Fugate. But, unlike most serial killers, there is nothing in Starkweather's upbringing that suggested he would be murderer. In fact, he had no excuse. He was undoubtedly born in hard times, in the town of Lincoln, Nebraska, in November, 1938, but his parents, Guy and Helen always managed to provide for their seven children and Starkweather did not have to face the kind of struggle that some people had at the time just to survive. He was not a victim of abuse, there was no absent father, no booze and no drugs. In fact, his family was clean-living and strong. The only cloud on the horizon was his father's crippling arthritis that sometimes led to periods of unemployment but his mother Helen was a hard-working mother who worked as a waitress to bring in a little extra money.

School was another matter for young Charles, however. He was teased remorselessly for how he looked – he suffered from *genu varus*, a mild birth defect that caused his legs to be bowed – and they laughed at a speech impediment from which he suffered. He was also a slow learner and schoolwork was neither his forte or something he was interested in. To make matters worse, in his teens he was diagnosed with severe myopia – short-sightedness – that rendered him almost blind.

Charles escaped from all his problems at the gym, building up his body until he was strong enough to bully the bullies and what had been a well-behaved boy from a good family turned into one of the town's most troubled and troublesome young men.

It was around the time that James Dean was single-handedly inventing the moody American teenager on celluloid and Starkweather began to imitate Dean, dressing like him, and becoming rebellious. In reality, however, he was a seething mass of self-loathing. He felt like a failure, a loser with few prospects.

Caril Ann Fugate was just thirteen when she met Charles in 1957. Like Charles, she had a rebellious nature and was not a great scholar. She was a pretty girl with dark brown hair and an unpredictable temper and Starkweather fell for her immediately, even quitting school to work loading and unloading trucks at the Western Newspaper Union warehouse that was situated close to her school.

Meanwhile, the relationship between Charles and his father was deteriorating and when Caril crashed Charles's hotrod – insured by his father – Guy threw his son out of the house.

He moved into a rooming house and Caril became even more the centre of his world. He told friends that they were getting married and made up a story that she was pregnant. Her parents were not pleased when the story made its way back to them.

Starkweather took a job on a garbage truck, a job which only added to the desperate pessimism he felt about his life. He began to think of crime as his only way out of a life of poverty and disappointment and he passed his time on the garbage truck planning bank robberies. During this time, a simple mantra ran through his head: 'Dead people are all on the same level.'

On 30 November 1957, while visiting a petrol station, Charles did not even have enough money to buy a stuffed toy dog for Caril. Robert Colvert, the twenty-one-year-old attendant, refused him credit and Charles resolved to take revenge.

At three the next morning he returned to the petrol station with a shotgun, leaving the gun in the car when he went in to buy a pack of cigarettes from Colvert who was working on his own. Starkweather then drove off, but turned the car round and went back to buy chewing gum. Again, he left the gun in the car. He drove off again, but stopped the car a short distance away, put on a bandana and a hat to cover his red hair and walked back to the petrol station with the gun in a bag. Taking out the gun, he held Covert up and took a hundred dollars from the cash register. He then made Colvert get into the car and drove him to a piece of wasteland. Colvert jumped him, trying to grab the gun, but it went off and Colvert fell to his knees. Starkweather blasted him in the head, killing him outright. Telling Caril about the robbery later, he claimed that someone else had killed Colvert but she did not believe him.

The story of the murder made big headlines in the papers, but police believed the perpetrator to be a transient and it looked like Charles had got away with it. He began to think of himself as beyond the normal laws and standards by which we live our lives. He felt like he could get away with anything.

But things remained much the same. He lost his job as a garbageman and became homeless when he was locked out of his room by his landlady after failing to pay the rent. Meanwhile, Caril's family, as well as his own, were trying to persuade Caril to dump him. He was getting desperate.

On 21 January 1958, he drove to the squalid hovel that was Caril's house, taking with him a borrowed .22 rifle and some ammunition. He later claimed that he had planned to go hunting with Caril's stepfather, Marion Bartlett, with the aim of patching up their relationship. He also brought along a couple of discarded carpet samples he had found for Velda.

Velda opened the door. Also in the house were Marion and the couple's two-year-old daughter, Betty Jean. But it was not long before the talk developed into the same old argument. Velda did not want him to carry on seeing her daughter and Marion literally kicked him out of the house.

A plan formed in Starkweather's head. Finding a payphone, he called Marion's work to tell them that he was ill and would not be back for a few days. He then returned to the house to wait for Caril to go come home from school. She argued with her parents on her return and, hearing the raised voices, Starkweather went back into the house. He claimed that Velda began hitting him, screaming that he had got Caril pregnant. Starkweather went out to the car and returned with his gun. When Marion threatened him with a claw hammer, Starkweather shot him in the head. Velda rushed him with a knife, he later claimed, and he shot her in the face. The baby was crying and when Velda, still alive, tried to reach it, he slammed the butt of the rifle into her head a couple of times. He went to the baby's bedroom to try to quieten her, but, unable to do so, threw Velda's knife at her, hitting her in the throat and killing her. He then returned to the room in which Marion was still moving around. Starkweather said later: '…I tried to stab him in the throat, but the knife wouldn't go in, and I just hit the top part of it with my hand and it went in.'

He dragged Velda's body to the outhouse and stuffed her down the open toilet. Meanwhile, the baby's body was put in a box in the outhouse and Marion was left in the chicken coop. Then Charlie and Caril cleaned up the mess and spent the remainder of the evening drinking Pepsi and eating crisps. For almost a week, they stayed there, the corpses rotting outside. Visitors were frightened off by a note Caril had pinned to the door telling them everyone inside had flu.

Eventually, people became suspicious and the police were called but Caril fobbed them off with the flu story. When Caril's grandmother asked the police to visit again, they searched inside the house but found nothing untoward. Later that day, Officer Bob van Busch and his brother made a search of the property and discovered the grisly remains of Velda, Marion and Betty. By this time, however, Charlie and Caril were long gone.

They had driven to a farm, twenty miles from Lincoln, that belonged to a Starkweather family friend, August Meyer, arriving there on 27 January. Sometime that day, Starkweather shot Meyer in the head, claiming later, as he did for many of his killings, that it was in self-defence. They grabbed his money and guns, had a meal and fell asleep.

Next morning, however, their car got bogged down in mud as they left the farm and they hitched a ride from seventeen-year-old Robert Jensen and sixteen-year-old Carol King. Starkweather decided to rob them and pulled his gun, demanding money. Back at the Meyer farm to which he had ordered them to drive, he shot Jensen six times in the head. He shot Carol once and then stabbed her repeatedly in the abdomen and pubic area. The couple would disagree later about Caril's role in the killings. She claimed she was sitting in the car all the time but he said she actually shot the girl while he was absent from the scene and was so jealous of the attention he had been paying to Carol that she helped in the mutilation of her body.

They next did a strange thing, driving back to Lincoln and even cruising past Caril's house which was a hive of police activity. At least they now knew that the bodies had been found. They parked in another part of town and went to sleep and by the time they opened their eyes again on the 28 January, the other three bodies had been found and they had become the subject of a huge a huge manhunt.

Forty-seven-year-old C. Lauer Ward, was a company president and a good friend of the governor of Nebraska. That morning, his wife Clara was at home with Lillian Fencl, their hard-of-hearing, fifty-one-year-old maid.

There was a knock at the door and Lillian opened it to find Charlie Starkweather with a gun in his hand. He soon realised Lillian could not hear very well and wrote notes to tell her what he wanted. When Clara came into the kitchen to see why breakfast had not been served, Charlie assured her that nothing bad was going to happen. He called Caril in and she had some coffee and fell asleep in the library while Charlie ate.

Later, when Clara went upstairs to change her shoes, Starkweather followed her. He claimed she took out a gun from a drawer a gun and she fired it, missing him. He threw a knife at her which stuck in her back and he followed that by stabbing her her repeatedly in the neck and chest.

He then called his father and told him to tell Bob van Busch that he was going to kill him because he had been interfering in his relationship with Caril and followed that with a badly spelled letter addressed to 'the law only', an attempt to justify his and Caril's actions. 'I and Caril are sorry for what has happen,' he wrote. 'Cause I have hurt every body cause of it and so has Caril. But I'm saying one thing every body that came out there was luckie there not dead even caril's sister.'

They loaded Ward's black 1956 Packard, with food and got ready to leave, but first waited for C. Lauer Ward who they shot dead when he came home from work that evening. They tied Lillian Fencl to a bed and stabbed her to death, Charlie later claiming that Caril killed her but Caril blaming him. The bodies were discovered the next day and Ward's friend, Governor Anderson, called out the National Guard. Jeeps, armed with mounted machine guns, began to patrol the streets of Lincoln and parents carried guns as they took their children to school. Meanwhile, spotter planes scrutinised the roads in the surrounding area for the black Packard.

They were on their way to Washington State, crossing into Wyoming on the morning of 29 January.

Seeing a Buick parked at the side of the highway, they decided it would be a good idea to change vehicles. It was a fatal decision for the car's driver, Merle Collinson, a travelling salesman from Montana who was asleep in the car. He was killed with shots to the head, neck, arm and leg. Charlie, courteous as ever, later blamed Caril for it.

But he was unable to work out how to release the car's emergency break and when a young geologist innocently stopped to offer help, Charlie thanked him by pulling his gun on him and telling him if he did not find out how to release the break, he would be killed. The geologist realised that the man seated next to Starkweather was, in fact, dead and tried to wrestle the weapon away from Starkweather. Just then, by a strange coincidence, a young Wyoming deputy sheriff, William Romer, pulled up in his car to see what was going on. Caril jumped out of the back seat of the car, shouting that she wanted him to take her to the police, that it was Charles Starkweather in the car and that he was a killer. Charlie, by this time, had jumped back into the Packard and sped off in the direction of the nearby town of Douglas. The deputy set off in hot pursuit, radioing in that he was chasing a black Packard and ordering that a roadblock be set up. Douglas police chief, Robert Ainslie, and Sheriff Earl Heflin of Converse County happened to see

Starkweather's car fly past them at speed and also set off in pursuit. Heflin took careful aim and shot out the back windscreen of the Packard. To their surprise, however, Starkweather came to an abrupt halt in the middle of the highway.

They pulled up behind him, cautiously waiting for him to get out. When he did, they told him to lie on the ground. It turned out that he had stopped because he thought he had been shot. But the blood was merely from a cut around his ear made by the broken glass of the windscreen.

He did look the part, though, when photographed later. Shaggy, swept back hair, cigarette dangling, in the manner of James Dean, from his lips, black leather motorcycle jerkin, tight black denims, cowboy boots – the very image of teenage rebellion.

Their choice following their arrest was stark. They could have the gas chamber in Wyoming or the electric chair in Nebraska. They chose Nebraska and he and Caril were extradited in January 1958 and were both charged with first-degree murder and murder while committing a robbery.

Starkweather's lawyers entered a plea of 'innocent by reason of insanity', but Charles insisted that he was sane. He also said initially that Caril was innocent. He changed his tune, however, when he learned that Caril was saying that she had actually been held hostage by him and began to implicate her, claiming she was responsible for some of the murders and all the mutilations.

Caril was found guilty, but at fourteen she was too young to be executed and was instead sentenced to life imprisonment. Still claiming that she was innocent, she was paroled seventeen years later in 1976.

It took the jury only twenty-four hours to find Charles Starkweather guilty and, as expected, he was sentenced to die in the electric chair. His father raised money for his appeal by selling locks of his son's hair, but it was futile. The sentence was carried out on 25 June 1959.

In 1982, Bruce Springsteen released an album entitled Nebraska on which the title song is about Charles Starkweather. He sings, 'I can't say that I'm sorry for the things that we done/At least for a little while, sir, me and her we had us some fun'.

PERRY SMITH AND RICHARD HICKOCK

(THE 'IN COLD BLOOD' MURDERS)

At 9 am on the morning of Sunday 14 November 1959, a car drove up the avenue of fruit trees leading to River Valley Farm and parked in front of the house. It was a gleaming white, two-storey residence a mile and a half from the main road, adjacent to which stood several large barns and a few outhouses. The owner was Herbert William Clutter, a highly successful forty-eight-year-old farmer and respected pillar of the local community, the town of Holcombe in Kansas. Clutter was a wealthy man with four children, two of whom were married and lived away from the farm. At home still were his daughter, the pretty sixteen-year-old Nancy and his fifteen-year-old son, Kenyon. Bonnie, his wife, ill for some time with depression, spent a great deal of time in bed.

The car that pulled up was driven by Clarence Ewalt. Every Sunday, Ewalt dropped his daughter, also called Nancy, off at the Clutters so that she could accompany them to church. She and Nancy Clutter were best friends.

She rang the doorbell and waited for an answer. She rang again, but the sound of the doorbell echoed through what seemed like an emptiness inside. She looked over at the garage, the doors of which lay open showing the Clutters' two cars still inside. Turning round to her father, he indicated that she should go round the side where there was a door into Mr Clutter's office. She walked round and knocked on the door, but again there was only silence. However, the door was slightly ajar. She pushed it open a little more, stepped half inside and shouted out a nervous 'Hello!'

She returned to the car where her father suggested they drive to the next homestead, the Kidwell house, to see if they had any idea where the Clutters might be. From there they tried telephoning, but again there was no answer. They returned to River Valley Farm, this time accompanied by Susan Kidwell, a mutual friend of the two Nancys and the two girls went round the side and entered the house, having again knocked loudly on the front door.

They noticed immediately that the Clutters had not eaten breakfast; there were no dishes out and the stove was cold. Strangely, Nancy Clutter's purse was lying on the floor, open.

They walked through the dining room and climbed the stairs. At the top they saw that Nancy's bedroom door lay open. A piercing scream rang out as Nancy Ewalt suddenly caught sight of her friend Nancy lying on the bed, her face to the wall, the back of her head blown away.

The previous night, Nancy's boyfriend, Bobby Rupp, had come to see if she wanted to drive to McKinney Lake with him, but Herbert Clutter refused to give his permission, suggesting instead that Bobby stay and watch television with them. Bobby left around 10.30, barely needing his headlights, the moon was so bright.

As he left, he failed to see a black 1949 Chevrolet glide up towards the River Valley Farm. Inside it sat Perry Smith and Richard Hickock, two men newly released from prison who were intent on robbing a safe they had been told Herbert Clutter kept behind his desk.

Half-Irish, half-Cherokee Perry Edward Smith had been born in Nevada in 1928 to parents who were rodeo performers. His father was abusive and his alcoholic mother consequently left him taking her four children to live in San Francisco when Perry was seven years old. When he was thirteen, his mother died and he spent the rest of his childhood in a Catholic orphanage where he was abused by the nuns for bed-wetting, a problem that did not leave him as he grew older. He lived an itinerant life with his father for a while and spent time in detention homes until he returned to his father's care. Meanwhile, two of his siblings committed suicide.

He joined the army in 1948, serving in Korea but he was forever in trouble for fighting other soldiers and the indigenous population. Nonetheless, he received an honourable discharge in 1952, finding work as a car painter. His life was changed when he bought a motorcycle and was involved in a serious collision with a car. He spent six months in hospital but, having suffered serious injuries to both legs, would spend the remainder of his life disabled and in constant pain that he treated by swallowing fistfuls of aspirin. In March 1956 he was sent to Lansing Prison for robbing a store.

Twenty-eight-year-old Richard Hickock was from Kansas City. He had graduated from high school and had stayed out of trouble and worked hard as a mechanic for a while, marrying a woman when he was nineteen and having three children. He and his wife soon found themselves in financial trouble, made worse by a car accident that left his face slightly disfigured and made their money problems even worse while he was not working. When he got another woman pregnant, he left his wife to go and live with her and his wife divorced him. By this time, he was passing dud cheques to get money for which he was arrested and imprisoned in 1956. His second wife divorced him while he was inside.

The two ex-cons had met up again in Olathe in Kansas where Hickock's parents lived after Hickock had contacted Smith to say that he had a 'sure fire cinch' for them to get their hands on a lot of money. He explained to Smith that while he was sharing a cell with a burglar called Floyd Wells, Wells had told him about a large farm where he had worked. He described to Hickock the safe that the owner kept behind the desk in his office. It was Herbert Clutter's River Valley Farm.

The two men set out for Holcomb, Hickock's .12 gauge Savage shotgun in the boot of his car. They bought rubber gloves en route to avoid leaving any fingerprints and further down the road purchased a roll of duct tape. They ate a large meal and pushed on towards Garden City, the nearest big town to the hamlet of Holcomb.

They drove down the drive that led to the farm, stopping far enough away not to be seen and waiting in the dark until the lights went off in the main house and in the other house on the property, located on the other side of the barns, where farmhand Alfred Stoecklein lived with his family. After the buildings had been dark for a while, they put on the rubber gloves and slipped quietly out of the Chevy, Smith with the shotgun, Hickock with a torch and a knife.

Hickock had memorised the layout of the house from Floyd Wells' description and they made their way to the side door that led into Herbert Clutter's office, expecting to have to pick the lock but pleasantly surprised when the door swung open; it had not been locked. They stepped inside, closing it behind them.

They switched on the torch, directing its beam at the desk behind which they had been told sat the safe and the answer to all their problems. But there was no safe, just bookshelves and pictures on the wall. It must have been moved and there was nothing for it but to wake up Herbert Clutter and get him to lead them to it. They crept across the living room and up the stairs to the room they thought must be Herbert Clutter's. As they opened the door, Clutter sat up, thinking it was his wife who, since she had become ill had slept in another bedroom. They dragged him out of bed and took him downstairs to the office where he told them there was no safe in the house but they were welcome to any money they could find. The problem was, he told them, he did not keep a lot of money at home as most of his business was done by cheque.

They took him back upstairs where they pulled

some bills from his wallet. Asked if his wife had any money, he told them that she was sick and begged them not to disturb her, but they paid no heed, forcing him to lead them to her bedroom where she awoke, startled. There was little money there either so they decided to lock the couple in the bathroom to prevent them escaping or raising the alarm.

They went to Kenyon Clutter's room where again they did not find any money, but as they were pushing him towards the bathroom to lock him in with his parents, his sister Nancy walked along the corridor, drying her hair. The two teenagers were pushed into the bathroom.

The two ex-cons had a conference, deciding to separate the family, tie them up and scare them into revealing where they had hidden the money and valuables that Smith and Hickock were sure they must possess. They tied their wrists in the bathroom and Smith first of all took Herbert Clutter down to the basement where he ordered him to lie on an old flattened cardboard box on the floor. Smith then tied his hands and feet together. Kenyon was brought down next and his hands were tied to an overhead steam pipe.

Upstairs again, Smith led Bonnie Clutter back to her bedroom, gagging her with duct tape, silencing her please to them not to touch Nancy. Smith later claimed that Hickock had bragged earlier in the day that he was going to have his way with the girl and indeed when he went into Nancy's room he found Hickock sitting on the edge of her bed talking quietly to her. However, Smith claimed, he stopped when he entered and they tied the terrified girl to her bed. Outside the room, the two men argued about Nancy. The tension was building.

They decided to leave the house – there was obviously no money there – but decided to first check up on Herbert and Kenyon in the basement before they went. As he wrapped more tape around Mr. Clutter's face, Hickock boasted about how the family were lucky to be allowed to live. Smith seems to have cracked at this point, reaching out the knife to him and telling him that if he was so hard why didn't he kill them. Instead, Smith lunged forward and himself cut Herbert Clutter's throat. As he lay there, hideous gurgling sounds coming from his wound, Smith raised the gun and shot him almost point-blank in the face. In quick succession, Kenyon was also shot in the face, Bonnie Clutter in the side of the head and Nancy in the back of the head.

Smith and Hickock had killed the four family members for a grand total of around $50.

Although a huge effort was put into finding the killers, developments were slow. Nothing seemed to be missing apart from a Zenith transistor radio to which Smith had taken a fancy. Furthermore, there was little evidence. The killers – investigators were convinced that it would have taken more than one man to carry out such acts – had worn gloves. However, there were boot prints that showed up under an infra-red light – one had the print of a cat paw on the heel and the other had diamond shaped markings.

Around Christmas, however, there was a big break in the case when Floyd Wells in Lansing Prison told the authorities about Hickock's unhealthy interest in River Valley Farm and the Clutter family. At last, it became clear who they were looking for. They began to ask around about Richard Hickock. When they visited his parents they learned that Perry Smith had turned up in November and that the pair had made a trip to Fort Scott to collect some money owed to Hickock by his sister. They had left on Saturday 15 November and would have had plenty time to drive to Holcomb and back by Sunday night when they had returned.

Smith and Hicock, meanwhile, had gone on a joyride through Mexico and Acapulco, driving back into the United States to spend Christmas in Miami. By December 30, they were in Las Vegas picking up a box of belongings that they had shipped from Mexico, reasoning that it would be too heavy to carry as they stole cars on their way north. In the box were the two pairs of boots – one with cat's paw markings, the other with diamond shaped markings.

As Hickock sat in their latest stolen car – a black and white 1956 Chevy – outside the building where Smith was collecting the parcel, two police officers in a patrol car took an interest in the Chevy's out of state plates. When they radioed in to have it checked they found it matched a car that had been stolen in Kansas. A few minutes later, Smith and Hickock were staring down the barrels of two police revolvers and were being handcuffed.

The two men confessed eventually. After blaming each other for the killings, Smith claimed that he had actually killed all four Clutters. Police were not sure if this was the truth, believing he might have been saving Hickock's parents from further anguish. Nevertheless, they were tried, found guilty on all counts of murder by the jury after deliberations lasting a mere forty minutes, and sentenced to death by hanging.

It took a while. Four execution dates came and went but finally, on 14 April 1965 Hickock went to his death saying en route to the gallows, 'You people are sending me to a much better place than this has been.' Perry Smith followed shortly after saying, 'It would be meaningless to apologise now. But, I do apologise.'

Joseph 'Mad Dog' Taborsky

His first crime was the theft of a bicycle when he was just seven. He moved on to shoplifting and burglary and by fourteen he was locked up in a home for juvenile delinquents. It was hardly a surprise, therefore, that he ended up on the Death Row of a Connecticut prison. What was a surprise, however, was that he spent time there not once, but twice. It would result in the state of Connecticut taking a long hard look at its death penalty statute.

In the month before what have become known as the 'mad dog' killings there was a real chance that the state was going to abolish the death penalty. Governor Abraham Ribicoff was in favour of it ending and there was both political and popular support for the move. However, when Joe Taborsky and his sidekick Arthur Culombe were arrested in 1957 for a string of murders while robbing stores and petrol stations, Taborsky already having escaped the electric chair once, Governor Ribicoff changed his mind. Suddenly capital punishment did not seem to be a deterrent. As one magazine, previously supportive of abolition, put it, capital punishment 'is like putting out a fire, or killing a mad dog.'

They nicknamed him 'The Chin', so prominent was his jutting jaw, and he was a big and ungainly man – six feet four inches tall, with massive hands, deep-set eyes, a thin mouth with a hint of cruelty about it and an oddly stiff walk. He spent much of his young adult life in and out of prison, usually for breaking and entering.

It began on the night of 23 March 1950 when Joe asked his brother, Albert, if he wanted to go out and get some money. What Joe had in mind was a spot of robbery with Albert acting as driver and lookout while he got it. They drove around looking for a likely place to rob and decided on a West Hartford liquor store that was owned by forty-year-old Louis Wolfson.

While Albert remained in the car, Joe ran into the store, re-appearing a short while later and ordering his brother to get away from there fast. It was only the following morning, Albert claimed, that he read in a newspaper that Joe had actually shot Louis Wolfson who was now fighting for his life in hospital.

Three days after the incident, Wolfson lost his struggle and died. He had managed to provide police officers with a description of his attacker, however – young, white, baby-faced, wearing a long coat and in serious need of a haircut.

In January 1951 the police were surprised when Albert confessed to driving the car that night ten months previously. He informed them that his brother Joe had killed Wolfson and added that he had earned just $32 for his trouble. The two brothers were arrested and Albert was sentenced to life. Joe, as expected, was sentenced to die in the electric chair.

It was not to be, however.

Albert, who had always been a sensitive individual, suffered a breakdown in prison, claiming to be Jesus Christ and rambling incoherently. He ended up in an asylum, diagnosed as incurably insane. Taborsky immediately put in an appeal and the state of Connecticut found itself in an awkward position because Albert was the only witness to the crime. Joe Taborsky could not be tried again without witnesses and so he was freed, leaving Death Row in October 1955, having spent fifty-two months there, watching other men go to their execution and moving closer to the chair every day.

He milked it following his release, claiming that he had found God during his incarceration and warning that 'You can't beat the law. From now on,' he claimed 'I'm not even going to get a parking ticket.' In a magazine interview, he said that he believed in capital punishment but thought that it should be carried out swiftly after sentencing. 'I say this because I have compassion for condemned men,' he said. 'They suffer supreme agony in the living grave of a death cell.' If it had been carried out quickly after his sentence, a number of people would have lived.

Taborsky left Hartford and moved to Brooklyn in New York.

He had grown up in Hartford's North End, his bedroom ironically overlooking an old jail. He was impressed, he said by the swagger of the inmates and as he grew up wanted to inherit some of that swagger for himself.

He had met Arthur 'Meatball' Culombe in 1948 when the two men worked for a delivery company. The same age as Taborsky, Culombe was mentally deficient but this did not prevent him from indulging in his hobbies – gun-collecting, hunting and breaking into houses and shops. Taborsky and he had committed several burglaries together but he had not been around when Taborsky had decided to rob Louis Wolfson's store.

The pair made each other's acquaintance again when Taborsky was released from prison and picked up where they had left off. It was the beginning of a crime and murder spree that would end in Mad Dog's execution four years later.

In early December 1956 they robbed a hotel in Hartford, the clerk escaping unharmed, and then hit a Hartford liquor store, brutally beating the store's owner, Jack Rosen. Peter Baron, owner of another liquor store in Rocky Hill was also severely beaten when they robbed his store.

The first bullet was fired on 15 December when the two entered a Hartford tailor shop just before six in the evening. Nickola Leone was shot in the face, the bullet lodging in his neck, but he survived.

One hour later Taborsky and Culombe drove up to a petrol station in New Britain. Taborsky distracted the owner, thirty-year-old Edward Kurpewski, by asking if he could use the toilet. Culombe, meanwhile, pulled his gun and marched Kurpewski into the toilet where he ordered him to get down on his knees and shot him in the back of the head, killing him.

Just then, Daniel Janowski pulled into the forecourt. Taborsky ordered him out of his car at gunpoint and inside. He told him to kneel and pulled the trigger, firing a bullet into his head and then pumping another one into him, just to be sure. Meanwhile, Janowski's tiny daughter lay asleep in the back of the car, to be found an hour later by a bus driver who stopped for petrol.

Six days later, on 21 December, Taborsky and Culombe walked into a grocery store in Coventry. Taborsky struck the sixty-four-year-old owner and his wife on the head with his pistol, rendering them unconscious, but not shooting them. However, when Taborsky saw their three-year-old granddaughter, Lorry, running around the store, he became annoyed and ordered his partner to take her somewhere and shoot her. Culombe took her and hid her underneath a counter, telling her to be quiet, before firing his gun into the floor, pretending to have killed her.

On Boxing Day it was the turn of Samuel Cohn, owner of an East Hartford liquor store who was found dead beneath the counter on which stood his empty cash register. Sixty-five-year-old Cohn had died from two bullets to the head.

Their next crime would be the one that would lead to their capture, all because of Joe Taborsky's huge feet.

On 5 January, they entered Casco's Drive-In Shoe Outlet in North Haven just after seven in the evening. Frank Adinolfi was immediately suspicious of them, but Taborsky asked for a pair of shoes in a size twelve. When Adinolfi turned to check his shelves for the correct size, he felt the barrel of a gun being pushed into his back. Culombe took him into a back room and pistol-whipped him until he was unconscious with blood pouring from his wounds. He left him, thinking he was dead.

Tragically, at that moment, just as Taborsky was

emptying the cash from the register, a couple walked in, visiting the shoe shop to buy shoes for their son. Bernard Speyer and his wife Ruth were beaten about the head with pistols before being ordered to kneel. Each received a bullet behind the right ear. They crumpled to the ground dead while Mad Dog and Meatball fled.

Frank Adinolfi, although seriously injured, was still alive, and he was able to provide descriptions and the vital information that one of the men had size twelve feet. When the police checked their records of ex-convicts with size twelve feet, Taborsky's name jumped out.

As the police carried out their checks, Taborsky had one last fling, not realising that he and his partner in crime were close to being caught. On 26 January 1957, he shot sixty-nine-year-old John Rosenthal twice in the chest in his drug store on Maple Avenue in Hartford just after 9 pm. His son Henry had been working in the basement and came running upstairs to be confronted by a large man rifling through the cash register with a gun in his hand. Henry Rosenthal picked up a bottle and threw it at him and Taborsky ran out of the shop onto the street, turning to fire at Henry but narrowly missing him.

Taborsky and Culombe were arrested on 23 February and after three days of intensive questioning,

Culombe cracked and confessed, providing full details of each robbery and murder. They were charged with first-degree murder.

There was little doubt that the pair would be found guilty and sure enough, they were sentenced to death on 27 June 1957, their sentences being upheld shortly after by the state Supreme Court. Culombe, however, took his appeal to the US Supreme Court and it was found that the police had been too aggressive in obtaining his confession. He made a plea bargain, pleading guilty in exchange for a life sentence. He would die in prison.

Joe Taborsky opted to waive his right to appeal and even confessed to the 1950 killing that had provided his first experience of Death Row.

On 17 May 1960, he ate a banana split, drank a cherry soda and smoked a few cigarettes before taking the walk he had avoided five years previously. At the age of thirty-five, he became the 73rd man to be executed in Connecticut since 1894 and the last in the whole of New England until 2005.

16TH STREET BAPTIST CHURCH BOMBING

George C. Wallace, Governor of Alabama, told the *New York Times* in a 1963 interview that to stop integration of blacks and whites Alabama needed a 'few first-class funerals'. Just a week later, Alabama got them.

The explosion smashed a hole through the back wall of the church, brought down the rear steps and blew out all the stained glass windows apart from one. It depicted Jesus Christ, the glass that made up his face damaged by the blast, leading young children. It was 10.22 am on Sunday 15 September 1963, and the bomb had gone off just as twenty-six black kids were walking into the church's basement assembly room to take part in the closing prayers of a sermon entitled 'The Love that Forgives.' Following the explosion, four little girls tragically lay dead – Addie

Mae Collins, aged fourteen, Denise McNair, aged eleven, Carole Robertson, aged fourteen, and Cynthia Wesley, aged fourteen. Another twenty-two people were injured. Shortly before the explosion, a white man had been spotted climbing out of a white and turquoise Chevrolet, carrying a box that he placed under the steps of the 16th Street Baptist Church in Birmingham, Alabama, a church that had become a rallying point and meeting place for civil rights demonstrators.

Birmingham, the most segregated city in a stridently segregated South, was home to the South's most violent chapter of the white supremacist organisation, the Ku Klux Klan, and this was another of dozens of bombings that had terrorised the city's black community since the end of the Second World War.

In 1963 the city had become the focus of the struggle for civil rights when Dr Martin Luther King, Jr, through his organisation, the Southern Christian Leadership Conference, had decided to launch a crusade for equal rights there. In his effort to win over the white community by occupying the moral high ground, he was opposed by an ideal opponent – the truculent Commissioner of Public Safety, Eugene 'Bull' Connor. Connor was more than happy to present a national and international television audience with scenes of brutality as his officers dealt with protestors. King went to prison himself for the cause and while in a Birmingham jail penned the eloquent 'Letter from Birmingham Jail', criticising moderate whites who were more interested in order than in justice.

Meanwhile, Bull Connor was turning dogs and fire hoses on demonstrators and hundreds of school-children were arrested, the city having to take them away in buses, there were so many. President Kennedy himself lobbied Birmingham businessmen to try to reach an accommodation. Finally, in May 1963, white city leaders had agreed that public facilities would be desegregated.

To some sections of the white community, however, the move was not welcomed. The following day bombs exploded at the headquarters of King's organisation's offices and at his brother's home. The black community rose up, rioting leading to serious damage on nine blocks of Alabama. Alabama State Troopers were called in and as they attacked the rioters, bottles and missiles rained down on them. Although the riots were damaging to Dr King's cause of non-violent protest, the seriousness of the situation struck home with Kennedy and his administration, fearing that blacks in the South could become uncontrollable. Ironically, it was the threat of violence that galvanised the government into taking action.

Demonstrations and protests broke out across the South as blacks in other cities tried to emulate what had been achieved in Birmingham. Almost 15,000 people were arrested in 758 civil rights demonstrations in 186 cities. The President made a televised broadcast in which he called civil rights a 'moral issue' and gave his support to the idea of federal civil rights legislation. Tragically, however, it went down badly in some quarters and later that night, Mississippi civil rights activist, Medgar Evers was shot and killed on the driveway of his house as he got out of his car.

On 28 August, Martin Luther King delivered his famous 'I Have a Dream' speech in Washington before a crowd of quarter of a million people.

However, the shadow of political violence was never far away as the bombing of the 16th Street Baptist Church amply demonstrated. Thousands of blacks poured onto the streets of Alabama and fought with police for two hours following the bombing, police firing into the air in efforts to disperse the crowds. Afterwards, there were sporadic scuffles and shooting throughout the afternoon and into the night. Police were sent in by Governor George C. Wallace with orders to break up all gatherings of both whites and blacks. Meanwhile, five hundred National Guardsmen were on standby.

The investigation into the bombing was launched

immediately but the head of the FBI at the time, J. Edgar Hoover, disliked Martin Luther King and all he stood for. Nonetheless, the FBI knew the identities of the bombers by 13 May 1965 when a memo to Hoover listed them as former Ku Klux Klansmen Robert E. Chambliss, Bobby Frank Cherry, Herman Frank Cash and Thomas E. Blanton, Jr, 122 sticks of dynamite had been used in the bombing and they had belonged to Robert E. Chambliss, also known as 'Dynamite Bob'. He was initially charged with the murders but was not convicted. Instead, he was successfully prosecuted for owning the dynamite without a permit. He was fined $100 and given a six-month jail sentence. It would not be until 1977 that he would be prosecuted by Alabama attorney Bill Baxley for the four murders. At last he was convicted and sent to prison for life. He died there in 1985.

Many years later, it emerged that the FBI had a quantity of evidence against the bombers, but on Hoover's orders, it was not shared with prosecutors. He feared that a white jury would never convict and liked to proceed only with cases where he knew he would win. He would also have to come clean in court about his use of a wiretap in the investigation as well as reveal his sources.

Blanton, for instance, was under surveillance, closely watched and listened to by the FBI who had planted a microphone in his apartment in 1964. He had watched the civil rights demonstrations with a mounting sense of anger as he realised that they were beginning to win the argument. He feared the change that was about to come. On one occasion Blanton is heard to say, 'I like to go shooting, I like to go fishing, I like to go bombing,' and on another he is heard telling a friend that he was finished with women. 'I am going to stick to bombing churches,' he says.

In July 1997, the Justice Department and the state of Alabama announced that they had re-opened the investigation into the bombing, having just re-located vital tapes that had long been lost in the FBI archives. It was another step in righting the wrongs of those dark days of the fifties and sixties. Byron de la Beckwith had been convicted in 1994 for the 1963 assassination of Medgar Evers and former Ku Klux Klan imperial wizard Sam Bowers was convicted in 1998 of the 1966 firebomb-killing of an NAACP leader. Thomas Blanton, now aged sixty-two, was finally convicted of the murders on 9 July 2001, thirty-eight years after the incident. It took the jury a mere two and a half hours to reach its verdict and Blanton was sent away for life.

Bobby Frank Cherry was supposed to be tried at the same time as Blanton but claimed to be suffering from vascular dementia that would prevent him from assisting his own defence. Eventually, however, he was declared mentally fit to stand trial. He denied any involvement but was said by an ex-wife to have bragged about having taken part in the bombing. She claimed that he had told her that he lit the fuse. He was sentenced to life, dying in the Kilby Correctional Facility in Montgomery in 2004.

A third man, Mitchell Burns, an associate of the bombers and a fellow member of the Ku Klux Klan, became an informant for the FBI, taping conversations and writing down everything he heard.

The fourth bomber, Herman Frank Cash, died in 1994 without facing charges.

UNIVERSITY OF TEXAS MASSACRE

The tower at the University of Texas at Austin stands 307 feet tall, the centrepiece of the campus and a well-known landmark at the heart of the city of Austin. On 1 August 1966, it became better known as the location in which for ninety-six terrifying minutes student Charlie Whitman fired the shots that killed fourteen innocent people in the very first of America's grisly catalogue of school shootings.

To the outside world Charlie Whitman was upstanding and reliable. His family were fairly wealthy and respected by the inhabitants of Lake Worth, Florida where they lived. Although everything appeared to be fine, however – Charlie was a good student, a fine pianist and had been one of the youngest ever Eagle Scouts – behind the closed doors of the Whitman home there were problems. Charlie's father, C.A. Whitman, was a plumber and had done very well for himself by working hard over the years.

But he ruled his home with a rod of iron, often beating his wife and exercising rigid discipline over his three sons. This discipline involved beatings with belts and fists and was meted out whenever one of the boys showed weakness of any kind or failed to live up to their father's high expectations. At the same time, however, they were all well provided for – the boys were bought guns, motorbikes and many other things their father thought would help them to become men.

It had all become too much for the eighteen-year-old Charlie in 1959 when he was severely beaten by his father after coming home drunk. C.A. nearly killed him by throwing him into the family swimming pool where he almost drowned. Afterwards Charlie immediately enlisted in the United States Marine Corps.

Trying to prove himself, he worked hard. Based at the Guantanamo naval base in Cuba he studied and passed a number of exams. He was awarded a Good Conduct Medal and the Marine Corps Expeditionary Medal.

Chillingly, he also proved himself to be a very good shot.

Eventually, he was awarded a scholarship through the Naval Enlisted Science Education Program which was designed to teach engineers who had prospects of later becoming officers. He was admitted to the

University of Texas at Austin but before long was getting into trouble. He and some other students were arrested for poaching deer and he was gambling, running up large debts with some very unsavoury characters. His college work was suffering, too, although there was some improvement after his marriage to a fellow student, Kathy Leissner in August 1962. It was too late, however, and the Navy withdrew his scholarship. He returned to active duty at Camp Lejeune in North Carolina at the beginning of 1963, leaving Kathy to finish her studies in Austin.

He was dismayed to learn that his time at university did not count towards his active duty enlistment and began to detest the navy. In November 1963 he was court-martialled for gambling and loan-sharking as well as for the unauthorised possession of a gun with which he had threatened another soldier who owed him money. Found guilty, he was sentenced to thirty days confinement and ninety days hard labour. He had made the rank of Lance-Corporal and was stripped of this promotion and reduced to Private again.

At last, after his father had pulled some strings to obtain an early release for his son, Charlie received an honourable discharge in December 1964 and, embarrassed by his failures as a student and a soldier, returned to Austin determined to make a fresh start.

He enrolled at the university to study architectural engineering, supporting himself with a job as a bill collector for a finance company. He then moved on to become a teller in a bank. His leisure hours were taken up with activities with a local Boy Scout group.

On the surface, he was a fine upstanding person who helped out in his local community. The journals he wrote, however, told a different story. He still felt inadequate and he details countless self-improvement schemes in his writings, desperately trying to become a better person, the kind of man his father would respect. Like C.A., he had been violent towards his wife at the beginning of their marriage, but now wrote how caring and considerate a husband should be. Also like his father, however, he was the victim of a terrible temper.

He was financially dependent on Kathy who taught at an Austin school but C.A. still sent him money and expensive gifts. He felt like a failure who had achieved nothing in his life and was dependent on others. His self-loathing grew so bad that his wife suggested he see a counsellor.

Just to make matters worse, C.A. and his wife finally split up around this time, his mother, Margaret, moving to Austin and providing him with a permanent reminder of the bad times. The couple divorced later that year. Charlie seemed to become even more depressed, finally agreeing to see a doctor who prescribed Valium and recommended that he see a university health centre psychiatrist, Dr Maurice Heatly.

Heatly recognised immediately the anger that was bubbling up inside Charlie. Their conversations were mainly about his father and his own inadequacies. At one point he told the psychiatrist about a fantasy that he had about going up to the top of the tower on the university campus with a deer rifle and taking pot shots at the people below. Heatly, however, did not believe that Charlie was a real danger to people; he had been talking for years about doing this, comments that were dismissed. He had one session with Dr Heatly but ominously did not return for a second.

Charlie had used drugs before and by the summer of 1966 was using the amphetamine, Dexedrine, to get him through his job as a research assistant and keep him awake while he studied. Nonetheless, his studies were flagging, as was his self-esteem. Everyone agreed that he was trying to do too much. The only thing that changed, however, was that his violent fantasies became even stronger.

He took the first step towards mayhem on 31 July, buying binoculars, a Bowie knife and a supply of canned meat. The day progressed more or less normally. He collected Kathy from work – she was working a summer job as an operator at South-western Bell – and they went to see a film. Afterwards they visited some friends, John and Fran Morgan, who later said that all seemed normal, although Charlie was unusually quiet. Kathy went back for her evening shift at six o'clock and Charlie went home. He had some letter-writing to do.

He wrote as if he had already committed the acts he was describing. 'I don't quite understand what it is that compels me to type this letter. Perhaps it is to leave some vague reason for the actions I have recently performed.' He talked about the 'many unusual and irrational thoughts' he had been having. He asked for his body to undergo an autopsy after his death to discover if there had been some physical reason for his behaviour and his thoughts. He then chillingly detailed the plan he had devised for the next twenty-four hours including his intention to kill his wife. He said that he would pick her up from work and then kill her because he did not consider this world worth living in and he did not want to leave her to suffer alone. He cited the same reason for killing his mother.

While he was writing this letter, he was interrupted by a knock at the door. It was a couple of friends, Larry and Eileen Fuess. They had a pleasant visit, buying ice cream from an ice cream vendor before leaving.

At 9.30 pm, Charlie went to pick up Kathy. Returning home, she talked on the phone to friends for a while. He called his mother asking if they could come over to share her air conditioning but went alone as Kathy was tired and decided to go to bed. He left for his mother's house close to midnight.

The carnage began.

He strangled her from behind with a length of rubber tubing as they entered the apartment, before stabbing her with a knife. She was also bludgeoned on the back of the head but it is unknown what he used to do this.

Having killed his mother, he sat down to write another letter.

'I have just taken my mother's life,' he wrote, 'I am very upset over having done it . . . I am truly sorry that this is the only way I could see to relieve her sufferings but I think it was best.' He put her to bed and wrote a note to the building's janitor, pretending that it had been written by his mother and asking him not to disturb her.

Returning home, he quickly dispatched his wife, as she lay in bed asleep. Pulling back the covers, he stabbed her in the chest five times. He returned to the letter he had begun the previous evening. '3:00 am,' he added to it in blue ink, 'Both dead.' He went on to blame his actions on his father. He wrote notes to his brothers and to his father before re-visiting his diaries, highlighting entries where he had written favourably about his wife.

Charlie Whitman was nothing if not organised. He had dug out his old Marine footlocker and had already begun to fill it with supplies. He had a radio, water, gasoline, a notebook and pen, a compass, a hatchet, a hammer, food, two knives, a torch (with batteries) and a lot more. His arsenal consisted of a 35 caliber Remington rifle, a 6mm Remington rifle with a scope, a 357 Magnum Smith & Wesson revolver, a 9mm Luger pistol, and a Galesi-Brescia pistol. That would not be enough, however, and he added to it later that morning with the purchase of a 30 caliber M-1 carbine and a 12-gauge shotgun.

To take care of business, he telephoned his wife's company and told them that she was ill and would not be coming to work.

In order to transport the footlocker, he hired a two-wheeled dolly and then bought ammunition from a variety of outlets to reduce suspicion. He was home again by 10.30 when he called his mother's employer to tell them that she would not be coming to work that day. He sawed the barrel of the shotgun he had bought and by 11 am he was ready.

His job as research assistant allowed him to bring large objects onto campus and so he passed through security without question. By 11.35, he had unloaded the footlocker and was wheeling it on the dolly into the tower's lift. He travelled to the 27th floor.

Edna Townsley was on duty at reception. Charlie hit her on the back of the head and dragged her behind a couch. Still alive at that time, she would be dead in a few hours. Shortly after, two people, Cheryl Botts and Don Walden, came into the reception area. They saw Charlie leaning over the couch, guns in his hands. They were not unduly worried, for some reason, and left, making it to safety.

Around this time, Michael Gabour, his wife Mary, their two sons and William and Margeurite Lamport came up the stairs but could not open the door – it was blocked by a desk. The men put their weight into the door, pushing it open to be confronted by Whitman who opened fire, spraying them with shotgun pellets. Mark Gabour was killed instantly, Mike was seriously wounded and Marguerite Lamport died as Charlie poured fire down the stairwell. Mary Gabour fell to the ground, critically wounded. It would be more than an hour before the survivors were rescued. Meanwhile, William Lamport and Michael Gabour ran downstairs looking for help.

In the area around the tower people were diving for cover at the sound of gunfire. Charlie, meanwhile, got down to business. He unpacked his supplies and his guns and ammo. He took out his 6mm rifle, the most accurate he had, and aimed at a girl in the South Mall. Claire Wilson, a pregnant eighteen-year-old, screamed and fell to the ground. She was wounded, her unborn baby was dead. A nearby friend, Thomas Eckman, looked across and asked what was wrong but just as he did so was hit in the chest. He fell across her, dead. A moment later, Dr Hamilton Boyer, a visiting physics professor, also fell to the ground dead.

Thomas Ashton, a Peace Corps trainee, took a fatal bullet in the chest and the area quickly began to be covered in wounded people lying still on the ground terrified of another bullet.

The police arrived and sealed off the tower. They also managed to evacuate the wounded.

Charlie, meanwhile, focused on Guadalupe Street whose shops and businesses looked like providing rich pickings for him. Alex Hernandez, a newspaper delivery boy was picked off as he rode his bicycle. Seventeen-year-old Karen Griffin fell to the ground a moment after him and would die a week later from her wound. Thomas Karr fell wounded but with only an hour to live. People rushed into the shops and stayed well away from the windows.

Police officer Billy Speed was hit as he hid behind a statue and fell to the ground dying. Thirty-eight-year-old doctoral student Harry Walchuk was hit as he bought a newspaper. His six children would never see their father again. Paul Sonntag, a student, was killed instantly by a bullet in the mouth. Claudia Rutt, hiding beside him behind a construction barrier, was fatally wounded an instant later.

It was a fire-fight. Police officers aimed at the tower but could see nothing. People arrived on the scene with guns they had brought from home and also joined in. Still Charlie picked off his targets. Two electricians unloading their truck five hundred yards away thought they were safe. Roy Dell Schmidt was hit in the abdomen and killed.

Some officers succeeded in getting inside the tower and brought down Mary and Mike Gabour who had been lying in pools of blood on the 27th floor for over an hour. Officers Martinez and Crum crept up the steps to the reception area. Two others, McCoy and Day followed close behind. Whitman had wedged the door to the observation deck shut with his trolley but Martinez kicked the door open and emerged carefully onto the deck. Followed by McCoy, with the other two men guarding the door, he made his way towards the southern part of the deck, from where the firing had come. Meanwhile, bullets from down below continued to whiz past them.

Martinez rounded the corner, opening fire with his .38. Whitman tried to turn but was too slow. McCoy fired twice from his shotgun into the sniper's head and he collapsed to the floor. Martinez grabbed McCoy's shotgun, ran up to Whitman's convulsing body and shot him at point-blank range. It was 1.24 pm and Charlie Whitman was dead.

Fourteen others were dead down below and dozens were injured.

Charlie got the autopsy he had requested in his note and they did indeed discover something. He had a small tumour in his brain which some of his friends and family have since seized on as the reason for the madness of 1 August 1966. Experts disagree, however.

The tower at the University of Texas at Austin was eventually closed to visitors in 1976, but was reopened in September 1999. It has security guards, a stainless steel lattice to prevent suicide leaps and visitors have to pass through a metal detector to get in.

THE NEPTUNE MURDERS

Fred Cowan was dressed to kill. Military boots, khaki trousers, a US Army field jacket and a beret sporting the death's head insignia – the symbol worn by the SS in the Second World War. Beneath the jacket, he wore a T-shirt, the chest of which bore the logo of the White supremacist National States Rights Party – a thunderbolt and the words 'White Power'. He carried a keenly sharp 9-inch hunting knife at his waist as well as two .45 automatic handguns and two other 9mm automatics. They were all fully loaded. Around him in the GTO that he was driving were hundreds of rounds of ammunition.

He was a large man, 250 pounds and more than six feet tall. Tattoos, many of them depicting Nazi themes, covered his eighteen inch biceps and huge barrel chest. He was en route to the Neptune Worldwide Moving Company in the small city of New Rochelle to do serious damage that Valentine's Day morning in 1977.

Frederick William Cowan was thirty-three. He had been born in New Rochelle in 1943 and had been outstanding as a child, a pleasure to be around or to have in your classroom if you were one of his teachers at the Blessed Sacrament Elementary School. He excelled at high school and on graduation enrolled in an engineering college.

In 1962, however, he abruptly dropped out and joined the Army. Three years later he was court-martialled following an incident in which, in a feat of some strength, he lifted up a Volkswagen car and turned it over before smashing it up with his bare hands. He was sent to Army prison. More trouble followed the next year when he left the scene of an accident. He was discharged and repatriated.

It was a different Fred Cowan who returned to New Rochelle in March 1965. He had become fascinated by Adolf Hitler and the Nazis, assembling a collection of Nazi memorabilia and reading everything he could find about them. He had also assimilated the Nazi philosophy, often expressing to anyone who would listen, his hatred of blacks and Jews. His hero was Reinhard Heydrich, head of the Gestapo during the Second World War and he took to calling himself Reinhard. By this time, he had found at job at Neptune.

That morning, at around 7 am, Cowan parked his

GTO in the car park in front of the building in which Neptune was based. He went round to the boot of the vehicle, lifting out an assault rifle before walking towards the entrance to the building. Inside, he immediately confronted two men having a conversation, sixty-year-old Joseph Hicks who had been a Neptune employee for twenty-five years and his colleague, fifty-five-year-old Fred Holmes. Without a moment's hesitation, Cowan raised the rifle and fired at the two men who fell to the floor, killing them on the spot. Both were black.

There was panic in the building immediately. Other employees in the hallway fled as fast as they could. The police were summoned within seconds of the first burst of gunfire.

Cowan headed down the hallway to the room in which the company's drivers rested. Forty-five-year-old African-American James Green had come in early to study his route for that day. Cowan stood in the doorway and shot him dead with a bullet in the back. The others in the room ran in all directions to evade the shooter.

The dispatcher's office was next. Cowan sprayed bullets all around the room, striking twenty-four-year-old Joseph Russo in the stomach and chest. Russo would die of his wounds six weeks after the shooting.

Ronald Cowell had been a good friend of Cowan

and he ran right into him as he tried to escape from the company cafeteria. Cowan grabbed him at the door, put the rifle to his head and hissed, 'Go home and tell my mother not to come down to Neptune.' Cowell did not need telling twice.

As the occupants of the cafe scattered in all directions, he shouted 'Where is Norman Bing?' – Bing was Cowan's supervisor – 'I'm gonna fuckin' blow him away!' he took a combat stance just outside the door and fired randomly into the room. Someone managed to lock the door but he reached inside, cutting his hand badly in the process on the broken glass and unlocked it. Throughout the building, people who had been unable to escape, cowered in locked offices, behind upturned desks and tables, frightened for their lives.

Still screaming that he wanted Norman Bing, he carried on along the corridor. Tragically, Pariyarathu Varghese, a thirty-two-year-old Indian who had only arrived in America the previous year to get married, ran across his path. Cowan raised the rifle, took aim and shot him, killing him instantly. Norman Bing, meanwhile, was understandably keeping his head down, hiding behind a desk.

Bing and Cowan had fallen out two weeks previously when Bing had suspended the big man for refusing to move a refrigerator. When Cowan was supposed to return to work three days previously he had failed to show. It had not helped that Norman Bing was Jewish.

Cowan climbed the stairs at the back of the building up to the first floor, making for the office of the company president, Richard Kirschenbaum. It was empty, however. He removed the guns from the holsters at his waist and looked at the windows, pleased to see that they were tinted which meant that he could see out but no one could see in. His hand hurt and he wrapped it before beginning to re-load his weapons. As he looked out the window, he saw the flashing lights of a police car pulling into the car park in answer to the calls about a gunman being on the loose at Neptune.

Patrolman Allen McLoed saw people running in every direction as he arrived and for the first time since he had received the call, began to think that maybe this was the real thing. He climbed out of the car, little realising that the gunman was watching his every move from up above. Cowan calmly put his rifle to his shoulder, took careful aim and fired through the window. McLoed fell to the ground dead with bullets through his head, chest and heart. Cowan was not finished, however, and as the officer's body lay there, he pumped more rounds into him. Police officers were also high on his list of enemies due to the protection he believed they provided for Jews and blacks.

Other police cars, responding to calls were now swinging into the car park. As Officer Ray Saltiro leapt from his car to go to McLoed's assistance, Cowan opened up with his semi-automatic, dozens of bullets ricocheting off the tarmac. A cop car pulling into the car park was sprayed with bullets, shattering its windscreen and wounding the officer driving it in the arm. Officer Saltiro, too was wounded, taking a bullet in the leg as he rushed out to try to bring back McLoed, not realising that his colleague was already dead. The police officers, now pinned down behind their vehicles, radioed in for back-up.

A terrible firefight was now raging between the officers and Cowan, over one hundred bullets being fired in just a few minutes. Soon, however, police snipers moved in, taking up position in an abandoned office building across the street from the Neptune building. They were unable to see Cowan, however, because of the tinted glass. The New Rochelle Police Commissioner, William Hegarty, was also on the scene, issuing instructions from a command centre that had been established. They tried to gain information from fleeing Neptune employees, to ascertain whether there was more than one gunman.

As ambulances began to arrive, Cowan opened fire

on them, the police snipers, meanwhile, trying desperately to get into good firing positions. Astonishingly, crowds were gathering, curious to see what the noise was all about, but in grave danger as bullets ricocheted off the pavements and buildings.

They tried to establish how many employees were left in the building and were horrified to realise that there might be as many as thirty. Meanwhile, they commandeered a couple of trucks, backing them into the car park in order to effect the rescue of the wounded officers trapped behind their cars. Cowan was now taking potshots at the snipers and shooting randomly, smashing windows and hitting parked cars several blocks away. By now there was a huge crowd and hundreds of police officers from neighbouring police departments.

At 10.30, a distant rumble could be heard and a twenty-ton armoured personnel carrier trundled down the street. It rolled into the car park, stopping next to the body of Officer McLoed. Under the cover it afforded them, a couple of his colleagues picked him up and pulled him into the vehicle.

A team of FBI agents and police officers was now dispatched to clear the Neptune employees from the building, entering through a rear door that Cowan could not see. They found the bodies of Green, Holmes and Hicks in the foyer and helped fourteen others, still alive, out of the building. One described it as looking like a war scene.

Suddenly, at 12.13, a phone rang on an open line on the switchboard. Lieutenant Tom Perotti was amazed to find himself talking to Fred Cowan when he answered. Astonishingly, the guman asked for some potato salad and hot chocolate, telling Perotti he got mean when he was hungry. He promised not to hurt anyone and asked for it to be left at the door. He hung up.

In siege situations communication with the person inside is absolutely vital and the command centre did its level best to establish a link to Cowan, speaking to him continuously through a loudspeaker that had been rigged up. His parents were brought in to try to reason with him, but still he ignored their efforts.

At 2.15 in the afternoon, a Neptune employee, Sal DeBello, who had been trapped in a toilet in the building, managed to escape but told the police that there was another man, William Hill, locked in another toilet on the same floor as Cowan and too afraid to try and come out. As another, Nicholas Siciliano emerged, it became obvious that there were still people hiding in the building. For all the cops knew, they might even have been taken hostage by Cowan.

A small assault team was assembled under the command of forty-three-year-old veteran, Sergeant

Bill Augostini, its mission to sweep the first floor where Cowan was hiding out, looking for employees.

Just before they entered the building, a single shot rang out from somewhere inside the building.

The team, wearing flak jackets and steel helmets, entered the building, cautiously making their way up the blood-covered stairs to the floor above. Gradually, hugging the walls, they negotiated their way to the president's office. The door was ajar and, as they peered anxiously inside, they could see a body lying on the floor. Cowan lay on his front, blood pooling under his head. In his hand was the .45. It was almost ten hours since he had walked into the Neptune building.

When they searched his house, they were astonished not only by the amount of Nazi memorabilia; they also found eleven cans of gunpowder, shotgun shells, primers, three antique muskets, one rifle, shell casings and equipment to make bullets, thousands of rounds of ammunition, a machete, at least twenty knives and eight Nazi bayonets.

Fred Cowan had meant business.

THE HUNGERFORD MASSACRE

'I wish I had stayed in bed' he shouted as helicopters hovered noisily overhead and police sharpshooters nervously gazed down their rifle sights, their guns aimed at the third floor window of John O'Gaunt Community Technology College where he had once been a student. Twenty-seven-year-old Michael Robert Ryan might well have wished he had stayed in bed that morning of 19 August 1987, but not as much as the inhabitants of the small English market town of Hungerford where he had gone on a murderous rampage earlier that day, killing fourteen people to add to the victim he had peppered with bullets in Savernake Forest at the start of his bloodletting.

It was 19 August and a lovely summer's day; thirty-five-year-old Susan Godfrey had taken her two children, Hannah, aged four and James, aged two, to the forest for a picnic. She was just getting ready to leave around noon when she saw a man walking towards her. Michael Ryan was dressed in dark clothing and, alarmingly, was carrying a gun. She did not know but he had been watching her for some time from his car. He often watched women but something made him want to do more this time.

He ordered her to put the children in the car and, anxious that nothing should happen to them, she fastened their seat belts, telling them that she would be back in a few moments to take them to their grandmother's house to help her celebrate her 95th birthday.

Ryan picked up the mat on which they had been picnicking and ordered her into the woods with him. A moment later the children heard a number of shots. He had pumped thirteen bullets into her. He returned, climbed into his car and drove off.

Ryan next appeared at the Golden Arrow petrol station where he filled up his tank as well as a five-litre can. Mrs Kakoub Dean, wife of the owner, seated behind the protective glass of the kiosk, watched as Ryan went to the boot of the car and took out a semi-automatic rifle. She was amazed to see him crouch in a shooting position and aim directly at her. She ducked and the bullet missed her, ricocheting around her work-station. He was annoyed and came into the shop pointing the weapon at her as she pleaded for her life. He pulled the trigger but, luckily for her, the gun failed to fire. He tried again and again it did not fire. He looked at her, turned and walked back to his car. He drove off, leaving her astonished to still be alive. She pulled herself together and telephoned the police only to learn that they had already been alerted by a man who had thought a robbery was in progress. It was 12.45.

Ryan, meanwhile, had driven home to 4 South View, a terrace house in a cul-de-sac in Hungerford where he lived with his sixty-three-year-old mother, Dorothy. She had been widowed two years previously when her eighty-year-old husband had died of cancer. A dinner lady at a local school, Dorothy, was reported to have spoilt her only child, paying for whatever he wanted. Michael had grown up with few friends, was described as sullen and, small for his age, was often bullied at school. Lately, things had got worse. He had become even more irritable and tense than usual, a state of affairs not helped by the fact that he was unemployed again. He had been a failure at school and had dropped out of a technical college where he had tried to obtain the necessary qualifications to become a building contractor. He ended up as a caretaker in a girls' school and had even lost that job.

He had one obsession – guns. Dorothy had given him his first gun, an air rifle and as soon as he was old enough, he began to collect other weapons, keeping them in a cabinet in the house. The guns undoubtedly made him feel powerful, making up for the weakness that had led to him being bullied. He also told lies about himself to help his self-esteem and became irrationally angry if someone doubted what he was telling them, whether it was that he had been in the army or that he owned a gun shop. To bolster the swaggering gun-owning macho man that he wanted to be – in imitation of his hero, the Sylvester Stallone character, Rambo – he began to dress in military clothing, purchasing survival equipment and camouflage jackets. He also obtained a special licence that permitted him to own even more powerful guns and he put together an impressive collection consisting of a Zabala shotgun, a Browning shotgun, a Beretta 92 semi-automatic pistol, a CZ ORSO semi-automatic .32 pistol, a Chinese copy of a Kalashnikov AK-47 semi-automatic rifle and an M1 Carbine semi-automatic rifle.

He went into the house, ignoring the neighbours standing chatting outside. They were used to being ignored by him. A short while later they heard what sounded like muffled shots from inside. Ryan had shot his two dogs.

He came out again, dressed in a flak jacket and wearing a band around his head, just like Rambo. He was carrying a bag that he had filled with food. Sliding into his silver Vauxhall Astra, he turned the key, but the engine did not respond. He tried again, but again the engine failed to turn over. It was one of the most significant engine failures in history.

He was furious as he clambered out of the car, taking his anger out on it by firing four bullets into the boot. He opened it and took out the petrol tank he had filled earlier and went back into the house. There he doused the downstairs rooms with the petrol and tossed a lit match into it. The house began to burn.

With the AK-47 over his shoulder and the Beretta in his hand, he emerged onto the street again. Immediately, he spotted a couple of neighbours, Roland and Sheila Mason, in their garden and shot them, killing both. He shot another neighbour through her window before running up and down the street a few times, looking for other neighbours. Meanwhile, he shot randomly at anything that moved. He warned some children to get off the street and then was confronted by Dorothy Smith who had come outside to find out what the noise was. He did not shoot her, however, merely turning and walking away.

Not far away he shot and wounded fourteen-year-old Lisa Mildenhall, apparently smiling at her before pulling the trigger. He killed Ken Clements who had been innocently walking with his family. The other family members huddled down out of sight as Ryan walked past.

The police were now moving into the area and a helicopter hovered overhead. Roadblocks had been established to prevent people from entering the danger zone. A fire engine could not get through to put out the fire in South View.

Ryan's next victim was a police officer, Roger Brereton who drove his patrol car into a hail of bullets that killed him. His car crashed into a telephone pole. He fired at another car, injuring its occupants before killing a man gardening on the corner of South View and Fairview Roads. Abdul Khan, a neighbour who had come home to make sure his family was safe ran into Ryan at this point. He had been a friend and had even helped Ryan to build his gun cabinet. It did not seem to matter – he was shot three times, but lived.

An ambulance was trying to reverse into South View but Ryan saw it and opened fire, sending the driver speeding off in the opposite direction.

Ivor Jackson whose wife had telephoned him as Ryan was taking aim at her, arrived on the scene, driven there by a work colleague. Ryan saw them approach and fired into their vehicle. Jackson was hit three times in the chest and once in the head. The driver was killed instantly and their car crashed into Roger Breteton's patrol car.

Just then, Ryan's mother, Dorothy, arrived home from shopping. She was, of course, horrified to see her home ablaze and the bodies of her neighbours littering the streets. In front of her stood her son, Michael, a gun in his hands. They tried to hold her back but she pushed through, shouting his name and asking him why he was killing people. She stopped next to the car in which Ivor Jackson sat, seriously wounded. He heard her say, 'Don't shoot me,' just before two shots rang out. Hit in the leg and the stomach, she collapsed to the ground. Then, with people watching from the houses around him, Michael Ryan walked up to his mother's prostrate body and shot her a further two times in the back, killing her.

The police, meanwhile, were waiting on specially trained officers of the Tactical Firearms Unit to arrive before making their move. They realised that with a man as heavily armed as Ryan an intervention could prove costly. They followed his movements from above and warned people to remain indoors.

Ryan walked across the school playing fields firing off random shots as he did so. He wounded an elderly woman and then killed twenty-six-year-old Francis Butler who had been walking his dog. He threw away the M1 carbine and began using the Beretta and AK-47. He took a shot at a boy on a bicycle but missed.

A taxi driver, Marcus Bernard, drove past on his way to see his newborn son in hospital. He would forever regret slowing down to see what was happening when Ryan fired a bullet at him that blasted off a piece of his head. Ryan continued, wounding another two people. He then killed a man and wounded a woman in a passing car. With extraordinary irony, they turned out to be the parents of the police officer who had checked Ryan out a few months previously that led to him being given the licence to own more powerful weapons. Another vehicle was attacked, the driver being hit and crashing his car into a pole.

Eleven people were now dead. The twelfth was van driver, Eric Vardy, and the thirteenth was twenty-year-old car driver, Sandra Hill. Suddenly, Ryan went into a house on Priory Road where he found Victor and Myrtle Gibbs. Myrtle was in a wheelchair and Victor threw himself across her to protect her, taking the full force of a volley of shots from Ryan's Beretta. Myrtle was seriously wounded and would die a few days later in hospital. He opened fire on some neighbours from the house and then shot and killed Ian Playle, passing with his young family in his car.

In the last fifteen minutes Michael Ryan had killed fourteen people and fatally wounded one other.

It was almost at an end. He left the house on Priory Road and made for the place where many of his problems had begun – John O'Gaunt College. He still took time to shoot George Noon who was working in his garden in the shoulder and the eye. He is also said to have pointed his gun at Noon's next-door neighbour and said 'Bang!' without firing.

By 2.30 in the afternoon, the school building was surrounded. The police opened a dialogue with him and at first he was belligerent but he began to change as the hours passed, expressing his regret at killing his mother and his dogs.

At 6.52, officers heard the sound of a muffled shot. After three hours during which there was no movement from within the building, they went in. They discovered him barricaded in an office, behind a filing cabinet, his gun between his knees.

He had died where he had suffered most.

GEORGE BANKS

Seasoned detectives were sickened by what they found at 28 School House Lane in Wilkes-Barre, northeastern Pennsylvania. When one detective asked how many were dead another replied that he'd lost track. Blood spattered the walls and ceilings of the rooms in the house and children as young as one-year-old lay dead, bullet holes blasted in their young bodies. They were about to find out that their killer had not restricted his rampage to just this house. There were more bodies at a trailer park in the nearby Pennsylvania township of Plains.

They should have seen it coming, really. George Emil Banks had been spinning out of control for some time. He had been ordained by mail order by the Universal Life Church, expecting as a result to be subject to religious tax exemptions. When the IRS rejected his application, he picketed city hall. He was also keeping a diary of his thoughts and ideas, meticulously noting down whatever was running through his addled brain. He began to develop an

Although Adolf Hitler was the most prominent man in the Nazi regime, many of his loyal supporters were just as guilty of crimes against humanity. Hermann Goering (above) was a prime example. Goering failed to convince the judges at his tribunal and he was found guilty of conspiracy to wage war, crimes against peace, war crimes and crimes against humanity.

Karl Adolf Eichmann was head of the Department for Jewish Affairs in the Gestapo from 1941 to 1945. He was responsible for the deportation of three million Jews to extermination camps. He was tried in an Israeli court on fifteen criminal charges, including crimes against humanity. He was convicted and hanged in 1962.

Doctor Wouter Basson is a South African cardiologist and former head of a secret chemical and biological warfare project during the apartheid era. Despite being acquitted in 2002 of sixty-seven separate charges, he was still labelled with the nickname 'Doctor Death'.

Slobodan Milosevic, the former president of Serbia and of Yugoslavia, was charged with crimes against humanity, violating the laws or customs of war, grave breaches of the Geneva Conventions and genocide, for his role during the wars in Croatia, Bosnia and Kosovo.

Charles Raymond Starkweather (above) was an
American spree killer who murdered eleven victims
during a road trip with his underage girlfriend, Caril
Ann Fugate (top left). Their story fascinated the world
and became an inspiration for many films.

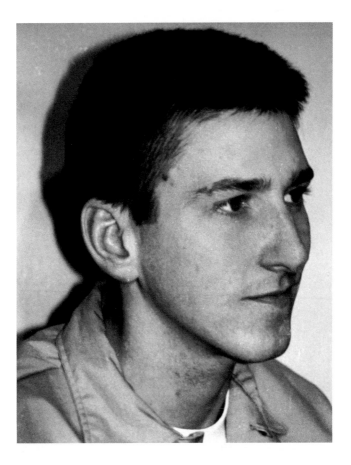

When his sentence was read out in court, Timothy McVeigh showed no sign of remorse for the 1995 Oklahoma bombing which killed 168 people and injured more than 500. The resulting shockwave was enormous, especially as this so-called 'homegrown' terrorism had been carried out by the kid nextdoor.

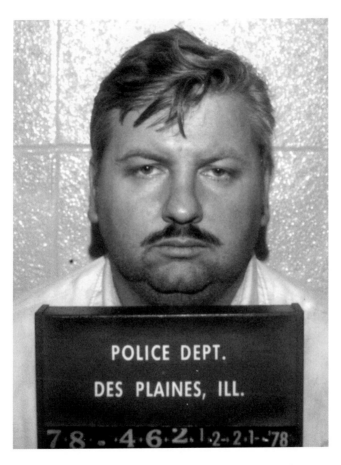

John Wayne Gacy was a popular community member, often dressing as a clown to amuse children at local hospitals. What people didn't know was the darker side of his character – the mass killer! He was eventually convicted and executed for the rape and murder of thirty-three boys and young men.

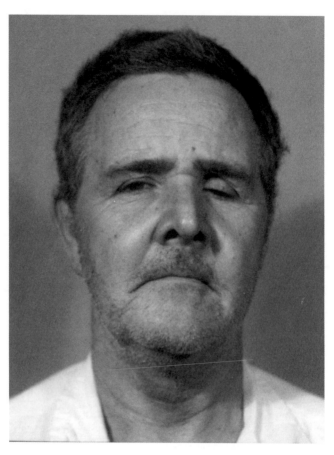

Henry Lee Lucas held the title as 'the most infamous man on death row' in the mid-1980s. Lucas wanted police to believe he was the ultimate mass killer, and he confessed to murder after murder, closing more than 200 cases. Unfortunately, his enthusiasm left many real murderers free on the streets to kill again.

unhealthy admiration for men such as Jim Jones who forced his followers to commit mass suicide in Guyana, mass murderer Charles Manson and serial killer John Wayne Gacy. As often seems to be the case with people who murder, he was fascinated by survivalist magazines and literature and subscribed to paramilitary publications such as *Soldier of War*. He collected guns and ammunition and rambled on to anyone who would listen about starting a war. His increasingly erratic behaviour peaked in 1982 when he started telling fellow guards at the State Correctional Institute in Camp Hill, where he worked, that he could commit mass murder and that he was preparing his children for warfare. He also told them he was going to blow his brains out.

As he wandered through the School Lane house, pumping bullets into young bodies, did he think of his own childhood, getting angry at the memory of the racism he claimed to have suffered as a result of his mother being white and his father black? He was born in 1942 and was followed by trouble of some kind or other all his life, underachieving and blaming everyone else for it. He was bullied at school because of his mixed race parentage, he claimed, abused by black and white alike. It got no better as he got older and he decided that the army was probably the best way to escape and make a clean start. He enlisted in 1959 but was discharged just two years later because he found it difficult to take orders.

He turned to crime, taking part in the robbery of a bar in Scranton, Pennsylvania in September 1961. When the owner of the bar refused to cooperate, Banks pulled out a gun and shot him in the chest. Banks got away with nothing apart from a six to fifteen year prison sentence in the State Correctional Institute in Graterford.

He escaped, however, while out on a work detail, only to be recaptured three hours later. They added eighteen months to his sentence and he was paroled in March 1969, after spending seven and a half years behind bars. On his release, he married a woman named Doris Jones whom he had known for a long time, and worked in a number of jobs.

In 1971, he found a good, well-paid job as a technician with the Bureau of Water Quality of the State Department of Environmental Resources in Wilkes-Barre, the first decent job he had. He also succeeded in getting his sentence commuted and his days on parole were over.

At home, though, things were not good – Banks's adultery not helping – and he and Doris separated in 1976. Around this time, he moved into the School Lane house along with several young, white girlfriends, some of whom had been homeless and two of whom were sisters. Regina Clemens had his daughter, Montanzima, in 1976, Sharon Mazzilo had a son, Kissamayu, the same year and Regina's sister, Susan Yuhas, had George's son, Bowendy, in 1978.

As his mental state began to deteriorate, his work began to suffer and the Department of Environmental Resources asked for his resignation in 1979. At home, too, he was facing problems. He lived in a white neighbourhood that did not look kindly on a black man living with a white woman, a situation not helped by the fact that he was living with more than one. They even firebombed his house once and windows were broken. Once in downtown Wilkes-Barre, he was attacked with a beer bottle and a nasty altercation was avoided only by the intervention of the police.

His neighbours accused him of being the one causing problems, prohibiting his women from talking to the neighbours and not allowing his children to play with the local kids.

Despite his prison record, he was employed in 1980 at the State Correctional Institute in Camp Hill. Meanwhile, another white woman, Dorothy Lyons, joined the Banks household, bringing her daughter, nine-year-old Nancy. Soon, Dorothy was pregnant and their son Foraroude was born in January 1981 while Susan gave birth to another daughter, Mauritania.

Sharon Mazzillo had had enough, however, and moved out to go and live with her mother.

In September 1982, Banks was sent home from work after his superiors heard about his wild ramblings about mass killings and preparing his children for war. They wanted him to undergo a psychiatric evaluation following which he was put on sick leave.

At the time he was also suffering stress from a custody dispute he had entered into with Sharon over Kassimayu. He won the dispute, being awarded custody as the child's primary care-provider, but Sharon refused to comply and held on to Kassimayu. Banks was furious. Too many things were going against him and he was close to breaking-point.

The night of 24 September, he had taken a pile of prescription drugs, washed down with straight gin. He woke up at 11.30 pm feeling a little fuzzy. Next to him lay his AR-15 semi-automatic rifle and sleeping beside him was four-year-old Bowendy. His women, Regina, Susan and Dorothy were asleep in chairs in the room, Susan cuddling one-year-old Mauritania who woke up just as Banks did.

He picked up his gun, the feeling of anger that had been eating away at him for weeks still burning inside him like an ulcer. Without warning, he raised it, pointing it at Regina and pulled the trigger. She was shot in the right cheek, the bullet travelling down through her sleeping body and into her heart, killing her. He turned to Susan and pumped five bullets into her chest as she pleaded with him for mercy. He dispatched little Mauritania with a single bullet in the head and Dorothy was shot in the chest and the neck before falling to the floor. Bowendy took a bullet in the face and slumped forward. Suddenly, there was silence. Only seconds had passed and there were five bodies in front of him. It was far from over, however.

He walked now towards the bedrooms of the other children. Montazima, six years old, was sitting on her bed. She died with a bullet to the chest, a second in her head making sure. Eleven-year-old Nancy Lyons was sitting up on her bed and in her arms was one-year-old Forarounde. Banks climbed up onto the bed and took aim, firing three rapid shots and hitting Forarounde in the back of the head and Nancy on the arm and in the face.

In his own bedroom, he changed out of his blood-soaked clothing, putting on a T-shirt with the words 'Kill 'em all and let God sort 'em out' printed on it.

Twenty-two-year-old Jimmy Olsen and twenty-four-year-old Ray Hall Jr had been across the street when they heard the gunfire. They decided not to hang around too long to find out what was going on and headed for their car. They were too late, however. Banks was by this time out in the street. He ran towards them, screaming that they would not live to tell anyone about the incident. He aimed and fired at them, hitting them both in the chest.

He jumped into his car and drove the four miles to Heather Highlands trailer park in Plains where Sharon and Kissamayu were living with her mother, Angela, and her two sons, Angelo and Keith. On this day, they had a visitor – Angela's nephew Keith.

Banks approached the building and Sharon, seeing the rifle in his hands, tried to close the door to the house. He was too strong for her and forced his way in, immediately raising the gun and firing. She died instantly as the bullet severed the main blood vessel to her heart. He spotted five-year-old Kissamayu asleep on the couch, placed the barrel up against the child's forehead and fired. Alice, meanwhile, was trying to phone for help. He went up to her, placed the gun under her nose pointing upwards and literally blew her head off.

Keith was watching from a cupboard, trying not to make a sound as Scott ran down the hall into the room. Banks grabbed him and pushed him to the ground, kicking and punching him. He then raised him up, placed the barrel of his gun to his head and pulled the trigger.

He walked out the door screaming, 'I killed them all!' before driving off, eyes wild.

As the police began to arrive at School Lane, Banks was driving towards the house of his mother, Mary Banks Yelland. Meanwhile, two policeman had now arrived at Heather Highlands and discovered that George Banks was the shooter. An all-points bulletin was issued and another victim, Ray Hall Jr., had now died in hospital.

He arrived at his mother's house at around 5.30 am, having slept in his car for a while. When she opened the door, he was in tears, telling her that he had killed everyone. At first she did not believe him but she soon realised this was more than just the drink talking, even though he stank of booze. She telephoned the School Lane house to find out for sure and a detective picked up the phone at the other end. Banks snatched the receiver out of his mother's hand and told the man who he was, asking how his kids were. The detective told them they were all alive and fine, hoping to keep the other man on the phone in order to locate him. Banks told him he knew he was lying, however, and threw down the phone.

He asked his mother to drive him to an empty rented house that he knew and he packed a bag with hundreds of rounds of ammunition. At 24 Monroe Street, she dropped him off, returning to her own house to find it surrounded by police cars. By 7.20 the Monroe Street house was sealed off. Inside Banks had barricaded all the windows and doors. They tried to negotiate with him, using a loudspeaker, but he shouted back that he hadn't wanted his kids to be brought up in a racist world.

They tried to persuade him that the children were still alive, even getting a local radio station to broadcast a phony news bulletin to that effect, but Banks was having none of it. Even his mother failed to talk him out.

It was a friend and former co-worker, Robert Brunson who managed to talk him round. After he had spoken with him, Banks was silent for a while and then, at 11.17 am he handed his gun through a broken window to an officer and walked out the front door with his hands in the air. It was finally over.

Banks insisted that he was not insane and, indeed, he was deemed fit to stand trial. He took the stand himself, talking about a police conspiracy against him and about the racism he encountered in his everyday life. He claimed that the children had been alive when the police arrived at School Lane and that they had shot them to get him for murder. He demanded that the bodies be exhumed.

The jury found him guilty of twelve counts of first-degree murder, one of third-degree murder and also of attempted murder, aggravated assault, robbery, theft and endangering the life of another person.

On his forty-first birthday, George Emil Banks was sentenced to death. He appealed his case until 2000, his death warrant being signed twice in that time, but rescinded by the appeals court. Since his conviction, he has attempted suicide four times and has had to be force fed while undertaking hunger strikes. A psychiatric report describes how he thinks he is engaged in a spiritual struggle with the Antichrist in New York, he believes that Pennsylvania is controlled by Muslims and in the 1990s he was involved in what he called 'a private war with President Bill Clinton and Monica Lewinsky.'

George Banks is now dying of liver cancer in the State Correctional Institute at Gaterford, Pennsylvania.

STANDARD GRAVURE
SHOOTING

He had been 'argumentative and confrontational for a number of years' according to a police officer who knew him. A fellow employee at Standard Gravure said, 'This guy's been talking about this for a year. He's been talking about guns and *Soldier of Fortune* magazine. He's paranoid and he thought everyone was after him.' He had made threats against the company and on 14 September 1989, forty-seven-year-old Joseph 'Rocky' Wesbecker made good on his threats, killing seven fellow employees and wounding twelve.

It was 8.30 in the morning as he parked in the car park in front of the factory's main entrance. Standard Gravure was a major printing company in Louisville, Kentucky. Founded in 1922, it had been sold in 1986, but times were tough and many of its customers, principally retailers, were going out of business. This impacted upon the company workers as they experienced the stress of not knowing how long they were going to have a job. He got out carrying a Chinese-made semi-automatic AK-47 imitation, a SIG Sauer 9mm handgun and a bag containing two MAC-11s, a .38 Smith & Wesson revolver, a bayonet and an arsenal of ammunition.

The company's reception area was on the third floor above the print works and that was where he was headed, looking for the bosses he hated so much and who he thought had treated him so badly. An elevator took him up and just before the doors slid open, he made himself ready.

On the third floor, the receptionists, Sharon Needy and Angela Bowman were settling themselves down behind their desk for another day, the first calls beginning to light up the switchboard. The lift doors opened and suddenly gunshots rang out killing forty-nine-year-old Sharon instantly and hitting Angela in the back. She would be left paralysed by her wound.

He was on a hunt for the Standard Gravure President, Michael Shea, although if he could find any of the management or supervisors, he would be happy.

He set off down the corridor, killing forty-seven-year-old James Husband and injuring Forrest Conrad, Paula Warman and John Stein, a maintenance supervisor. Next, he walked down towards the pressroom where he had spent so much of his life. He shot and killed fifty-nine-year-old Paul Salle and wounded two others. Tossing his bag under a stairwell, he made his way to the basement. John Tingle had heard the noise and came out to find out what was going on. He said, 'How are you, Rock,' but Wesbecker just growled at him, 'Hi John. I told them I'd be back. Get away from me.' He was not going to kill his friend. Tingle pressed himself against the wall and let Wesbecker continue on his murderous way to the basement. Seeing a figure up ahead, he fired a bullet into him, killing him. However, fifty-four-year-old Richard Barger was another man that he had not wanted to kill. Recognising him, he walked over and said sorry, but, of course, it was too late for that

He went back up to the press floor where he shot randomly at everyone he came across. Fifty-six-year-old James Wible and forty-two-year-old Lloyd White fell to the ground dead. He strolled into the small room where workers took their breaks. He shot all seven people in there, killing forty-six-year-old William Ganote with a bullet in the head.

He was out of bullets now and had to re-load, but was soon firing again, hitting forty-five-year-old Kenneth Fentress and fatally wounding him. Suddenly, however, Wesbecker walked out of the pressroom and took out his SIG Sauer pistol. He quickly put it under his chin and pulled the trigger, killing himself.

Thirty minutes of horror had left eight people dead, including Wesbecker, twelve wounded and one person who had suffered a heart attack as a result of the shock.

It is sometimes hard to say what drives a person to commit the kind of acts that Joseph Thomas Wesbecker committed, but in his case there were numerous contributory factors. His life, for instance, had been one disappointment after another. From birth he seemed to have been fated, his father, a construction worker, dying in a fall when he was just thirteen months old. His mother was only sixteen years old at the time and he was passed from carer to carer, ending up in an orphanage for a year at one stage. The one steadying influence in his life was his grandfather, but he died when Wesbecker was just four.

He dropped out of high school early and in 1960, aged eighteen, he started work at a printing works. A year later, he was married. He had two sons but even that failed to bring him much joy. His younger son suffered from scoliosis – a condition where the sufferer has an abnormal curvature of the spine – and his elder son was repeatedly arrested for exposing himself to strangers. His marriage would end in divorce and a bitter custody battle over the boys. A second marriage lasted only a year

In 1971 he moved to Standard Gravure where he

would remain until his death. But his job, too, was a problem. He hated it, especially when he was made to work on 'the folder', a cramped space surrounded by switches that controlled seven three-storey-high presses. It was horrendously noisy and terrifyingly stressful. He begged to be moved to less stressful duties but his bosses' only response was to make him work there more.

He had started buying guns in 1988 and several years before had made threats about hurting his second wife's first husband and daughter. He purchased an AK-47 assault rifle, several semi-automatic pistols, hundreds of rounds of ammunition and told a friend that he was collecting them in case he had to use them on his bosses. 'I could come in and wipe the whole place out,' he told one union boss. He threatened to bomb the plant and is said to have thought about hiring an assassin to kill several of the company's managers. His threats, like Wesbecker himself, were laughed at.

He was not a well man, making twenty-one visits to a psychiatrist who prescribed the anti-depressant Prozac. He already had a long history of psychiatric problems and was treated at least three times for them between 1978 and 1987. He had tried to kill himself several times – some sources suggest he had tried to kill himself as many as fifteen times – and suffered from alternating bouts of depression and manic depression. When asked on one occasion by a doctor if he had ever felt like harming anyone, he replied 'my foreman' and on being asked when, replied, 'at work'.

However, Wesbecker became ever more lonely and suicidal, especially after the break-up of his second marriage. He now did not see members of his own family and had no friends. Work was all he had and he hated it.

After the management's refusal to redeploy him, he became angry and bitter towards them. He complained to them about changes to factory policy, especially after the sale of the business in 1986. He complained about the relocation of the workers' car park to a site further away from the plant and a ban on workers using the lift to the administrative offices, the very one he used on that fateful day. He also told them that because of exposure to the solvent toluene he was suffering from blackouts, memory loss and dizzy spells.

He took his complaints to the Jefferson County Human Relations Commission in May 1987 and when he was examined they did find that he was suffering from depression and manic depression, supporting his claim of discrimination.

He was put on long-term disability leave in August

1988 on the understanding that he would be re-employed as soon as he was well enough. On 13 September 1989, however, he received a letter informing him that his disability income was being cancelled. The next morning, he put his guns in his car.

The Prozac that had been prescribed to Wesbecker became the subject of a lawsuit brought by twenty-seven survivors, relatives and executors of the estates of those who died. It was claimed that Prozac, made by the company Eli Lilly, had nasty side effects that might have caused Wesbecker to behave in the way he did. His doctor had wondered if he should take him off it – he noticed that Wesbecker was agitated and suffering from sudden mood swings. He begged the doctor not to take him off it, claiming that it had helped him remember an incident in the factory when a foreman had forced him to perform fellatio on him while being watched by another worker. The doctor was uncertain whether this was true, but immediately ordered Wesbecker to stop taking it and booked him in for further hospital treatment.

Three days later, the lift doors opened at Standard Gravure and Rocky Wesbecker claimed his place in the grim pantheon of mass killers.

ECOLE POLYTECHNIQUE MASSACRE

On 6 December 1989, several thousand students at the Ecole Polytechnique in Montreal were enjoying the last day of term, presenting their final work and looking forward to the Christmas break. Tragically, a number of them would not live to enjoy the imminent festivities.

A young man in a white baseball cap, a grey parka and heavy boots had been sitting outside the registrar's office that afternoon. Beside him was a green plastic bag that he put his hand in every now and then, as if making sure that its contents were still there. He seemed nervous, avoiding eye contact and sitting stiffly. Eventually, when one employee asked him if she could help him, he got up and immediately walked away as if her words had broken the spell.

It was five o'clock and the college was beginning to close down for the day, people locking their offices and starting to make their way to the exits. The boy, whose name was Marc Lepine, reached into his bag and took out a lightweight Sturm Ruger Mini-14 .223 calibre semi-automatic rifle, ideal for shooting small game which is the reason Lepine had given for its purchase to the shop assistant who had sold it to him. Attached to it was a magazine containing thirty rounds that could be fired in rapid succession. He threw away the bag and started walking towards classroom 230.

He turned the door handle and strode into the room which contained about sixty students. The two lecturers paid little attention to him, thinking he was just a student arriving late for class. They turned towards him, however, when he said, a grin spreading across his face, 'Everyone stop everything.' Then, speaking in French, he ordered the ten women in the room to stand up and move across the room where they were isolated from the men whom he ordered to leave. For a moment, no one moved. As happened several times that late afternoon, they thought he was playing an end-of-term prank. When he fired a couple of rounds into the ceiling, however, they realised that this was no joke and began to go out the door, some hesitating, wondering if they should try to overpower him. No one dared, however.

'You're all a bunch of feminists,' he shouted to the

women now herded into a corner of the room, 'and I hate feminists.' He then proceeded to explain his reasons for being there and for what he was about to unleash. As he had told them, he hated feminists and believed that women were stealing men's jobs. Their place was in the home, he said, and it was time that women were taught their place in society.

One woman, Natalie Provost, argued with him that they were not feminists who marched and agitated for women's rights, but her protests only irritated him and he raised his gun and began firing at them, calmly sweeping across them from left to right. The women screamed and begged for mercy, but he carried on firing until every one of them had been shot and had crumpled to the floor. The walls were splattered with blood and six of them were dead.

Outside, the men raised the alarm and looked for help, but Lepine strode out of the room and walked past them, raising his rifle at them, but not firing. They backed off, not daring to try to stop him. He walked along the corridor, shooting at other students that he saw, hitting another three, two of whom were women.

Ambulances began to arrive, but the police, already on the scene, would not permit them to enter the building while the gunman was still on the loose. They waited outside while people inside bled to death. Meanwhile, word was spreading throughout the college that a madman was on the loose. Doors were locked and barricaded and people cowered behind whatever cover they could find. As they saw him go past they noticed that he was smiling, One boy described him as looking like he was having a good time.

One woman had a particularly lucky escape. Lepine walked into the room in which she was trapped. He aimed at her and pulled the trigger, but he was out of ammo. He looked at her, turned and walked away, reloading as he went. As soon as he had gone, she jumped to the door and locked it with trembling hands. Just then, he returned and finding the door locked, tried to shoot his way in, but was unable to break the lock. He turned again and walked away.

He stood at the top of an escalator leading from the second floor to the first, taking aim at a young woman walking down it. She fell down the steps to the bottom. Then, still on the second floor, he saw a woman locking the door of her office from the inside. As she did so, he took aim and fired, turning as she fell to the floor. He returned to the escalator and descended to the floor below, making for the cafeteria where around one hundred people were enjoying dinner and the free wine the Ecole Polytechnique was providing for students on this last day of term.

Frightened students had already run through the cafeteria, shouting to those seated there that they should flee, that there was a gunman shooting people. However, once again it was thought to be a last-day practical joke and many had remained seated at their tables, enjoying their food. He looked for women but saw mostly men in the room. If he did see a man with a woman, however, he was fair game and as he shot at the women he also wounded their male companions. Everyone now realised that this was serious and that fact was confirmed when he shot a woman queuing at the food counter. He turned and shot two other women as the diners stampeded out of the area, knocking over chairs, tables and other students in their haste.

Police officers waited for twenty minutes before entering the building while Lepine took the escalator to the third floor, firing at a woman and two men. He arrived at a classroom where, remarkably, the lesson was still in progress. No one had warned them what was happening outside. Inside were twenty-six students and two teachers. A presentation was in progress, being delivered from a platform at the front of the class by two male students and twenty-three-year-old Maryse Leclair, daughter of the Director of Communications for Montreal's police force.

When Lepine walked in, everyone was momentarily

stunned. He shouted at them twice to get out, but they were all so shocked that no one moved. He brought them back to dreadful reality by raising his rifle and shooting Maryse who was standing on the platform. She was hit in the abdomen and fell to the floor. He turned to face the class as they all dived for cover under their desks. This was no joke, they now realised. He saw two women trying to make an escape through a door near the platform and opened fire on them. Others were trying to get out through another door. They, too, were gunned down. He now began walking up and down the rows of desks, firing until he had run out of ammunition and then re-loading again. The horror was unimaginable as people screamed and the ones who had been hit, lay moaning in pain.

Maryse Leclair, meanwhile, was still alive, lying on the ground begging for help. He heard her and went back over to her, sitting down and pulling a six-inch knife from a sheath strapped to his body. To everyone's horror, he plunged it into her heart. As she screamed, he plunged the knife into her a further two times. Even on a day filled with such violence, this was an act of unbelievable horror. The students went silent, determined not to draw attention to themselves. 'Trapped like rats' was how one student later described it.

Lepine next stood up and walked over to the

teacher's desk as they all held their breath. He took off his hat and put it on the desk. As he took off his parka and wrapped it round the barrel of the rifle, the fire alarm went off, set off by someone in the building a little too late. Everyone jumped at the sound. Lepine turned the rifle so that the barrel was pointing at his face. 'Ah shit,' he said, before pressing the end of the weapon against his forehead and pulling the trigger. The bullet blew away a part of his skull and he dropped to the floor, dead at last. He was the fifteenth person to die at Ecole Polytechnique that day.

Where had it come from this terrible bloodlust? What had made Marc Lepine into one of Canada's most notorious killers? The answers undoubtedly lay somewhere in his past.

He was born Gamil Gharbi to an abusive Algerian father, Rachid Liass Gharbi, and a French-Canadian mother, Monique. His father abused not just his wife but also his children, beating them for the smallest infraction. Gamil was terrified of him, knowing that even if he failed to greet him properly in the morning he would suffer a beating.

Eventually, when Gamil was seven, the abuse proved too much for his mother and she sued for divorce, citing his violence and being supported in her allegations by her sister, although Gharbi denied that he was abusive.

Even though his hatred for his father was intense – so intense that he changed his name to Marc Lepine when he was thirteen years old – he still espoused Rachid's twisted views about women and it became an obsession. He hated the fact that women – including his mother who obtained a university degree – were being educated. It evolved into a belief that women were the reason he was so unsuccessful, that they were taking jobs that he should be getting and it is true that he was having little success in the job market. He had been rejected by Ecole Polytechnique and blamed his rejection on the fact that the college was trying to enroll more women students. He had tried a number of things – a computer programming course and a science programme for instance – but had never stuck at any of them. He had also tried to join the Canadian army but had been rejected because of his antisocial tendencies. He had also lost a job where he claimed he was fired by a woman and replaced by a woman, although this was untrue. However, he was a difficult person to work with and to employ. He was anti-authority, rude and disruptive.

He never fitted in, was never able to really make lasting friendships throughout his life. He had had a few girlfriends but his attitude to women meant that they did not stick around for very long. All he was interested in were computers, electronics and weapons.

He had planned his action well in advance. He had stopped looking for work because he knew he would not be around very much longer. He had spent time in the school, learning its layout, making his plans for that fateful 6 December.

A few days after the bloodbath, the pearl-white coffins of Lepine's victims were on view in a chapel at the University of Montreal. Tens of thousands of people queued to pay their respects. The deaths were not over, however. A number of students committed suicide in the months and years following the incident, at least two of them citing the stress they suffered as a result of it as reasons for taking their own lives. In Canada, stricter gun controls were introduced in response to the ease with which Lepine obtained his weapon.

A year after the massacre, the police issued a suicide letter found in Lepine's pocket in which he wrote about his hatred of feminists and cited nineteen prominent Quebec women that he had wanted to kill. He wrote, 'I have decided to send the feminists, who have always ruined my life, to their Maker. For seven years life has brought me no joy and being totally blasé, I have decided to put an end to those viragos.'

JULIO GONZALEZ: THE HAPPY LAND FIRE

Twenty-five-year-old Cuban Army deserter Julio Gonzalez got to America the hard way. Taken at gunpoint from a Cuban prison on 15 May 1980, along with hundreds of others he was pushed onto a rickety boat and sailed across the Straits of Florida to be thrown off on American soil at Key West, Florida, with no possessions and no money, to make his own way in the land of the free.

East Tremont, in New York City's Bronx neighbourhood, has been through a lot of changes over the years. It used to be home to Irish and Italian immigrants but after the war, in the fifties and sixties, African-Americans began moving in. Then, in the seventies and eighties, it became a haven for Central Americans – people from Mexico, Honduras, Puerto Rico and Ecuador.

East Tremont is where Julio Gonzalez ended up, given a helping hand on the way by the American Council for Nationalities. He worked in a series of badly paid jobs but found a girlfriend – forty-five-year-old Lydia Feliciano – four years after he arrived in America and moved in with her.

Lydia worked in a social club named Happy Land, just one of the hundreds of such clubs that were located in east Tremont, near Southern Avenue. These clubs reflected the culture and origins of their clientele. They were illegal, violating many of the city's ordinances for fire, safety, hygiene and many other things. But they offered a chance to meet friends and dance and drink amongst your own.

Happy Land, located at 1959 Southern Boulevard, just off East Tremont Avenue, was primarily a meeting place for Hondurans and Dominicans in the area, people not only from Honduras, in fact, but, more specifically, from the country's northern region, close to neighbouring Nicaragua. They were poor in America but not as poor as they had been back in their native land. At the weekend they came out, dressed in their finery, to forget about the troubles of the week.

25 March 1990 was the weekend of Punta Carnivale, the Honduran equivalent of Mardi Gras and Happy Land was bursting at the seams. Julio was

sitting at the bar with Lydia but things were bad. She had thrown him out when he lost his job as a warehouseman at a lamp factory and was no longer able to pay his rent. There were other issues between the couple that night. Julio hated Lydia working at Happy Land and was always trying to get her to quit. But she liked it and it paid the rent. They argued and drank beer, Lydia refusing to take him back and Julio, who had consumed a skinful of beer, becoming increasingly angry. Her family and friends did not like him and everyone had been encouraging her to finish completely with him. She told him she had lots of men interested in her as the argument increased in intensity.

Eventually she tried to stand up to get away from him, but he grabbed her arm, trying to stop her. A bouncer had been watching the escalating discussion and came over to intervene. Julio turned on the man, shouting at him that Lydia was his woman and it was nothing to do with anyone else. The bouncer quickly took control and shoved Gonzalez out of the club where he continued to argue at the door while people watched, smiling at how stupid he was making himself look. Realising he was getting nowhere, he wandered off into the night, still shouting.

He was furious and desolate. He had no job, no girlfriend and, frankly, no future. He wanted revenge on the world, but Happy Land would be a good place to start. He decided to teach them a lesson, heading for a petrol station at 174th Street and Southern Boulevard. By the time he got there, he was carrying a one gallon oil can that he had found on the street.

The attendant at the petrol station at first refused to serve him, even when Gonzalez told him his car had run out of petrol, but another customer who knew him, told the attendant that he was alright. The man filled his container and took a dollar in payment.

It was around 3.30 in the morning when he returned to the entrance to the club. Unusually there was no one around; they were all upstairs, grinding away to the pulsating music that echoed down the stairs. Gonzalez unscrewed the cap of the can and poured it onto the floor and the steps at the club's doorway. He stood back, took out a couple of matches, struck them on the side of the box and threw them into the fuel.

It went up in a great whoosh of flames, remaining at first within the confines of the entrance between the door that led upstairs and the door that led out onto East Tremont. Gonzalez calmly strolled across the street, leaned on a wall and watched.

Inside the club, someone noticed the flames and screamed 'Fire!' It was Lydia who was at the cloakroom area. Some others were picking up their coats at that moment and were horrified to see the flames licking at the downstairs walls. They thought their exit was blocked by the fire, but Lydia led the way to a door on the club's north side. There they found to their dismay that there was a metal gate preventing them from opening the door. One of the men reached between the door and the gate and managed to raise the metal barrier sufficiently for them to force the door open. They squeezed through and ran out into Southern Boulevard and safety.

The fire continued to burn in the doorway, the inside door beginning to turn red-hot. Suddenly the DJ, Reuben Valladarez, saw the flames and realised what was going on. He shouted to the crowd but could not be heard above the loud music pulsing out of the club's PA system. He looked down and saw the flames down on the ground floor. He stopped the music and threw the switches to put on all the lights and screamed at the crowd that they had to get out quickly. People immediately crowded around the doorway, but there was no way out through the smoke and the increasing heat. This floor was unventilated and did not have any windows. It began to fill with smoke. Reuben decided to make a break for it. He ran down the steps, shoving his way between the patrons of the club, sometimes having to crawl between their legs, made it to the inside door and crashed through it onto the street, the clothes burned off his back; badly injured but alive. He would be the sole survivor from the party-goers on the upper floor.

With the door opened, a huge draft was immediately created that fanned the flames and drew the fire up the stairs and into the room where the dancers were throwing themselves to the floor to get some oxygen as lethal, black smoke sought out every corner of the room. People died in the first few seconds, their bodies starved of air, some still holding their glasses. Others stumbled over chairs, tables and bodies, trying to get out. Within a minute or two, the sounds of panic began to fade and die, leaving just the sound of the fire roaring through the room. In the midst of it lay eighty-seven people, dancing just minutes earlier, but now dead.

Firefighters were on the scene by 3.41. They had no idea of the scale of the tragedy they were about to walk into as there was not a sound from the building. Pouring water into the hallway, they noticed a few bodies. Then they pulled nineteen bodies from around the door. They made their way up the stairs to the second floor. The room was dark and their footsteps were difficult until they realised that they were walking on a carpet of bodies. They were piled on top of each other. Even for hardened fire fighters it was a grim scene from which many took a long time to recover.

As they brought lights in, it got worse. The dead were dressed in their best party clothes, some holding hands, others grasping at their throats. In an area twenty-four feet by fifty, they counted sixty-nine bodies.

An immediate enquiry was launched into why clubs like Happy Land were allowed to exist, firetraps every one of them. Happy Land itself had been ordered to close in 1988 because of its lack of fire escapes, alarms and sprinklers. The Fire Department was supposed to follow up on the closure order but it was unknown whether this had happened. The recriminations began.

Julio Gonzalez, meanwhile, had watched the fire take hold and the first firefighters arrive, sipping a bottle of beer as the first bodies were carried out. He then walked to East Tremont Avenue and caught a bus home. Before climbing the stairs to his one-room apartment, he knocked on the door of Pedro Rivera, another tenant. The door was opened by Rivera's girlfriend and he told her that he had been involved in some trouble at Happy Land, bursting into tears. He told her that he had killed Lydia and burned down the club but she surmised that he was just drunk and did not believe him, telling him to go to bed. He went to his apartment, removed his clothes that stank of petrol, lay down on his bed and fell asleep.

He was awakened at around 4 pm that day. Detectives Kevin Maroney and Andy Lugo had finally spoken to Lydia Feliciano who told them she had had a fight with her boyfriend and that he had left the club in a foul temper. They thought Gonzalez was a suspect, at least, and drove round to his apartment building.

When he opened the door, the two detectives knew immediately that they had their man. The stench of petrol from inside the apartment was overwhelming. They escorted him to the police station and read him his rights in Spanish. He confessed almost immediately, telling them that he had wanted to take revenge on Lydia for dumping him. 'It looks like the devil got into me!' he said. They charged him with eighty-seven counts of murder, at the time the worst mass murder in American history. After his court appearance, he was held in a local psychiatric ward on suicide watch.

The scenes in the South Bronx in the next few days were indescribable as they buried their dead. The streets echoed with the plaintive grief of countless families. More than sixty of the dead were of Honduran descent and ninety orphans were created by the fire. It affected everyone in the community. As news of the tragedy spread to their home villages in Honduras, they too went into mourning.

Julio Gonzalez's trial started on 19 August 1991. The jury found him guilty on all charges – 174 of murder, two for each person killed in the fire. On 19 September he was sentenced to twenty-five years to life on each count, to run concurrently. As the sentence was read out, the gallery erupted into cheers – it was the maximum sentence permissible by law. Gonzalez, refusing to make any statement to the court, was sent to the Clinton Detention Centre in the town of Dannemora and will be eligible for parole in 2015.

A monument to the eighty-seven victims now stands in front of 1959 Southern Boulevard. In 1995 a law suit awarded $15 million to their families.

No one ever danced at Happy Land again.

ARAMOANA
MASSACRE

Locals call it 'The Spit', the small coastal settlement of Aramoana that lies twenty-seven kilometres north of Dunedin in New Zealand. Its population of 261 is boosted in the warm weather by visitors taking the chance to get out of the city and spend time in what New Zealanders call 'cribs' – modest holiday homes or beach houses, often made of cheap or recycled material.

On 13 November 1990, a resident of Aramoana shattered the tranquility of this idyllic setting when he went on the rampage with a rifle with a telescopic sight, killing thirteen people in the deadliest killing spree in New Zealand's history.

David Malcolm Gray was the son of Mary Elizabeth Gray who was known to her friends as 'Molly' and and David Francis Gray who had two other children, Joan and Barry. Gray had been sent to Port Chalmers Primary School and then Otago Boys' High School but although he was something of a loner, there was nothing about him, classmates say, that suggested that he would become a mass murderer.

He was, however, deeply affected by the deaths of his parents, his father in 1978 and his mother seven years later. Following the death of his mother, he moved from the family home in Port Chalmers to their holiday place at Aramoana.

Gray was an avid fan of military and survivalist books and magazines and had amassed a large collection of guns and ammunition at his house. He was barred from a shop from which he purchased them in January 1990 after allegedly threatening a shop assistant with what appeared to be a gun hidden in a cardboard box. He also loved animals, according to his sister, Joan, which caused problems in his relationship with his next door neighbour, Garry Holden, who had pets which kept dying.

The bad feeling between him and his neighbour erupted into violence during the evening of 13 November 1990. At 7.30 pm, Gray complained to Holden that one of his daughters had been trespassing on his property. The two men had an argument, as usual, after which Gray returned to his house. He re-emerged carrying a gun, a Norinco AK-47 assault rifle. He pointed it at Holden, pulled the trigger and shot him dead.

He next entered Holden's house, looking for Holden's two young daughters, nine-year-old Chiquita and eleven-year-old Jasmine, and Holden's girlfriend's adopted daughter, Rewa, who was also eleven. He found Chiquita and shot her, the bullet hitting her in the arm before travelling through her chest and into her abdomen. Blood flowing from her wound, she ran to the house of another neighbour, Julie Ann Bryson, passing her dead father's body while the other two girls hid in the house. She blurted out to Bryson what had happened, informing her that Jasmine and Rewa were still in the house. The woman jumped into her van and drove to the Holden house with the wounded Chiquita seated beside her. Gray had now set fire to the house and as Julie drove up, he was standing outside. He opened fire on her.

Gray was now shooting wildly at anything that came within range. A utility vehicle, its occupants seeing the blaze, pulled up to ascertain what they could do to help. Gray fired at it. A car was passing containing the Percy family and a couple of family friends who were returning from a day's fishing. He sent a fuselage of bullets into the vehicle, killing twenty-six-year-old Vanessa Percy and her six-year-old son, Dion and his friend, six-year-old Leo Wilson. Vanessa's daughter, Stacey, was seriously wounded by bullets to her abdomen. Her forty-two-year-old husband, Ross, who had been driving died in the hail of gunfire, as did forty-one-year-old friend, Alek Tali.

Gray went into the house of sixty-nine-year-old Tim Jamieson and shot dead both him and his friend, seventy-one-year-old Victor Crimp. Another neighbour, forty-five-year-old Jim Dickson was out looking for his dog, Patch. He was shot and fell to the ground dead.

The noise of all of this brought Dickson's mother, Helen, and another neighbour, sixty-two-year-old Chris Cole out into the road to see what was going on. Gray caught sight of them and opened fire, as they dived for cover. Cole was wounded. Helen, meanwhile, a recent recipient of a new hip, crawled on her stomach along a ditch in order to get back into her house to phone for help. Courageously, she then crawled back to her wounded neighbour to reassure her that help was on its way. They waited but no one arrived, so once again she crawled back to the house and dialled the New Zealand emergency number. Sadly, Chris Cole would later die from her wounds in hospital.

As darkness started to fall, police officers began to arrive at the scene, amongst the first of them Sergeant Stewart Guthrie who was in command of the Port Chalmers police station. He was armed with a .38 Smith & Wesson police revolver. The local fire chief, Russell Anderson, armed himself with a rifle owned by one of the residents and the two moved carefully towards David Gray's house. Telling Anderson to cover the front of the house, Sergeant Guthrie crept round to the rear. Meanwhile, other officers began to arrive and started to seal off the building, establishing a cordon around it.

Gray had sight of the gunman, watching him move around at the back of the house, but when he lost sight of him, he warned his fellow officers to be on alert. Hiding in some sand dunes behind the house, Guthrie saw Gray come out, shouted a warning to him and then fired a shot. Gray shouted back, 'Don't shoot!' and the policeman thought that he was surrendering and that this horrific incident was coming to a conclusion. Suddenly, however, shots rang out, one of which hit Guthrie in the head, killing him instantly.

New Zealand's Armed Offender Squad (AOS) had now arrived and sealed off the town, placing a roadblock on the only exit road. AOS units also began to arrive from other parts of New Zealand. The Special Tactics Group (STG), New Zealand's counter-terrorist force was also summoned and flew into Dunedin early next morning. A media circus awaited them at the airport before they boarded vehicles to take them to Aramoana where local people briefed them about the town and told them what they knew about David Gray.

STG personnel flew over the township in a helicopter, flying high to stay out of range of Gray's rifle. He had already taken a potshot at a news helicopter earlier that morning. Landing, they split into two groups, linking up with a team from the AOS who were already in position. Gray, in the meantime, had gone into another house, eaten and fallen sleep.

The STG crept past the bodies littering the street and, having checked neighbouring buildings, tossed a stun grenade and tear gas into Gray's crib. They found it to be empty and carried on along the street, clearing each house they came to. At one house they found a terrified woman who had been hiding under a table for twenty hours.

Gray was eventually spotted at the end of the day at a window of a crib on Aramoana's northeastern side. The officers threw a stun grenade through a window but Gray had placed a mattress against the window on the inside and the grenade bounced harmlessly off it and landed outside. They followed it with tear gas and a gunfight broke out when he opened fire on them. Gray was walking around inside the building, seemingly firing at random.

It ended at 5.50 pm, almost twenty-two hours after it started with the argument with Garry Holden. Gray suddenly ran from the house, screaming, 'Kill me!

Fucking kill me!' They obliged. Orders had already been issued that if he was armed he was to be shot. He was struck by five shots, once in the eye, once each in the neck and chest and twice in the groin. He was not yet dead, however, and, incredibly, fought with the officers who tried to restrain him with handcuffs. He cursed them for not killing him, but within twenty minutes he was dead from his wounds. Inside the house they found an armoury of weapons including a .22 Winchester rifle, fitted with a silencer, an air rifle, hundreds of rounds of ammunition for the Winchester and a hundred rounds for the Norinco rifle with which he had done his murderous work earlier in the day and that he had been carrying when he emerged from the house.

Eleven people had been shot by Gray and the bodies of Holden's daughter, Jasmine and his girlfriend's adopted daughter, Rewa, were discovered in the burnt-out house.

In the aftermath, many questions were asked and people wanted to know what had pushed him over the edge. It was reported that he had become increasingly unbalanced in the months before the attack, losing friends and becoming obsessively angry about a two-dollar bank charge that had been made against him for cashing a cheque.

Three days after the incident, Gray's crib was the

victim of an arson attack. Unsurprisingly, his family asked that there be no investigation into the attack. Gun control in New Zealand was tightened after a lengthy debate in the New Zealand media.

Sergeant Stewart Guthrie was awarded a posthumous George Cross.

LUBY'S MASSACRE

The town of Belton in Bell County, Texas, is located close to the massive United States Army base of Fort Hood. George Hennard lived there and hated the place. His father – also called George – had been an army surgeon and his numerous postings had meant that George Jr. had moved around a great deal during his childhood. It was perhaps for that reason that he failed to shine at school. He was in the navy for a while after high school and that seems to have been one of the happier phases of his life. Then in 1979, he enlisted in the merchant marines. By this time, however, he had taken a liking to marijuana and, being something of a loner, it did not help him to socialise any better. He was unpopular amongst his shipmates and eventually was dismissed from the service for being involved in a vicious fight.

He moved back to Belton to live with his mother – his parents had, by this time, divorced – at this time he gained a reputation as an unpleasant character displaying increasingly erratic behaviour. He was argumentative and aggressive towards his mother's neighbours, often shouting obscenities at them and would often run onto the front lawn and scream and shout at the top of his voice for no apparent reason.

Thirty-five-year-old George Hennard had hated women from a very early age and a roommate recalled him telling him that he was going to kill his mother. However, he seemed to have established a fantasy relationship with the two daughters of a woman who lived locally, stalking them wherever they went and even wrote a letter to them. In its rambling four handwritten pages he wrote, 'It is very ironic about Belton, Texas. I found the best and worst in women there. You and your sister are the one side. Then the abundance of evil women that make up the worst on the other side . . . I will no matter what prevail over the female vipers in those two rinky-dink towns in Texas. Please give me the satisfaction of some day laughing in the face of all those mostly white treacherous female vipers from those two towns who tried to destroy me and my family,' He added the sinister postscript, 'I will prevail in the bitter end.' Indeed, it would be bitter.

The girls' mother was naturally alarmed by the letter's contents and by the attention this odd man was paying to her daughters. She took the letter to the police but they were of little help, telling her that as he had not committed any crimes and had not harmed anyone, there was nothing they could do to help. She then took the letter to her father who worked in a Tennessee hospital. He passed it to a hospital psychiatrist who described the letter as evidence of an obsessional fascination with the two young women and that its writer was carrying a great deal of anger and humiliation that could ultimately prove dangerous.

The same roommate who heard Hennard say he wanted to kill his mother was not surprised by developments. He described how Hennard had talked about killing himself and never had any friends or girlfriends. He told how he worked nights as a shelf-stacker in a grocery store and even though he would come home exhausted and try to sleep, Hennard would get up at dawn and turn on the television or play music loud. 'He did whatever he wanted to do,' the man said.

Hennard was desperate to get back the seaman's licence he had lost when he had been kicked out of the merchant marines. But at the beginning of 1991 he heard finally from the US Coast Guard Tribunal that he would not be getting it back. His increasing use of drugs and alcohol probably did not help and it was to them that he turned when he received the bad news. A few days later, he went out and bought a gun – a Glock-17.

National Bosses Day was on 16 October 1991 and Luby's Cafeteria at 1705 East Coastal Texas Expressway in Killeen, the largest town in the area, was full of workers lunching with their bosses, as well as others enjoying lunch. There were around two hundred people – customers, waiting and kitchen staff – in the building. The car park was full and cars were having to turn round and go and find another place to eat.

Suddenly, at 12.45, a blue pickup truck drove at speed towards the restaurant and, failing to stop, ploughed straight through the glass window, showering glass in every direction and trapping one man horrifically beneath it. At the wheel was George Hennard and he had driven into the window intentionally. At last he was going to take his revenge.

He climbed out of the cab and in his hands diners were horrified to see his Glock-17 semi-automatic and a Ruger p-89 semi-automatic. 'As he got out, he yelled, 'This is what Bell County has done to me!' Without any warning he then started firing. The man who had been trapped beneath the truck managed to get free and started to try to get away. Hennard fired a bullet straight into his skull and he fell to the ground dead. Screams rang out throughout the restaurant as people scrambled for safety, cowering under tables and behind partitions. Hennard began to carefully and calmly cut them down, firing rapidly as he moved around the restaurant. His pockets were stuffed with ammunition and as soon as one clip was finished he swiftly replaced it with a fresh one. Sometimes he shot his victims at point-blank range. As he walked through the building, he spoke to his victims, saying 'Was it all worth it?'

One man, Tommy Vaughn, threw himself through a window and escaped and others followed him flooding breathlessly out onto the car park outside. Hennard allowed a woman and a four-year-old child to escape. One woman, Suzanna Hupp, told how she had actually brought a gun to Luby's that day but had left it outside in her car because at the time it would have been against the law to bring it in with her. Her father made a run at Hennard in an attempt to bring him down, but the gunman swung round and shot him. Her mother was also killed. Hupp would later campaign for a change in the gun laws that would allow people to carry concealed weapons. She was elected to the Texas House of Representatives in 1996 where she would remain for another five terms.

Police arrived on the scene and a gun battle with Hennard ensued during which he was wounded. He staggered into a hallway leading to the restaurant's toilets and shot himself through the left eye. His spree had lasted just ten horrific and terrifying minutes.

Outside in the carnage that he had created, twenty-three people had died in what was the most murderous shooting rampage in American history until the massacre at Virginia Tech in 2007.

Helicopters hovered over the restaurant, ready to ferry the wounded to hospital and a refrigerated lorry was used as an ad hoc morgue for the dead bodies.

No one ever knew what really made George Hennard go postal that day. His father tried to find a medical reason for it, suggesting he was possibly suffering from an aneurysm, but the coroner's report provided nothing to support his claim. Neither were any drugs or alcohol found in his bloodstream. George himself had given clues through the years that he might do something drastic, often warning people that one day they would see just what he was capable of. That October day they finally did see it and it was something the people of Killeen would never forget.

TIMOTHY MCVEIGH AND THE OKLAHOMA CITY BOMBING

He was a gun-nut, introduced to them by his grandfather, and came to believe you really needed five guns just to get by, like a set of spanners in a toolbox – one for every occasion: a semi-automatic, magazine-fed rifle that would be good for fending off large mobs; a bolt-action hunting/sniper rifle to shoot large game or to defend yourself against an entrenched attacker; a shotgun to hunt for birds; a .22 caliber rifle to shoot small game and to improve your skills as a marksman; and a pistol for close-quarters self defence. He harboured ambitions to be a gunshop owner when young and to impress other kids, sometimes took a gun to school. Guns were the first tool of freedom and would be necessary when the going got rough and vital supplies needed to be defended. He was so adamant about this that he resigned his membership of the right-wing National Rifle Association because he believed it to be weak.

He waged a war against the American federal government, considering it to be tyrannical and guilty of war crimes. It took too much tax from its citizens, he believed, and it had too much control.

On 19 April he lit fuses in the cab of a truck outside the Alfred P. Murrah building in Oklahoma City, igniting a massive car bomb that killed 169 people, many of them federal employees and a number of them children being cared for in a day centre in the building. It was an outrage that stunned America.

He had been bullied at school, retreating inside himself and becoming a loner but he was good with computers, even succeeding in hacking into government computers while still quite young.

His family was Irish Catholic and McVeigh was brought up in Pendleton, New York. His parents divorced when he was ten years old and he lived with his father while his sisters moved to Florida with their mother. After graduating from high school, he worked for an armoured car security service before deciding, in May 1988, to enlist in the US Army.

He was based at Fort Riley in Kansas before serving in the Gulf War as a gunner on a Bradley Fighting Vehicle in the 1st Infantry Division, being awarded a bronze star. He claimed that during his time in the

Gulf, he heard his commanding officer issuing orders to kill Iraqis who had surrendered. On his return from Iraq, he tried to join the Special Forces but was not considered to be fit enough. Disappointment at his failure persuaded him to leave the Army.

He worked for a while as a security guard again but quit his job, claiming that the Buffalo area was too liberal and took to the road, travelling round the country visiting former Army colleagues. He also wrote letters to newspapers complaining about the amount of taxes American citizens had to pay. In one of them, he wrote, 'Is a Civil War Imminent? Do we have to shed blood to reform the current system? I hope it doesn't come to that. But it might.'

He had only had one relationship with a woman in his life and found it difficult to communicate properly with women. This increasing loneliness, coupled with his lack of prospects and the transient nature of his life made him increasingly angry and frustrated. He began to gamble heavily and also lost heavily, running up large debts on credit cards. His anger was brought to a head when he received a bill from the United States government informing him that they had overpaid him $1,058 during his time in the Army and that they would like him to repay it. 'Go ahead,' he wrote back to them, 'take everything I own; take my dignity. Feel good as you grow fat and rich at my expense; sucking my tax dollars and property.'

In 1993, trouble broke out at a compound near Waco in Texas where David Koresh – leader of the Branch Davidian cult – and six followers became involved in a fifty-one-day siege with the FBI. McVeigh, fascinated by the incident and furious with the federal response to it, travelled to the area and handed out pro-gun fliers and bumper stickers. He was particularly infuriated by the end of the siege when federal agents stormed the building.

In the months following the Waco siege, McVeigh worked at gun shows. During this time, he was distributing cards on which were printed the name and address of FBI sniper, Lon Horiuchi, who had angered McVeigh by killing a woman, Vicki Weaver, during a siege at Ruby Ridge in Idaho in 1992. He had written hate mail to Horiuchi who was acquitted of the manslaughter of Mrs. Weaver. He even considered abandoning his plan to bomb a federal building to target the sniper instead.

He spent time in Arizona, living with a friend, Michael Fortier and his wife. He had considered buying land in Arizona, near Seligman, because he believed it would be untouched in the event of a nuclear war. He experimented with drugs at this time – cannabis and methamphetamine – but soon became disinterested and left Arizona, heading for a farm where his friend and future partner in the Oklahoma City bombing, Terry Nichols, lived.

Nichols and his brother knew how to make bombs and they taught McVeigh how you could make a bomb out of simple, everyday, household materials. It was around this time that the siege at Waco ended in bloodshed and McVeigh, outraged by what he saw as the government's aggression, using CS gas on the women and children in the compound, resolved to do something about it.

Becoming paranoid about government conspiracies and cover-ups, he visited places like the secretive US Air Force base at Area 51, taking photographs in a deliberate violation of government restrictions there. Meanwhile, he and Nichols responded to rumours of a ban on the sale of ammonium nitrate fertilizer – an essential ingredient in home-made explosive devices – by buying it in bulk and selling it to survivalists.

He was becoming more extreme in his beliefs, writing highly abusive letters to federal organisations such as the Bureau of Alcohol, Firearms and Tobacco. 'ATF, all you tyrannical mother fuckers will swing in the wind one day,' he wrote, 'for your treasonous actions against the Constitution of the United States. Remember the Nuremberg War Trials. But . . . but . . . but . . . I only followed orders . . . Die, you spineless cowardice bastards.'

He was now, he claimed, moving from the propaganda phase to the action phase and put together a list of candidates for assassination, including US Attorney General, Janet Reno, and other notable figures. Lon Horiuchi still retained his position in McVeigh's pantheon of hatred. Eventually, however, he concluded that he would make the biggest statement by striking at a federal building.

McVeigh worked out his priorities before deciding on the Alfred P. Murrah building. There had to be at least two of the federal law-enforcement agencies, the Bureau of Alcohol, Tobacco and Firearms, the FBI or the Drug Enforcement Agency in the building. The Oklahoma City building fulfilled this requirement but it also had a glass frontage that would prove extra-lethal in an explosion. Furthermore, its large car park would provide better opportunities for photography and filming of the havoc he was about to wreak. He selected 19 April as the day to explode his bomb – the anniversary of the assault on the Waco compound and also the 220th anniversary of the Battle of Lexington and Concord.

In October 1994, McVeigh obtained three fifty-four-gallon drums of nitro methane. Disguised as a biker, he claimed that he and some friends wanted it to race their bikes. He rented storage space and used it to hold the various elements of the bomb he and

Nichols were about to make. They had already stolen blasting caps and other explosives equipment from a quarry in Marion in Texas. They assembled a prototype and exploded it out in a remote corner of the desert. It worked.

On 14 April, McVeigh took a room at the Dreamland Motel in Junction City, Kansas. The next day, he rented a Ryder truck, using the name Robert D. Kling, the name a sardonic reference to the Klingon warriors in his beloved *Star Trek*.

On 16 April, he drove to Oklahoma City with Nichols. They parked a yellow 1977 Mercury Marquis a few blocks away from the Murrah building, to be used as a getaway vehicle. They removed the licence plate from the car and left a note saying that it had broken down and should not be towed away; it would be moved by 23 April, the note said. They headed back to Kansas.

On April 18, they loaded the bomb onto the truck – 108 fifty-pound bags of ammonium nitrate fertilizer, three fifty-five-gallon drums of liquid nitro methane, crates of the explosive Tovex, seventeen bags of the explosive ANFO, shock tubes and cannon fuse. They drove to Geary County State Lake where they nailed boards to the floor that would hold the thirteen barrels in place on the back of the truck. They then mixed the chemicals to make the explosive and arranged the thirteen barrels in a way that would cause most damage.

Holes were drilled in the cab of the truck allowing McVeigh to ignite the fuses from there. He put in a fail-safe second fuse to be used in the event that the first one failed. Originally, Nichols was going to accompany McVeigh on the trip to Oklahoma, but it was decided that it would only take one of them to deliver and ignite the bomb. Nichols returned to Kansas while McVeigh drove back to his motel in Junction City.

He had intended to set the bomb off at eleven o'clock on the morning of 19 April, but decided to bring it forward to nine. He entered Oklahoma City at 8.50 and as he approached the building, at 8.57, he lit the five-minute fuse. Three minutes after that, he lit the two-minute fuse. He parked in a drop-off zone that he was unaware was directly beneath the building's day centre that was filled with the children of employees. He jumped out of the cab, locked the vehicle and walked hurriedly towards his getaway car.

At 9.02, the truck exploded in front of the north side of the nine-storey building, creating a thirty-feet wide and eight-feet deep crater. A third of the building was destroyed and 324 buildings nearby were either damaged or destroyed. 168 people were killed, five per cent of them by flying glass, and 450 were injured. Amongst the dead were nineteen children who were being looked after in the day centre at the time of the explosion. McVeigh would later refer to the deaths of the children as 'collateral damage', although he did claim that had he been aware of the day centre he might have changed targets. In a characteristically callous statement, he later said, 'To these people in Oklahoma who have lost a loved one, I'm sorry but it happens every day. You're not the first mother to lose a kid, or the first grandparent to lose a grandson or a granddaughter. It happens every day, somewhere in the world. I'm not going to go into that courtroom, curl into a fetal ball, and cry just because the victims want me to do that.'

So powerful had been the explosion that, as he ran towards the getaway car, McVeigh had been lifted off his feet. He drove out of the city, heading north, but as he drove on Interstate 35 near the town of Perry, he was stopped by an Oklahoma State Trooper who noticed that his car was missing a licence plate. McVeigh alerted the trooper to the fact that he had a gun, but the weapon was not licensed in Oklahoma and he was arrested as a result, charged with having a concealed weapon. Soon, while he was in custody, they began to link him to the bomb. He was identified by the clerk at the Dreamland Hotel as Robert Kling and the van rental agency employees identified him as the renter of the van that had been found amongst the wreckage of the Murrah building and that had been discovered to have been the source of the carnage.

A few days later, as a desperate rescue operation continued in Oklahoma City, Terry Nichols gave himself up to the police and incriminating evidence was found all over his house when they searched it, such as books on bomb-making, ammonium nitrate and a hand-drawn map of downtown Oklahoma City.

The crime task force assembled to investigate the case before it came to trial was the largest assembled in the United States since the assassination of President John F. Kennedy. Nine hundred federal, state and local law enforcement officers took part, conducting 28,000 interviews and amassing an astonishing 3.5 tons of evidence. McVeigh, Nichols and Michael Fortier and his wife Lori were charged with the bombing.

Terry Nichols was tried twice. Found guilty of conspiring to build a weapon of mass destruction and of eight counts of involuntary manslaughter of federal officers, he received a sentence of life imprisonment without parole. He was then arraigned on 161 counts of first-degree murder of which he was found guilty in 2004. However, the jury could not reach a decision on a death sentence. He was given a life sentence for each murder and now languishes in the maximum-security Florence Federal Prison in Colorado.

Michael Fortier, who had helped McVeigh and Nichols sell stolen guns to raise funds and who had taken part in surveying the Alfred P. Murrah building, made a plea bargain, along with his wife by which he testified against his former partners. He was sent to prison for twelve years and on his release in 2006, entered the US government's Witness Protection Programme. His wife Lori was granted immunity from prosecution.

Timothy McVeigh was found guilty on 2 June 1997 and sentenced to death. He was executed by lethal injection on 11 June 2001 at the penitentiary in Terra Haute. He chose a poem, *Invictus*, by British 19th century poet as his final statement. The last stanza reads, 'It matters not how strait the gate/How charged with punishments the scroll/I am the master of my fate/I am the captain of my soul'. He remained in control until the end and never expressed a moment's regret.

THE DUNBLANE SCHOOL SHOOTING

13 March 1996 seemed like any other day in the Scottish city of Stirling. There had been a frost during the previous night and Thomas Watt Hamilton had to scrape ice off the windscreen of his white van, parked in the road outside his house in Kent Road. Around 8.15, a passing neighbour stopped to exchange a few words with him about the weather. She later reported that there seemed nothing untoward. They grumbled about the weather and she went on her way.

It was to be anything but a normal day in the life of Thomas Hamilton, however, or in the lives of the pupils and teachers of Dunblane Primary School.

Thomas Hamilton was born in a Glasgow maternity hospital in 1952. Like so many killers, he would never know his father. He had gone off with another woman when his wife, Agnes, had become pregnant. The couple were divorced after just eighteen months of marriage.

Agnes worked as a hotel chambermaid and with only her low income to keep her and her son, life was tough. To help make ends meet, she moved in with her adoptive parents who lived in Cranhill, a housing estate in Glasgow's east end. However, at the age of two, Hamilton's grandparents adopted him, believing he would have a better future if he thought they were his parents. His mother, they told him, was actually his sister. He was not told the truth about his origins until he was twenty-two.

As a boy, he was fascinated by guns, although some would later say it was more of an obsession than a fascination. He became a member of several local rifle clubs and in his mid-twenties obtained a firearms licence that permitted him to start collecting guns.

He had been a member of the Boys Brigade when young and in the 1970s he became involved with a local Boy Scout troop, in 1973 being appointed Assistant Scout Leader. However, there were a number of complaints made about him that cast a shadow over his activities. On one occasion, the van he was driving a party of boys in to Aviemore in the Scottish Highlands broke down, leaving them to huddle for warmth throughout a cold night. On another occasion, he led a group of boys on a winter expedition that was far too arduous for boys of their age. Most of them returned home suffering from mild hypothermia.

His actions were considered reckless by parents and other scout leaders and he was asked to resign. He refused, however, and responded by writing angry letters to the Scout Association, demanding an enquiry. Eventually, they forced him out.

Meanwhile, the business he had started in 1972 – a DIY shop called 'Woodcraft' – had started to fail. He decided to launch a business of a different kind – a string of boys' clubs, aimed at boys aged between seven and eleven years of age, in the Stirling and Dunblane area. Renting out space in schools and gymnasiums, he offered a wide range of activities such as football, swimming, gymnastics and target practice. They began well and it looked like he might be on to a winning formula. Before long, however, stories began to circulate about his odd behaviour. He would drill the boys in a military fashion and enjoyed disciplining them. He made them do things that made them feel uncomfortable such as rubbing suntan oil all over his naked body as he 'writhed and groaned in ecstasy'. He took photographs of them in skimpy bathing costumes that he demanded they wear and they were displayed all over his house.

Complaints started to flood in to the police. It was obvious that something was not quite right with Thomas Hamilton but when the police investigated they came to the conclusion that he was doing nothing illegal.

His activities with the boys and guns were equally disturbing, however. He would drop them off on an island with guns and tell them to shoot any living thing they came across. During the evenings on these expeditions, Hamilton allegedly whipped the boys with a steel rod and rubbed lotion into their bodies. He would then pay them to say nothing to their parents about what he had done.

One police officer wrote a report saying that Hamilton's gun permit should be revoked, but no action was taken as once again there was no evidence of illegal activity, just rumours of dubious behaviour.

Hamilton heard the rumours, of course, and wrote letters to leading lights in the community, telling them that he was not a pervert and that he was being victimised. Letters – of a vaguely threatening nature – also arrived at the homes of teachers and parents that he thought were behind the rumours. The Queen was even in receipt of letters protesting about his treatment.

It was building up inside Hamilton, the injustice the anger and indignation he felt at the wrong he was being perpetrated. Never mind the fact that two reports had been made about him. One said that he had rubbed a boy on the inside of his leg and another claimed that he had touched a twelve-year-old's private parts and anally assaulted him with his fingers. He felt hard done by and was intent on revenge, even up to two years before his anger boiled over in such a sickening way.

Hamilton had relentlessly quizzed one boy about the layout of his school – Dunblane Primary School. He asked the boy to describe the layout of the building, adding in details about fire escapes and what happened during a normal day, at what time did assemblies take place and how was the gym used and so on.

Meanwhile, he carried on as if nothing was about to happen.

Shortly after he had passed the time of day with his neighbour he got in the van and drove off in the direction of the town of Dunblane, about six miles to the north of Stirling. He arrived at his destination, Dunblane Primary School in Doune Road, at around 9.30, parking beside a telegraph pole in one of the school's car parks. Climbing out of the van, he took a pair of pliers from the boot and cut the telephone wires at the foot of the pole. He had made a mistake, however. These did not connect the school to the telephone network. They were, instead, linked to nearby houses.

Hamilton set off across the car park, carrying two 9mm Browning HP pistols and two Smith & Wesson .357 Magnum revolvers. He had 743 cartridges and that day would use 109 of them. Entering the school through a door on its west side, to avoid being seen, he made his way towards the gym, remembering the directions he had gleaned from the boy at his club.

Dunblane was a large school, with 640 pupils and this made morning assemblies for the entire school impossible. They were held in rotation, therefore, one each morning for a different year group. So on this day, all primary one, two and three classes, the classes in the school that contained the youngest children, had attended assembly from 9.10 until 9.30.

Primary 1/13 was due to have a PE session after assembly and had, consequently, changed in readiness prior to going into the assembly hall. It was a class of twenty-eight children, taught by forty-seven-year-old Gwen Mayor. Twenty-five of them were five years old and the remaining three were six. A PE teacher, Eileen Harrild was already in the gym with supervisory assistant, Mary Blake, when the class arrived and while the adults had a discussion about the lesson, the children were asked to wait in the centre of the hall.

As they were talking, Eileen Harrild heard a noise behind her and turned round to see what it was. What she was hearing were probably the random shots Thomas Hamilton was firing into the stage in the assembly hall and the girls' toilet, which was located just outside the gym. As she watched the door, he entered the gym, dressed in a dark jacket, black corduroy trousers and a woollen hat. He was wearing ear protectors and in his hand, to her horror, she saw a gun.

A couple of steps into the gym, Hamilton opened fire, shooting indiscriminately. Eileen Harrild was immediately hit in both arms, her right hand and left breast. She staggered into a storage area abutting the gym and a number of terrified children scrambled in after her. Gwen Mayor was shot and fell to the floor, dead. Mary Blake was also hit but made it to the storage area, ushering a group of the children in front of her. In the store, shocked and frightened children cowered, blood pooling on the floor from their wounds. Meanwhile, in the gym the children left behind screamed and sobbed.

Hamilton fired twenty-nine shots, killing one child and wounding a number of others. He walked up one side of the gym, firing at them. He then moved into the centre and, walking in a semi-circle, fired sixteen bullets into a group of pupils who lay on the floor, trying to hide or already wounded. Callously, he approached them and began to fire at them from point-blank range.

A pupil from another class, who was running an errand for his teacher, heard the commotion and looked into the gym. Spotting him, Hamilton opened fire. But the boy ran off, fortunately injured only by some broken glass.

Hamilton walked to the southern end of the gym and fired another twenty-four bullets. He fired through a window, probably at an adult who was walking past outside and then opened the fire escape door and let loose another four shots.

Stepping through the door he fired at the library cloakroom, wounding teacher Grace Tweddle in the head. He then turned his attention to a temporary classroom, firing nine shots into it. The teacher had already heard the noise and had instructed her class to get onto the floor, a decision which saved their lives as bullets rammed into seats and desks.

Hamilton returned to the gym and opened fire again. Then he suddenly drew a revolver from his pocket, placed the barrel in his mouth and pulled the trigger. He fell to the ground, dying.

Fifteen children and their teacher Gwen Mayor lay dead around him. One other pupil would die later in hospital.

The nightmare had lasted just four minutes.

THE PORT ARTHUR MASSACRE

He was described as 'a quiet lad and a bit of a loner.'
So quiet, in fact, that to this day, no one apart from
his lawyer knows what drove Martin Bryant to go
berserk in the Tasmanian tourist destination of Port
Arthur on 28 April 1996. During the biggest killing
spree in Australian history and one of the biggest
anywhere in the world in recent times, he killed
thirty-five people, seriously wounding another
twenty-one.

Bryant was a relatively wealthy young man. He
had befriended an elderly spinster eight years
previously when he was twenty, doing gardening and
odd jobs for her and when she died, she left him a
great deal of money, money that he immediately
began splashing around on foreign travel. Between
1993 and 1996, he visited visited Singapore, Bangkok,
Sweden, Los Angeles, Frankfurt, Copenhagen,
Sydney, Tokyo, Poland, and Auckland. He also visited

the United Kingdom on a number of occasions and journeyed all over Australia. Eventually, however, his financial adviser became concerned at the amount that he was spending and Bryant scaled back on foreign travel.

He had another indulgence, however. He had purchased an AR-10 rifle from an advertisement in a newspaper and also had a .30 caliber gun and a 12-gauge shotgun. Not long before the massacre, he went to a sports shop and bought a sports bag that had to be strong enough, he told the shop assistant, to carry large amounts of ammunition. He measured its length with a tape measure to ensure that it would be long enough to hold his guns.

On the morning of 28 April, Bryant woke up at six o'clock in the house he had inherited from his benefactor. It was unusual for him to get up so early as his inheritance meant that he did not have to work. His girlfriend left the house around eight to visit her parents and Bryant himself left at around ten minutes before ten. He made some stops on his journey, firstly buying a cigarette lighter, paying with a large denomination note and leaving without waiting for his change. He then purchased a bottle of tomato sauce, a strange act for someone with mass murder on his mind. He bought a cup of coffee at a Shell service station at Focett Village, telling the man behind the counter that he was going surfing. A little later he filled the petrol tank of his yellow Volvo at another service station.

At some point around this time, something seems to have snapped in Martin Bryant's head. It may have been the thought of the vicinity of the Seascape guest accommodation site owned by David and Noelene Martin. Bryant's father had tried to buy Seascape a few years previously but the Martins had snapped it up before Mr. Bryant senior was able to get the money together. He had become depressed, eventually committing suicide.

So, Bryant undoubtedly bore a grudge against the Martins and perhaps it was this that unhinged him sufficiently to create the carnage that was to follow.

He stopped at the property, disappeared inside, firing several shots with one of his guns. He gagged David Martin and then viciously stabbed him. He also killed his wife.

It had begun.

The Port Arthur historic site – scene of a brutal 19th century penal colony – is a busy place with cafes, restaurants and shops ready to separate tourists from their cash. It had become Tasmania's number one tourist destination and by lunchtime that day was thronged with visitors.

Bryant queued in a line of cars waiting to pay the

toll at the booth at the entrance to the site. After once driving out of the queue and going to the back, he paid his entrance fee and drove in, parking near to one of its most popular places, the Broad Arrow Café, close to the water's edge. He was asked to move by a security guard who told him that the area in which he had parked was reserved for camper vans. He drove to the designated area, but after sitting in his car for a few minutes drove back to his original parking space. He climbed out of the car carrying a large bag and a video camera and walked towards the café.

It was 1.30 and in the café the lunchtime rush was beginning to slow. It was still busy, however, with around sixty people lingering over their coffees and desserts. Bryant came in, carrying his bag, looking, with his long blond hair, like the ideal picture of a surfer. He sat down on the front balcony of the café to eat his lunch. He is reported to have said, 'There's a lot of wasps around today,' to no one in particular and commented on the lack of Japanese tourists before proceeding to eat his meal. The 'wasps' comment is likely to have referred to the acronym for 'White Anglo-Saxon protestants' rather than the insects.

Finishing, he stood up, picked up his bags and walked back into the main part of the café. He stared long and hard at a group of diners at one table before focusing on an Asian couple seated close to where he was standing. He quickly unzipped the sports bag, reached inside and pulled out his AR-15 semi-automatic rifle. Without a moment's hesitation, he shot the Asian man in the neck, firing from the hip and killing him instantly. He swung it round the dead man's partner and fired a bullet into her head. Swiftly, he turned to the other group, raising the rifle to his shoulder and firing a shot at Mick Sargeant who felt the bullet singe his scalp before he fell to the floor, looking on in horror as Bryant shot his girlfriend, seated next to him, in the back of the head. Three people were dead.

People began to dive for cover, under tables and behind the counter, but Bryant calmly selected his targets and shot them. People trying to protect their families died in the hail of bullets. Twenty-eight-year-old New Zealand winemaker, Jason Winter, threw a tray at him to try to distract him, but as his family – his wife and fifteen-month-old son – huddled under the table, Jason was shot. Three men with their backs to Bryant had no idea what was happening behind them, one of them commenting, 'That's not funny,' on hearing the shots. The three men were shot and killed. Others at their table fell to the floor bleeding profusely.

He headed for the exit, firing all the time. A couple of men seated at another table were next, shot dead from a distance of no more than a couple of metres. Their wives, hiding under the table were unhurt.

He turned round and shot and killed Mervyn Howard. Another shot hit his wife Elizabeth in the neck. Bryant walked over and finished her off with a shot to the head.

A woman, Sarah Loughton, rushed over to protect her mother, Carolyn, who had been crawling between the tables, trying to get away from Bryant. The mother pulled her down and lay on top of her. Bryant shot Carolyn in the back and then leaned down to shoot Sarah in the head. Carolyn would survive to learn of her daughter's death in hospital later.

About fifteen seconds after he had opened fire, twelve people lay dead and many lay wounded. The pleasant water's edge restaurant had become a charnel house.

He walked towards the gift shop part of the café, still shooting, as people dived under tables and tried to be invisible. People had tried to escape onto the deck through a door but it was locked. More people in this area were shot. At one point he walked up to Nicole Burgess, crouching in a corner of the room, and fired a bullet into her head. People were hiding behind a fabric screen. He shot two of them in the head, a man and a woman, killing them instantly.

For the next minute, he seems to have moved back

and forward between the café and the gift shop, probably re-loading at some point. He shot dead more people hiding in the corners of the gift shop. Then he left the building.

He had fired twenty-nine shots in ninety seconds. Twenty people now lay dead. Unfortunately, he was not yet finished.

Outside there was confusion. Some people had managed to escape from the café and were warning others to get out of sight. They hid behind coaches or in nearby shops and bars. Some actually believed that there was a historic re-enactment of some kind going on and converged on the area. He moved amongst the coaches, shooting a driver who would die later in hospital. He then opened fire on people hiding between a couple of coaches, wounding several.

Returning to his car, he changed weapons before opening fire again, but not hitting anyone. He got into the vehicle and sat there for a few moments before emerging again and returning to the coaches but again not finding a target. Then, he shot an already wounded woman lying on the ground – she would die later – before killing a woman hiding on a bus. Suddenly, seeing Neville Quin, husband of the woman he had shot while she lay wounded, Bryant chased him onto a coach. He pointed the gun at the cowering Mr Quin and chillingly said, 'No one gets away from me.' Quin ducked as Bryant squeezed the trigger and was hit in the neck, but survived.

He climbed back into his Volvo, put his foot on the accelerator and drove out of the car park. As he approached the toll booth, he spotted Nanette Mikac and her two young daughters – Alannah, aged six and Madeleine, aged three. He slowed down and she thought he was offering help to get away. Calmly, he ordered Nanette to get down on her knees and then shot her in the temple. He turned and shot Madeleine in the shoulder and then killed her with a bullet in the chest. Alannah had, meanwhile, made a run for it and was hiding behind a tree. He missed the terrified girl a couple of times before walking up to her, putting the barrel of his gun to her neck and killing her.

At the toll booth, he had an argument with a man before shooting him dead. Another driver got out of his car, possibly to intervene and was killed with a bullet in the chest. He went up to the man's car, a BMW, dragged the two female occupants out and shot them dead before transferring all his equipment from the Volvo to the BMW and driving off, shooting at another approaching car as he did so.

At a service station close to the toll booth, he stopped a Toyota Corolla and tried to pull the woman occupant from the passenger seat. The driver jumped out to help her and Bryant pushed him backwards, ordering him to climb into the boot of the BMW. He was taking the man hostage. Returning to the Toyota, he killed the woman passenger with three shots. He drove off in the direction of Seascape, where it had all begun, pursued now by the police.

He fired at a car en route and then when he had arrived at Seascape, shot into a passing Frontera, wounding a woman. Another vehicle arrived on the scene and he shot at that, too, but they managed to rescue the inhabitants of the Frontera and escape.

At the house, Bryant handcuffed his hostage to the banisters and then poured petrol on the BMW and set fire to it.

It was 2 pm and the police were arriving and making the area secure. Meanwhile, Bryant fired on them. A couple of officers who had been pinned down in a ditch near the house, were rescued by the Tasmania Police Special Operations team.

They made contact with him through a cordless phone in the house and calling himself 'Jamie', he requested a helicopter to take him to a plane that would fly him to Adelaide. He threatened that only if this was done would he release the hostage. During the night, however, the phone's battery died and communication stopped.

The next morning, police saw flames coming from the house and watched as Bryant ran out, ripping his burning clothes off. He was taken to the same hospital in which many of his victims lay seriously wounded.

During his interrogation by investigating officers, he denied everything, that he had shot anyone or that he had even been at Port Arthur that day. The guns were not his, he claimed, apart from the shotgun that he had left behind in the Volvo.

He initially pleaded not guilty to the thirty-five murder charges – he laughed hysterically as the judge read them out to him. However, he later changed his plea to guilty, although he never provided a confession.

He was sent to prison for life, thirty-five times, and had another 1,035 years added to his sentence for numerous other charges arising from the events of that day. He will never be released.

COLUMBINE HIGH SCHOOL

Going to school in America would never be the same again.

On that April day in 1999, an anger was unleashed that would continue to resonate through schools for the foreseeable future. Two disturbed boys, furious with the world, rampaged through Columbine High School in Jefferson County, Colorado, demonstrating a callous disregard for life and leaving in their wake twelve dead and twenty-three wounded. There would be many questions in the aftermath of the killings as to why they had felt the need to remove themselves from the everyday reality of being human. Was it the social isolation they felt, a feeling that would undoubtedly have engendered a feeling of helplessness and depression in them and made them feel like caged animals who felt the need to strike out? Or were they just seeking attention in the most extreme way possible? They may also have been responding to a climate of bullying and many schools across the United States initiated anti-bullying programmes in the wake of the shootings. Some characterised the two as outcasts, 'Goths' and 'nerds' who spent an unhealthy amount of time in front of their computers. Others, however, said that they actually had a close circle of friends and were not excluded from wider social networks at the school.

There had been signs, however. Eighteen year-old Eric Harris's website, originally created to host new levels for the computer game *Doom*, created with the help of his friend, Dylan Klebold, seventeen, featured a blog, launched in early 1997, that provided instruction on how to make bombs. The blog also presented Harris's thoughts about parents, teachers and school friends and it became increasingly obvious that he was developing a dangerous hatred for the society in which he lived and the people with whom he mixed.

Few people visited the site, of course, but when it began to feature death threats aimed at a Columbine pupil, Brooks Brown, as well as violent messages about students and teachers at the school, it was brought to the attention of the authorities. An order was actually issued for Harris's home to be serched for explosives, but it was never executed.

The two boys had already been caught stealing tools and were ordered to attend various classes and were put on probation. In the meantime, Harris was also seeing a psychologist, continuing to do so until shortly before the massacre. He had been put on a course of medication, anti-depressants, including the drug, Luvox, the side effects of which included increased aggression, loss of remorse, depersonalisation and mania. For a young man at war with society it was perhaps not the best course of treatment.

As their murderous ambitions began to escalate, the two boys began to compile journals in which they wrote about beating the death toll of the 1995 Oklahoma City bombing when 169 people had been killed by a bomb planted by Timothy McVeigh. They talked about hijacking a plane and crashing it into a building in New York City, but eventually they settled on an elaborate plot to massacre as many of their classmates and teachers as they could.

The plan was to set off a couple of bombs in the school cafeteria and then as students and teachers fled the bombs they would pick them off outside. They would then enter the school and shoot as many as they could find. After that, they would turn their attention to the people in the houses on the perimeter of the school.

On the morning of Tuesday, 20 April 1999 – significant because it was Adolf Hitler's birthday and one day after the anniversaries of Oklahoma City and the deaths of David Koresh's Branch Davidians in the fifty-one-day siege at Waco – the boys made a dramatic video in which they said farewell to friends and families, apologising for what they were about to do. They then loaded their cars with the explosive devices they had constructed and the arsenal of weapons they had acquired in the previous few months – two 9mm firearms and a couple of twelve-gauge shotguns. They climbed into their cars and drove separately to Columbine High School.

Arriving at the school at 11.10 am, they parked in separate car parks. En route, they had stopped to set up a small incendiary device as a diversion in a field about half a mile from the school. It partially exploded at 11.14 and it is thought that they hoped emergency personnel would be called and would be busy there while they unleashed their mayhem at Columbine.

Harris and Klebold, wearing trench coats, met up and armed a couple of large propane bombs before carrying them in duffel bags into the school cafeteria. These were set to explode at 11.17, and they hoped that they would destroy the café and bring the library located above it crashing down. However, as the two boys waited by their cars for the explosions, the time passed and nothing happened. It became obvious the bombs were duds.

Around this time, they were approached by Brooks Brown, the boy Harris had threatened on his website but with whom he had recently settled his differences. He asked them why they had missed a test earlier that morning, but Harris, ignoring his question, calmly told him it would be best if he went home. The tone of his voice suggested to Brown that something was seriously wrong and he did, indeed, set off for home.

The bombs having failed to detonate, they changed their plans, climbing, fully armed and carrying duffel bags filled with ammunition, to the top of the school's west entrance steps. It was now 11.19 and they had a view of the side entrance to the cafeteria, the school's main west entrance and the athletic fields. Harris yelled 'Go! Go!' and the carnage began.

The first victims were Rachel Scott and Richard Castaldo, seated on the grass to the left of Harris and Klebold, enjoying lunch. Scott, hit four times, died instantly and Castaldo, hit eight times, was seriously wounded. It is reported that, as well as targeting the school's 'jocks' – athletes who wore white caps to mark their status at the school – who, according to some theories, had been bullying Harris and Klebold and making homophobic remarks about them, they also wanted to target Christians. To this end, it is reported that the killers first asked Rachel Scott if she believed in God and when she innocently replied 'Yes I do', they opened fire on her.

Harris now pulled out his semi-automatic and shot Daniel Rohrbough and two friends, Sean Graves and Lance Kirklin, who had been standing on the west staircase, wounding all three. They then shot at pupils seated on the grass next to the steps, hitting Michael Johnson on the face, arms and leg. Johnson escaped and Mark Taylor, hit in the chest, arms and leg, collapsed to the ground pretending to be dead. Klebold walked down the steps, pausing to shoot the wounded Lance Kirklin in the face. Daniel Rohrbough was shot again in the back and died. Anne-Marie Hochhalter was wounded in the chest, arm, abdomen, back and left leg as she tried to get away at the entrance to the cafeteria. Harris and Klebold now began to make their way to the West Entrance, throwing pipe bombs as they went.

Teacher Patti Nielson was on her way outside to find out what the noise was, but was shot and hit in the shoulder by shrapnel. She ran back inside, making for the library where she ordered the students there to hide beneath the desks. She also called the police.

At 11.24, a sheriff arrived and began shooting at Harris and Klebold who returned fire. He called in for backup. The two boys entered the school, shooting Stephanie Munson in the ankle in the North Hallway, before heading for the library. Coach William Sanders met them en route and was shot in the chest. He struggled into a science classroom where students tried to staunch the flow of blood. They put a sign in the classroom window, saying '1 bleeding to death'. Sanders died a few hours later.

Harris and Klebold threw bombs into the cafeteria as they approached the library. This time they exploded. At 11.29, they entered the library where fifty-two students, two teachers and two librarians were hiding. Harris screamed at everyone to get up, but when no one did, he changed his order to, 'Everyone with a white cap or baseball cap, stand up!' meaning the school athletes. Again no one stood and Harris shouted, 'Fine, I'll start anyway!'

The massacre in the library was horrific in the extreme as the two wandered round, firing randomly or leaning down to look at the terrified students huddled together under desks before shooting them. At one point, Harris banged a desktop twice with his hand and then bent down to see Cassie Bernall cowering in terror. 'Peek-a-boo!' he sneered, before shooting her in the head. Unfortunately for him, the recoil of the gun sent it back hard into his face, breaking his nose.

Ten students died in the library and a further twelve were wounded.

Passing the library windows, they fired at police outside who were working to evacuate teachers and students. The officers returned fire.

At 11.37, as they re-loaded their weapons, Klebold spoke to a student he knew, John Savage. When Savage asked Klebold what they were doing, he replied nonchalantly, 'Oh, just killing people.' He then allowed the boy to leave the library.

The two killers were now heard to remark how the novelty of shooting people had worn off. Klebold suggested it might be more fun to knife their victims. They then left the carnage of the library. It was 11.42.

They wandered the corridors, firing randomly and entered the cafeteria again, shooting at the propane bomb, trying, unsuccessfully, to detonate it. They threw a pipe bomb, which exploded and headed back up the stairs. Passing a number of classrooms, they stared in the windows at the students cowering inside, but did not enter.

At 12.02, they returned to the library, now empty of all but the dead students. They shot at the police outside again but then, at 12.08, they turned their weapons on themselves. Eric Harris shot himself with a single shot in the mouth and Dylan Klebold shot himself in the head.

It had lasted forty-nine minutes.

THE JONESBORO MASSACRE

It is a community in which guns are an everyday thing. Hunting is the sport of choice and kids are brought up to use weapons, graduating from BB guns to rifles and pistols at an early age. Drew Golden's family were no different. Drew's grandfather's kitchen was like a gun shop. Rifles lined the walls on a twelve-foot rack and ammo sat on top of the cupboards. Drew had been taken hunting by his grandfather, Doug, and had just killed his first duck. Now, he longed for the moment he could get a deer in his sights. His father, Dennis, who worked for the Post Office, was on the committee of the Jonesboro Practical Pistol Shooter's Association and his eleven-year-old son was beginning to compete alongside him in competitions. He was a good shot, too.

Drew Golden's cousin, Mitchell Johnson, was a bad kid. He was thirteen years old and already smoking pot. His behaviour had resulted in frequent suspensions from Westside Middle School and he was often violent. His parents had divorced and Johnson had taken it badly, self-harming and taking a shotgun into the woods to shoot squirrels, pretending they were the teachers he hated so much.

Ludicrously, Johnson also claimed to be a member of a gang – the Treetop Piru – that was affiliated to the South Central Los Angeles street gang, the Bloods. The hardcore 'gangsta' world of Minneapolis, Memphis and South L.A. seemed a million miles from the sleepy town of Jonesboro with its Baptist, Church of Christ and Methodist churches every couple of blocks and its beautiful old houses – Johnson's fantasies were believed by nobody. Rather they were attempts by a socially inept boy to find some respect in a world that seemed to be ignoring him.

Both boys were outsiders and despite their age difference, travelled together on the school bus and hung out together. One girl reported how they made fun of her for wearing glasses and others told how they would talk about taking drugs, smoking weed.

On Monday 23 March 1998, they talked about other things on the bus. They said they were going to kill someone. One girl remembered Mitchell Johnson saying, '. . . tomorrow you will find out if you live or die. Everyone that hates me, everyone that I don't like is going to die.'

Johnson had been angry because an eleven-year-old girl, Candace Porter, had broken up with him. It was rumoured that she had insulted him and he had taken offence, determined to take revenge in some way. However, as usual, no one believed him. It was just more big talk from a kid with an inferiority complex, they thought.

Johnson later claimed that the whole thing was Golden's idea, although it is not known if this is true. He said his cousin had approached him just before Christmas 1997 with a plan to scare people at the school who had been picking on him. Johnson said that at first he told Golden he must be mad but he said no one would get hurt and that Johnson's role would be to find them transport. Golden said he would provide the guns.

The next morning, Mitchell Johnson was absent from school. He had told his parents that he had pains in his stomach and they let him stay home. As soon as they went to work, however, he left the house, got into their grey Dodge van and, after a stop at Drew's grandfather's house, drove it up a side road close to the school. In the back was survival equipment, a tent, a portable radio and some food. There was also an arsenal of weapons.

Doug Golden, Drew's grandfather, believed his array of guns was secure against robbery. A length of aircraft cable passed through their trigger guards, one end fixed to the wall, the other fastened by a heavy-duty padlock. The only problem was, however, that his grandson knew where to find the key.

At Drew's house, the two boys had loaded the van with all their gear, sleeping bags, a bow and arrows, a machete and a blowtorch. It was Johnson's intention that once they had carried out their deed, they would hide out in the wilderness until the heat had died down. They tried to break into a gun safe that Drew's parents owned, but were unable to do so. Nonetheless, he was still able to find a couple of pistols lying around in the house. They travelled then to his grandfather's house, stopping to fill the van's tank en route, although it took them three petrol stations before they could find anyone willing to sell them petrol.

At Doug Golden's house, Johnson kept watch while Drew broke in a basement door with a crowbar. It was a house with which he was very familiar, having virtually been brought up there while his mother worked long hours at the local post office. He had to be quiet because his great grandmother, Nora Golden, lived next door and was home that morning. A path had been worn between the two neighbouring houses when he had been younger, so much time did he spend there. The previous night he had eaten dinner there. Now, he emerged with an armful of weapons that he had taken from the rack. They had ten guns and a number of very large hunting knives. Johnson took a particular fancy to a Remington 30.06 semi-automatic deer hunting rifle with a gun-sight. It was almost impossible to miss your target with one of those, even if you were an inexperienced marksman.

Meanwhile, at Jonesboro school, the yellow school buses drew up just before eight o'clock and began to disgorge their passengers, kids chattering and shouting to each other. The first bell rang at 8.10 and the second, ten minutes later, let the students know that it was time to make the daily Pledge of Allegiance. They then got on with the lessons of the day.

The two boys had driven to the school where at 12.40 Golden climbed out, went inside and set off the fire alarm. Johnson, meanwhile, had gathered up the arsenal of weapons they had assembled and carried them into the woods near the school. Golden ran out and joined Johnson at the edge of the woods, pulling on a camouflage vest filled with ammunition. It contained nineteen .44-caliber shells and thirty-four .357 shells in the middle front pockets, seven more .357 shells in an upper right pocket, a lower left pocket packed with forty-nine .380 shells, sixteen .30 special shells, twenty-six .357 magnums shells, six .30-caliber shells, and three .30-caliber 30-shot clips in a back pocket. He was carrying a .30-caliber carbine rifle and three pistols. Johnson had the Remington, four pistols, two knives and a similarly huge amount of ammunition in his pockets, including a couple of speed loaders for a .38 revolver.

As the alarm sounded in the school, teachers and pupils followed the well-rehearsed procedure, lining up in single file in their classes. The process was for the first pupil in the line to hold the door open and let the others pass through. Once everyone had exited he or she had to turn over a sign that hung on the door that read 'all clear' before joining the others. They then walked down the corridor out of the back door and on to the lawn which at the time was muddy from construction work

Suddenly, there were strange noises – popping sounds, like firecrackers or perhaps noise from the construction site. Then the bullets began to come thick and fast and everyone realised this was more than just firecrackers. Two construction workers described seeing the boys firing from the woods, recalling how they were mowing down everything in sight.

They fired twenty-six shots in about fifteen seconds. Eleven-year-old Brittheny Varner was hit and died almost instantly. Shannon Wright, a thirty-two-year-old English teacher with a young child, lunged across the girl next to her to protect her and was hit in the chest and fell to the ground. As she lay dying she asked those around to tell her husband and son that she loved them very much. Twelve-year-old Paige Ann Herring, twelve-year-old Stephanie Johnson and eleven-year-old Natalie Brooks also died. A teacher and nine other pupils lay injured, one of them Candace Porter, the girl who had recently dumped Mitchell Johnson. She was wounded slightly by a bullet in the ribs.

Emergency calls began to flood the Craighead County Sheriff's office and soon ambulances and patrol cars were speeding to the school, followed by anxious parents who had begun to hear the news of the incident.

Meanwhile, Golden and Johnson had taken off into the woods but were caught by pursuing officers and lay down on the ground quietly.

They were amongst the youngest people ever charged with murder in American history. But they were lucky in their youth because it meant that they would not be subject to the death penalty to which they would almost certainly have been sentenced had they been a few years older.

In August 1988 they received the maximum sentence Arkansas law could give them – confinement until the age of eighteen. They were actually held in prison until twenty-one due to additional weapons charges – the federal crime of bringing a gun into a school – the authorities brought against them. Mitchell Johnson left prison on 11 August 2005 and Andrew Golden was released on 25 May 2007.

Golden was rumoured to have returned to Arkansas where he lives and works under an assumed name.

Johnson, meanwhile, went with a friend to Columbia, South Carolina where he worked and began attending a Seventh Day Adventist Church, incredibly thinking about becoming a minister. Life was difficult and as soon as employers found out who he was they would fire him. He moved to Fayetteville where he hooked up with a prison acquaintance, another juvenile killer, twenty-two-year-old Justin Trammell who had killed his father with a crossbow in 2000. On 1 January 2007, Johnson was in a car with Trammell that was stopped by police for a traffic offence. In the car they found marijuana and a loaded gun. Johnson was charged with possessing a gun while a user of or addicted to a controlled substance and in September 2008 he was sentenced to four years in prison. He then received another twelve-year sentence for credit card theft.

THURSTON HIGH SCHOOL MASSACRE

The cafeteria was busy. It was just before eight in the morning and some students sat at the tables eating breakfast while others milled about talking and laughing. There were more people than usual in there that Thursday morning, 21 May 1998, at Thurston High School in Springfield in the Williamette Valley in northwest Oregon, because the school library, another popular hang-out before classes began, was hosting an early-morning breakfast honouring a few senior boys' contributions to the school. The atmosphere in the cafeteria was relaxed. The next day, Friday and the following Monday were holidays and everyone was eagerly anticipating the break from the routine that would provide.

Meanwhile, fifteen-year-old freshman Kipland P. Kinkel was making the twenty-minute drive to school in his mother's Ford Explorer from his home in the town's Shangri-La suburb. Behind him he left his parents, William and Faith, two popular teachers of Spanish, whom he had shot dead the previous evening. Hidden beneath his coat that morning were three weapons – a sawn-off Ruger 10.22 rifle, a Ruger .22 pistol and a 9mm Glock 19. He also had two knives and 1,200 rounds of ammunition. His father, who had enrolled him in gun safety classes when he saw that his son had an interest in guns, had bought him the Glock. However, his parents were unaware that he had purchased the rifle from a neighbour.

The previous day had been catastrophic for Kip Kinkel. He had been arrested and suspended from school after being caught with a .32 pistol that he had purchased from another student. Korey Ewert had stolen the gun from the father of one of his friends and had arranged the sale with Kinkel the previous night. It was a Beretta .32 handgun and Kinkel paid $110 for it following which he had put it in a paper bag and left it in his locker at school. The owner of the gun reported its theft to the police and he also provided a list of names of students whom he believed might have taken it, amongst them Korey Ewert, but not Kip Kinkel. It soon emerged, however, that he was involved and he was summoned to the principal's office. He told them the weapon was in his locker and he was expelled and arrested. His father drove him home following his release from police custody.

He later told police that they had gone to a Burger King in town before driving home. His father had then lectured him about his behaviour, telling him how embarrassed and ashamed he was of his behaviour and how upset his mother would be when she got home from work. It was all too much for the fragile Kinkel's temperament. He fetched the Ruger 10.22 rifle from his bedroom and went down to the kitchen where William Kinkel was standing with his back to him having a drink. The boy raised the rifle, took aim and shot his father in the head from about ten feet, before dragging his body into the bathroom and covering it with a sheet.

For a while after that, Kinkel was on the phone to friends who called him to talk about what had happened at school. Around six, his mother came home, driving her car into the house's basement garage. She walked up the stairs from the garage to find her son waiting for her. He said, 'I love you' and then shot her six times – twice in the back of the head, three times in the face and once in the heart. He dragged her body down into the garage and, as with his father, covered her with a white sheet. He then claimed to have considered killing himself and told police that he put the Glock to his head several times with that intention, but could not go through with it. He sat in the house listening to music through the night, especially the piece *Liebestod* from the sound-track of the film, *Romeo and Juliet*, which he listened to repeatedly and which was still playing when police arrived at the house later in the day.

When he arrived at the school, he parked off campus and climbed out of the car. He was wearing a trench coat that reached down to his ankles and on his back was a backpack. Kinkel was a strange kid and he had often talked about creating mayhem and killing people. On this Thursday his words became more than just talk and by the end of the morning, apart from his parents, another two would be dead and twenty-four would be wounded, many seriously.

He made his way to the school foyer where he immediately fired two shots, one fatally wounding Ben Walker and the other wounding another student, Ryan Attebury. He then strolled calmly into the crowded cafeteria, knowing that was where everyone would be at that time in the morning. He carried on walking – described as having a blank look on his face by one of the students who was present that morning – and firing randomly as he passed, swivelling from side to side.

As is often the case in such situations, the students in the cafeteria could not believe that what was happening was real, presuming it must be some kind of prank. Others who heard the noise but had not yet seen the gunman, merely thought someone was letting off firecrackers.

One student had been surprised when he saw Kinkel walk in, knowing that he had been suspended for the previous day's serious incident. He watched him pull a gun from inside his coat and open fire. The boy fell to the ground and tried to hide.

People screamed as they lay on the ground or stampeded for the doors, leaping tables and scattering chairs in their wake. Students watched in horror as he walked up to one wounded boy lying on his front on the ground. He put his foot on the boy's back and fired into his body four times at point-blank range. The scariest thing was that his face was expressionless, 'like it was something he did every day,' said one student.

In many instances of shootings in schools, people are afraid to tackle a gunman but at Thurston there were some courageous students who brought Kinkel's rampage to an end as he stopped momentarily to reload.

A boy who wrestled for the school team, six foot four inch Jake Ryker, had already been wounded in the chest but decided to have a go, as did Adam Walburger. Ryker shouted at Kinkel and launched himself at the five foot five inch gunman, knocking him to the ground, taking another bullet from the

Glock in the process. His younger brother, Josh, and another wounded student, Tony Case, joined him and Walburger in helping to restrain Kinkel until police officers arrived on the scene, without any doubt saving the lives of many more students.

Ambulances were beginning to arrive and paramedics leapt from their cabs to attend to the many wounded. They set up a triage centre in the cafeteria to treat the most seriously hurt who were then taken to hospital if they were well enough to travel. Within fifty-three minutes all of the wounded had been evacuated from the school to hospital. At last it was over.

Kipland P. Kinkel was a difficult child who had been prescribed Prozac to manage the irrational anger he often felt that would make him lash out at anyone near to him and to deal with the clinical depression with which he had been diagnosed. He had attended counselling sessions also intended to manage his erratic behaviour. While still young, his teachers considered him immature and lacking physical and emotional development. As if that was not bad enough, he had a low IQ and was diagnosed with dyslexia. He was put in a remedial class and had to repeat a year.

To some Kip Kinkel was just a clown, but others saw a dark side to him, especially when they considered the obsession he had with bombs and violence. At one time he is reported to have boasted of how he was going to plant a bomb in the teachers' seating area of a school assembly. He had on one occasion read out in class from his journal – it spoke of killing people. On another occasion, he had given a short talk in class about how to make a bomb. He listened to the music of Satanic rocker Marilyn Manson and lived his life, some said, as if he was in a video game. That video game became real when he bought a 9mm Glock pistol with his earnings from helping out around the house.

When they got him to the police station, Kinkel pulled a knife that had been strapped to his leg and that they had missed when they had arrested him. He charged one officer with the knife, shouting 'Shoot me! Kill me!' hoping, he later claimed, that the officer would shoot him dead. He was restrained and disarmed without any harm, however.

In September 1999, Kinkel, abandoning his previous plea of not guilty on grounds of insanity, pleaded guilty to murder and attempted murder. He was sentenced to 111 years with no possibility of parole. At sentencing, he apologised to the court for the murder of his parents, the two students and for his bloody rampage.

Now twenty-seven years of age, Kipland P. Kinkel

is held at the Oregon State Correctional Institution where he will spend the remainder of his life.

VIRGINIA TECH MASSACRE

When Seung-Hui Cho had first arrived at Virginia Polytechnic Institute and State University, commonly known as Virginia Tech, he had found it difficult to talk to anyone, even failing to respond to greetings when he passed other students. On the class sign-in sheet on which pupils had to write their names, he wrote only a question mark and he even introduced himself enigmatically as 'Question Mark' when he met people. He became known as 'The Question Mark Kid'.

This type of behaviour was not new. A South Korean national with residential status, he had always been an odd, strangely menacing character, even when very young. His family which had arrived in the United States when he was eight years old, had long worried about him, some family members suspecting that he possibly suffered from autism. He spoke rarely and mumbled when he did. He also found it difficult to make eye contact with anyone to whom he was speaking and was never willing to embrace other family members. As a result, he became a victim of bullying schoolmates and retreated even further inside himself. Eventually, he was diagnosed with depression and selective mutism, a social anxiety disorder that prevented him from speaking. He received therapy, but discontinued it.

His father had been a bookstore owner in South Korea, but he had never managed to make much money from it and the United States seemed to hold greater promise for him and his wife and two children. They settled in Centreville in Virginia, twenty-five miles of Washington DC and the mother and started up a dry cleaning business. They went to church and raised their children as Christians.

He was bright, however, finishing his three-year course at elementary school in only one and a half years. He was good at maths and English and was popular with the other pupils. However, his parents' experience was somewhat different and they claim that he came home from school crying and throwing tantrums every day, saying he never wanted to go back. It was in secondary school that they began to diagnose him as having problems and that was also when he started to be bullied for the odd way he spoke. Around that time, the bullying became so bad that it was rumoured that he had a hit list of students he wanted to kill. Then, in 1999 when the Columbine School shootings occurred, Cho was transfixed by it. In a school assignment, he wrote that he wanted to 'repeat Columbine'. The school let his sister know what he had done and she informed her parents who sent him to a psychiatrist.

When he went to Virginia Tech to study English in 2003, his behaviour became even more erratic. He was obviously intelligent, but was an insecure loner who appeared arrogant and never removed his sunglasses, even indoors. Having taught him for only six weeks, poetry teacher, Nikki Giovanni, had him removed from her class in autumn, 2005, after he had photographed female students' legs under their desks and because of the violent, obscene poems he had been writing. She communicated her concerns to her Department Head, Lucinda Roy, who passed them to the student affairs office and the Dean's office, but, as he had made no overt threats against anyone, there was nothing they could do.

Roy made efforts to help the boy, working one-to-one with him, but became concerned with her own personal safety to the extent that she invented a code to pass to a colleague, if she felt threatened. She urged Cho to seek counselling, but he never did.

Meanwhile, Cho's previous mental health problems

were not divulged due to privacy laws and his failure to communicate with his fellow students was just put down to a quirk of his nature.

He never seemed to do any work, attend classes or read books. A roommate reported that he sat on a wooden rocking chair by a window staring out at the lawn for hours on end. He typed endlessly on his laptop and was once spotted riding his bike in endless circles around the dormitory car park. He was obsessed by the song *Shine* by rock band, Collective Soul, playing it continuously. Andy Koch, another roommate, reported receiving repeated mobile phone calls from Cho in which he claimed to be Koch's brother. He informed Koch that he had an imaginary girlfriend called Jelly, a supermodel who lived in outer space, travelled by spaceship and knew Cho by the pet name, Spanky. On another occasion, during a holiday break, Cho called Koch and claimed to be holidaying with Russian president, Vladimir Putin. His behaviour was becoming so bizarre that Koch and other roommates advised female students not to visit them in their room.

These concerns were exacerbated by the fact that he had been accused on several occasions of stalking female students, sending them unsolicited text messages and writing lines of Shakespeare on their doors. After his final stalking of a female student had met with no response from her, he texted Koch, 'I might as well kill myself now'. Koch, worried for Cho's safety, alerted the authorities.

On 13 December 2005, Cho was declared to be 'mentally ill and in need of hospitalisation' and was temporarily detained at Carilion St. Albans Behavioral Health Center in Christiansburg, Virginia, pending a commitment hearing before the Montgomery County, Virginia district court. However, the recommendation was simply that he undergo outpatient treatment for his condition and he was released. Critically, because he had not been involuntarily committed to a mental health facility, he could still legally purchase firearms under Virginia Law.

He purchased two guns – a .22-caliber Walther P22 semi-automatic handgun and a month later a 9mm semi-automatic Glock 19 handgun. Virginia law prohibited the purchase of two guns within a period of thirty days. On the morning of 16 April, he was ready to emulate his heroes, Dylan Klebold and Eric Harris, the perpetrators of the Columbine High School massacre in 1999, an event that had thrilled him.

That morning, at around seven o'clock, he gained access to West Ambler Johnston hall, a residential hall at Virginia Tech that housed 894 students. It is not known how he got in there at that time as he had a pass card that only allowed him entry after 7.30. He proceeded to the room of a nineteen-year-old freshman student, Emily J. Hilscher and shot her and a senior, Ryan C. Clark, dead. He then returned to his own room where he cleaned himself up before deleting all his email correspondence and removing the hard drive from his computer. An hour later, he was seen in the vicinity of a duck pond on the campus into which it is believed he might have thrown the hard drive and his mobile phone. However, no trace of either has ever been found.

Meanwhile, emergency services were responding to the earlier incident. Critically, however, in decisions that were later heavily criticised, the campus authorities and police did not order a lockdown of the university buildings. Neither did they cancel that morning's classes until the shooter was caught.

Carrying a backpack in which were chains, locks, a hammer, a knife, his two guns and almost four hundred rounds of ammunition, Cho next visited the local post office where he posted a package containing his writings and some video recordings of himself to NBC News. These would arrive at the television station the following day.

Shortly after, he arrived at Norris Hall where Engineering Science and Mechanics were taught. Inside, he chained the main doors shut, taping a message to them that a bomb would be detonated if they were tampered with. He then headed for the second floor of the building where a number of classrooms were situated.

He is said to have looked into a couple of classrooms before launching his first attack. It was an Advanced Hydrology class, taught by Professor G. V. Loganathan in Room 206. There were thirteen students in the room and after Cho had shot dead the professor he opened fire on the terrified students, killing nine of them and wounding two.

Across the corridor, in Room 207, Christopher Bishop was teaching a German class. Cho entered the room and opened fire, killing Bishop and four more students. In Rooms 204 and 211, he continued his spree, shooting more students and teachers. He went back to some of the classrooms more than once, firing, in total, more than one hundred and seventy-four rounds. In other classrooms, as soon as the gunfire was heard, students and teachers barricaded doors with whatever they could find.

In Room 204, Mathematics and Engineering Professor and Holocaust survivor, Liviu Libresco, succeeded in holding the classroom door until most of his panicked students had escaped via the windows, but Cho fired through the door killing him.

In a French class in Room 211, teacher Jocelyne Couture-Nowak similarly attempted to block the door, ordering her students to the rear of the class. Again, she was shot through the door. A student, Henry Lee, who had tried to help her, was also killed.

When Cho was seen heading towards Room 205, a student, Zach Petkewicz pushed a large table up against the door. After failing to gain entry and shooting several rounds through the door, Cho moved on.

Meanwhile, in Room 207, where Cho had already shot a number of people, some students barricaded the door and tended to the wounded, preventing him from re-entering the room.

By this time, thirty people, students and teachers were dead and seventeen were wounded.

Outside, the police were trying to get into the building but were being prevented from doing so by the chains with which Cho had locked them. One officer succeeded in shooting off a deadbolt on a laboratory door and they entered the building. As they made for the second floor, they heard Cho's last shot. When they found him, he had a single, self-inflicted bullet wound to the temple.

After the shootings, Police searching Cho's room, found a note that may go some way to explaining why he did it. In it he criticised 'rich kids' and what he described as 'deceitful charlatans'. He wrote, 'you caused me to do this'.

However, whatever his twisted motives, he had

more than emulated the Columbine killers. The Virginia Tech massacre became the deadliest school shooting in American history.

AMISH SCHOOL SHOOTING

2 October 2006 was just a normal day in the tiny Amish schoolhouse in the hamlet of Nickel Mines, in Bart Township, Lancaster County, Pennsylvania. Suddenly, however, at around 10.25 in the morning, a thirty-two-year-old man in a baseball cap appeared at the door of the schoolhouse. In his hand he held a clevis, a U-shaped chunk of metal with holes at the top of each end of the U. He asked the teacher if anyone had found one lying on the road outside. Twenty-year-old teacher, Emma Mae Zook went over to him, but found his manner slightly odd. He seemed to stand too close to her and nervously avoided making eye contact. She told him they had not seen the hook but charitably offered to interrupt the lesson she was teaching at the time – German and spelling – to allow the children to go out and help him look for it.

He turned round and walked back to the pickup truck in which he had arrived but to her surprise returned with a 9mm handgun. It was no longer a normal day.

Charles Carl Roberts IV had been born in Lancaster County in 1973, son of a police officer and a woman who worked for a Christian organisation that staged Bible plays. He was educated at home, through a home-schooling association from which he earned a diploma. In 1990, when he was seventeen he worked as a dishwasher at the Good 'n Plenty restaurant in Smoketown, Pennsylvania and by 2006, he was married to Marie and the couple had three children. He was employed by North West Foods, working as a commercial milk tanker driver.

That morning he and his wife had walked their children to the bus stop where they would catch a bus to school in Bart Township. He said goodbye to them all at 8.45 and went back home while his wife went into town. When she returned home at around eleven that morning she found four suicide notes, one to her and one to each of their children.

The one addressed to her said, 'I don't know how you put up with me all those years. I am not worthy of you, you are the perfect wife you deserve so much better. We had so many good memories together as well as the tragedy with Elise. It changed my life forever I haven't been the same since it affected me in a way I never felt possible. I am filled with so much hate, hate toward myself hate towards God and unimaginable emptiness it seems like every time we do something fun I think about how Elise wasn't here to share it with us and I go right back to anger.'

Roberts ordered the boys in the class to help him unload his truck. They brought in 12 gauge shotgun, a .30-06 bolt-action rifle, around 600 rounds of ammunition, cans of black powder, a stun gun, two knives, a change of clothes, an apparent truss board and a box containing a hammer, hacksaw, pliers, wire, screws, bolts and tape. He used 2×6 and 2×4 boards with eye bolts and flex ties to barricade the school doors before binding the arms and legs of the hostages.

Emma Zook's mother and some other family members were in the class that morning, visiting, and while Roberts supervised the boys, they quickly caught each other's eye and ran out the door, leaving Sarah, Emma's sister-in-law behind. Roberts was furious when he saw the women take off and immediately ordered one of the boys – Peterli Fischer – to run after them and tell them that unless they came back, he would start shooting. His sister, nine-year-old Emma, could only speak Pennsylvania German and probably did not understand when the gunman shouted at her, 'Stay here! Do not move! You will be shot!' She ran off with her brother, probably saving her life by doing so. Tragically, their two older sisters, thirteen-year-old Marian and eleven-year-old Barbie would both be shot that morning, Marian dying while Barbie would spend time in intensive care before undergoing several operations.

While Emma and her mother ran to the nearby farm of Amos Smoker to telephone the police, Roberts sent the remaining adults out of the schoolhouse, Sarah with her two young children, and a pregnant twenty-one-year-old woman. He also sent out the fifteen male students and began to line his remaining ten female hostages up in front of the blackboard.

The police had now been alerted, the first of a number of patrol cars arriving at 10.42. They immediately tried to speak to the gunman in the schoolhouse using their patrol cars' PA systems. Roberts was by this time barricading the doors, nailing boards across them and piling up desks against them. It is believed his intention was to sexually assault the girls which would explain the tub of KY Jelly that he had brought – it was a sexual lubricant.

Meanwhile, an Amish farmhand from Amos Smoker's farm had approached the back wall of the school, accompanied by his two large dogs. There were no windows on the wall and he was unseen. He crept quietly round to a side window where he flattened himself against the wall, listening. But when he saw a police car driving along the road looking like it was not going to stop, he ran out into the road, relinquishing what could have been a strategically vital position.

Inside Roberts was using plastic ties to bind the girls' arms and legs but he became aware of some troopers moving towards the building. He jumped up and shouted to them to move back at once or he would start shooting the girls. The patrolmen moved back immediately, but did not leave the area as he had requested. Through their PAs they told him to throw his guns out of the window and to come out. He refused.

Two of the older girls – the Fischer sisters, Marian and Barbie – started talking to him at this point, astonishingly asking him to shoot them first and to spare their classmates.

Suddenly, the officers and growing crowd that was gathering outside, heard a child screaming from within the schoolhouse at which point a group of police officers concealing themselves behind a shed that was joined to the building at the back, requested permission to approach the windows. Permission was denied for fear that they might incite an adverse reaction from the gunman. At 11.07, gunshots suddenly rang out from inside. Roberts had started shooting. The officers immediately rushed to the door and windows. Just as they got there the shooting stopped abruptly. He had shot himself.

When they entered the classroom they encountered a scene of unimaginable horror. Several of the girls had been shot, execution-style, in the back of head from close range. Three – Naomi Rose Ebersol, aged seven, Marian Stoltzfus Fischer, aged thirteen, and Anna Mae Stoltzfus, aged twelve – died at the scene and two others – Lena Zook Miller, aged seven and Mary Liz Miller, aged eight – would die in hospital the following day. Five others were in a critical condition. Six-year-old Rosanna King suffered severe injuries to her brain and was not expected to survive. She is still alive although she can neither walk or talk.

Roberts is reported to have spoken to his wife in a phone call while barricaded in the schoolhouse. He told her that he had molested two young female relatives when he had been twelve years old and that he was daydreaming of molesting young girls again. Strangely, however, the relatives in question later denied his claims but the presence of KY Jelly in the equipment he carried into the school would suggest that he did indeed intend to sexually molest the girls.

In his suicide notes, he also talked about the daughter, Elise, that he and his wife had lost shortly after birth nine years previously. He suggested that he was still angry at God for her death.

The response of the Amish community following the incident was extraordinary. The grandfather of one of the murdered girls said, 'We must not think evil of this man' and dozens of Amish neighbours of the Roberts family attended Charles Roberts' funeral on 7 October and one Amish neighbour had comforted Roberts' widow hours after the shooting. Incredibly, they set up a charitable fund for her and her children.

The West Nickel Mines schoolhouse was torn down ten days after the shootings, the site being left as quiet pasture. A new schoolhouse – the New Hope School – built at another location, close to the original site was opened on 7 April 2007.

NORTHERN ILLINOIS UNIVERSITY SHOOTING

It was a dramatic entrance. The door opened and a man, dressed entirely in black, walked onto the stage wearing a knitted cap and a sweatshirt. In his hands was a shotgun. In front of him the one hundred students in a geology class in Cole Hall looked up and wondered who the hell he was.

He was Steven Philip Kazmierczak, a twenty-seven-year-old graduate of NIU who had been born in Elk Grove Village in Illinois. However, he had problems while still young, being treated for mental illness at a psychiatric centre after his parents found him difficult to control at home. He studied sociology at NIU and remained there even when his family moved to Florida in 2004.

In September 2001 he enjoyed a brief stint in the US Army but was discharged before he had completed basic training when they discovered that he had not been entirely honest about his mental illness on his application form.

At NIU where he returned after his spell in the Army, he became an outstanding student and he seemed entirely normal to both teachers and fellow students. He became Vice-President of the NIU chapter of the American Correctional Association and was praised for work about the American prison system. In 2006, with two other students, he penned an academic paper entitled 'Self-injury in Correctional Settings: Pathology of Prisons or of Prisoners?' that appeared in the academic journal *Criminology & Public Policy*. He won at least two top awards, including a Dean's Award, before leaving the University in the spring of 2007. This accolade was given to only the brightest of students.

In 2007, he took a couple of courses at NIU – Arabic and Politics of the Middle East, doing a research paper on the Palestinian political organisation Hamas and its work in the area of social services. He left to become a part-time student at the School of Social Work at the University of Illinois at Urbana-Champaign (UIUC), where he would be studying mental health issues. Meanwhile, he found a job at the Rockville Correctional Facility for Women but left abruptly after just three weeks without giving a reason. By early 2008, he was enrolled as a full-time student at UIUC.

In the weeks leading up to the atrocity at NIU, Kazmierczak's behaviour had been increasingly erratic. His girlfriend at the time, Jessica Batty, confirmed later that he had stopped taking the medication his psychiatrist had prescribed – Xanax to deal with the anxiety he felt, Ambien to help him sleep and Prozac to stop him felling depressed. She, like many others was astonished by his actions, never having seen him be violent during the two years that they had been together. In fact, she described him as 'probably the nicest, most caring person ever.' After the incident, Jessica received a number of packages from this 'caring person', amongst which were a gun holster and bullets, a textbook on serial killers, Friedrich Nietzsche's book, *The Antichrist,* and a letter to her that read, 'Jessica, you're the best! You've done so much for me, and I truly do love you. You will make an excellent psychologist or social worker one day! Don't forget about me! Love, Steven Kazmierczak.'

On the whole, though, prior to the shooting, he seemed to be pretty normal, quiet perhaps – he did not have many friends – but showing not a trace of the behaviour that might suggest he was about to do something so terrible. Privately, however, he was seriously troubled. He had made suicide attempts and had shown an unhealthy interest in previous high school and university shooting incidents such as Columbine and Virginia Tech. On his arm was a tattoo of a doll from the popular horror movie, *Saw*, driving through a pool of blood on a tricycle.

A few days before the shooting, he had arrived at a Travelodge hotel not far from the NIU campus. He checked in paying in cash and signing only his first name, police later discovered. The room was left littered with cigarette butts, empty energy drink bottles and cold medicine containers. He left behind a duffel bag with its zip glued shut. The bomb squad, called to open it, found more ammunition inside, ammunition bought from the same website as the Virginia Tech shooter, Seung-Hui Cho.

Now it was just before three on the afternoon of 14 February 2008, and it was his turn.

He stood there for a couple of heartbeats, looking out at them, his eyes empty, as one recalled later. 'His face was blank, like he wasn't a person. He was a statue, aiming,' she said. Another described him as having 'a blank stare on his face, not a frown, not a grin, like there was nobody there . . . He was reloading his gun, like he's in the backyard, methodically going about it.' In his hand was a pump-action Remington 870 shotgun that he had managed to smuggle in to the university in a guitar case. He also had three handguns – a Glock 9mm, a 9mm Sig Sauer and a .380 Hi-Point. He had purchased the Remington and the Glock just a week previously.

Suddenly, as he opened fire, the noise was deafening. He was not aiming at anyone in particular, just spraying gunfire amongst them at their desks. Chaos erupted immediately as students screamed and threw themselves to the floor or pushed and shoved as they ran or crawled to the door. Twenty-year-old Dan Parmenter was unlucky enough to be seated in the front row. Parmenter, a sophomore finance major from Elmhurst, worked at the university newspaper, the *Northern Star*, who was looking forward to an internship at the Chicago Board of Trade in the coming summer, was shot in the head and died instantly. His girlfriend, seated next to him was also shot.

He ran out of ammunition in the shotgun and switched to one of the handguns. Then, just as abruptly as it had all started, he turned the gun round and shot himself, crumpling to the stage dead. In front of him, apart from Dan Parmenter, Catalina Garcia, aged twenty, Julianna Gehant, aged thirty-two, Ryanne Mace, aged nineteen and Gayle Dubowski, aged twenty, died, two of them with him in the hall and the other two in hospital. Fifteen others were wounded. Around Kazmierczak's body lay forty-eight shell casings and six shotgun cells.

The authorities were baffled by the shooting. Had it been set off by the fact that it was Valentine's Day or was that just coincidence? A weekend manager at a mental health treatment centre for teens where Kazmierczak was a patient for a year knew him well and described him as a quiet boy who liked to keep very much to himself. She remembered that he self-harmed and that when he got angry and violent it was difficult to tell because his expression remained the same. She also suggested that he never really admitted to being mentally ill which may be why he stopped taking his medication. Without it, however, there was nothing to put a cork on the violent urges he felt.

NIU campus had been shut down on 10 December 2007 following the discovery of graffiti on the wall of a restroom that warned of a possible shooting. The writing made a reference to the Virginia Tech shooting in which thirty-two died. It said enigmatically, 'What time? The VA tech shooters [sic] messed up w/ having only one shooter.' However, it seemed that the graffiti was probably not connected with Steven Kamierczak.

Cole Hall is be demolished in the near future to be replaced by a new building to be called Memorial Hall, at a cost of $7.7 million.

AKIHABARA
MASSACRE

On the morning of Sunday 8 June 2008, he made his intentions clear on a Japanese internet discussion board.

05.34 I can't get over this headache.

05.35 Rain is forecast. Bad.

06.02 I'm used to playing the role of good man. Everybody is so easily deceived.

06.03 Am I incapable of having friends?

06.10 It seems the road I planned to take is blocked. After all, everything is against me.

06.31 The time has come. Let's go.

06.39 It seems I'll be battling against my headache.

06.49 . . . against rain.

06.50 . . . against time.

07.30 What a dreadful rain . . . even though I prepared everything perfectly.

07.47 Even though the scale is small, I'll do what I decided to in the rain.

09.48 Into Kanagawa and having a rest. Things are going well at the moment.

10.53 Awful jam. Will I be in time?

11.07 Shibuya. It's awful.

11.45 Reached Akihabara. It's the day of 'pedestrians' paradise', isn't it? Just minutes left now.

Finally and chillingly, at 12.10 pm, 'It's time.'

Earlier posts on the discussion board by twenty-five-year-old Tomohiro Kato gave warning of his state of mind. He bemoaned the fact that he did not have a girlfriend and that he had quit his job, believing he was going to lose it anyway. 'Anybody with hope couldn't possibly understand how I feel' read one post. 'I don't have a single friend and I won't in the future,' read another, 'I'll be ignored because I'm ugly. I'm lower than trash because at least the trash gets recycled.' He also made his intentions clear when he wrote, 'I will kill people in Akihabara.'

People later described him as a cartoonist of some talent, a young man who would lose himself in cyberspace for hours on end. At karaoke evenings he would sing the theme tunes of the television animations he loved so much and although he claimed on the discussion board to be desperate to find a girlfriend, friends described him as only being interested in two-dimensional girlfriends.

Kato grew up in a nice suburban home in Aomori,

the capital of the prefecture that bears its name in Honshu in northern Japan. His father was successful, working as a manager in a financial institution. His parents were obsessed with their two sons' perform-ance at school, often making them re-do homework again and again until they believed that it was of a standard that would impress their teachers. For them – as for so many Japanese – educational success was vital because it would lead to financial success and respect in later life. To begin with, Kato responded well, performing exceptionally in his schoolwork and also proving to be a very good athlete. At his junior high school, he became president of the junior tennis club.

His behaviour began to change, however, when he enrolled at the elite Aomori Prefecture High School. Unpopular with his fellow students, the standard of his work plummeted until he was ranked number 300 out of the 360 students in his year. His parents' dreams for him were beginning to fall apart, but they had not helped. His brother recalled how on one occasion they made Tomohiro eat scraps of food from the floor and neighbours remember him being punished by being made to stand outside the house in freezing cold winter weather for a number of hours. His parents were even more disappointed, however, when he failed university entrance exams. Instead of university, he went to train to become a motor mechanic at

Nakanihon Automative College and following that he found employment, but only as a temporary worker, at a factory making parts for cars. By this time, he rarely saw his parents. He got himself into debt and had made a failed suicide attempt in 2006.

He was becoming paranoid as the day of the attack approached. Three days before, he randomly accused his workmates of hiding his clothes and immediately quit, believing he was going to be sacked soon anyway.

The Akihabara area of Tokyo, located just five minutes from Tokyo Station, is also known as Akihabara Electric Town. It is a destination for lovers of electronic goods, especially computers and video games and was a symbol of the gadget-loving Japanese society and especially the obsessive geeks of a subculture known as otaku; people·just like Kato. They are fanatical about manga comics, video games and animated pornography.

Many also suggest that it is a symbol of a society coming apart at the seams, where it is estimated that up to a million people simply shut themselves away in their bedrooms playing computer games and surfing the Web, emerging only at night to visit a convenience store. Thirty-two thousand people commit suicide every year in a country where it is becoming increasingly hard to survive, where once people had jobs for life earning good money, but now have to take on extra, part-time jobs just to make ends meet in their one room apartments in Japan's increasingly vast and expensive cities.

This once crime-free country was becoming used to shocking attacks and the authorities estimate that between 1998 and 2007, there were sixty-seven random attacks. Some say that it began with the June 1994 Matsumoto Incident, a sarin nerve gas attack by the Aum Shrinikyo religious movement that had killed seven people and hospitalised thousands. Then in 1996, a fourteen-year-old boy had killed a schoolgirl and placed her head on a stake outside the school they both attended. Seven years to the day before Kato's attack, on 8 June 2001, a man had killed eight children with a knife after walking into a school in Osaka in western Japan.

Two days before the attack, Kato visited a military supply shop in Fukui. He was in the shop for about twenty minutes, purchasing during that time a telescopic baton and a pair of leather gloves. He can be seen on CCTV footage laughing with the shop assistant as he demonstrates stabbing actions with the knives he was purchasing in the store. The following day, he visited Akihabara to sell his computer and a pile of software to raise sufficient cash to enable him to rent a two-ton truck with which to cause mayhem.

In the midst of the many messages he posted that

morning on the online forum, at around 8.45 that Sunday morning, Kato stopped at the house of a friend and handed him a bag filled with DVDs and video games. He told him he was driving to Akihabara to deliver the truck and after that was flying east.

At Akihabara, the main thoroughfare, Chuo Dori is closed to road traffic on Sundays and public holidays and on this particular Sunday it was thronged with pedestrians checking out the latest gadgets and gizmos in the surrounding stores.

Just before the attack, Kato posted his last message on the discussion board and then erased all the addresses and messages on his mobile phone so that none of his contacts would be bothered by the authorities after the attack.

At 12.35, the shopping crowd at a crossing on Chuo Dori was horrified when Kato's white truck suddenly roared towards them at speed, travelling on Kanda Myojin-dori. The truck ploughed into them, continuing for about thirty metres, killing three people and seriously injuring two. When it came to a stop, Kato leapt from the cab, knife in hand and began indiscriminately stabbing those around him, killing another four people and injuring eight. The horrified crowd panicked and ran in all directions to escape the onslaught of this madman. Police swarmed towards the scene and Kato ran south on Chuo Dori, finally being cornered in a narrow alley where an officer pulled his gun on him and he dropped his knife to the ground. He was then overpowered by several officers and some bystanders. Kato is reported to have said when they had secured him, 'I came to Akihabara to kill people. I'm tired of life. It didn't matter who they were. I came alone.'

Behind him, lit by the blue lights of the ambulances that had hurried to the scene, was a scene of horror, the road punctuated by bodies and pools of blood. By the end of the day, seven people were dead – six men between nineteen and seventy-four and a twenty-one-year-old woman – and ten were in hospital, seriously injured.

Kato was charged with the seven murders and subjected to psychiatric tests. He cooperated with investigating officers but at no point displayed any signs of regret for what he had done and at no point did he apologise.

Following the attack, several people were arrested trying to carry out copycat killings in other parts of Japan. One man made his intentions known on an online forum and was arrested before he could kill anyone. Two weeks after the attack, three women were injured in a knife attack at Osaka station. A man carrying a knife was overpowered at Akihabara on 26

June. Altogether twelve people were arrested and five warned for posting threatening messages. They were aged between thirteen and thirty.

Meanwhile, Tomohiro Kato was found to be mentally fit to stand trial. It seems likely that he will be found guilty and face the death penalty.

PART THREE

SERIAL KILLERS

WILLIAM
'THE MUTILATOR'
MACDONALD

It was a case that gripped and terrified the inhabitants of Sydney, Australia's largest city. A serial killer was on the rampage, killing his victims randomly with multiple stab wounds to the head and neck followed by the removal of their genitals. The police were baffled – the random nature of the killings rendering their job impossible and Sydney became a city of people who feared to leave their homes.

Born in Liverpool, England, in 1924, Allen Ginsberg was an odd, solitary child who often disappeared from home at night and had to be brought back by police. Like almost every other psychopath, he found it impossible to form relationships and had no friends.

Aged nineteen, he enlisted in the army and underwent what was probably the defining experience of his life when he was raped by a brutal corporal who told him he would be killed if he told anyone about the experience. However, Ginsberg found that rather than want to tell anyone, he wanted more. He had enjoyed it and realised that he was a homosexual.

He had been diagnosed as schizophrenic while young and the same diagnosis was made of him when he left the army. In 1947, his behaviour was becoming so erratic that his brother had him committed to an asylum. It was a horrific experience that ended when his mother obtained his release and took him home with her.

In those times, homosexuality was a criminal offence and men seeking such liaisons had to do so secretly. Like many men, Ginsberg solicited sex in grubby public toilets or in the undergrowth of public parks.

Meanwhile, his health was deteriorating. Suffering from frightening illusions and hearing voices, he sought medical help. Once again, he was sent to a mental institution, staying this time for three months. When he came out, nothing had changed and, if anything, he felt he was getting worse. He decided that only a major change in his life would help and took on a new name – William MacDonald – and emigrated to Canada to start a new life in 1949. In 1955 he moved again, following countless Britons to Australia.

His sex life was no different to what it had been in Britain, however, and before long he was arrested when he solicited sex with a man in a public toilet in Adelaide. The man turned out to be a policeman working undercover and MacDonald was given two years' probation.

Being a homosexual had always made his life difficult. In Britain he had been the butt of endless jokes and moved from job to job because of it. In Australia it was little different and on one occasion he was badly beaten by his fellow workers. He moved from state to state and from job to job, the taunts of his colleagues constantly ringing in his ears.

His first murder took place in the Queensland capital, Brisbane, in 1960. Fifty-five-year-old Amos Hurst got drunk with MacDonald in a hotel near the Roma Street railway station. The drinking session carried on in Hurst's hotel room, both men by this time extremely drunk. MacDonald suddenly began to strangle Hurst, claiming later that he had done it on the spur of the moment, had suddenly had an urge to do it. Blood spurted from Hurst's mouth and MacDonald punched him in the face before letting him slide to the floor, dead. He calmly removed the dead man's clothes, placed him in bed and washed the blood off himself before returning to his lodgings.

A few days later, MacDonald was amazed to read

an obituary that said that Hurst had died of a heart attack. There was no mention of him being strangled. He thought he had got away with murder but the truth was that although the death had been considered suspicious at the post mortem, it could not be established whether the dead man had been strangled or had received the bruising on his neck in a fight. The authorities decided to close the case.

Buoyed by his good luck, MacDonald bought a knife and set out to find another victim. Again he met a man in a bar and drank with him before buying a bottle of sherry and taking it to a nearby park. When his drinking partner fell to the ground dead drunk, MacDonald seized his chance, straddling the man's prone body and taking out his knife. Just as suddenly as the urge to kill had overtaken him, however, it left him. He sheathed his knife and went home leaving the fortunate man unharmed.

In January 1961 he moved to Sydney where he found work as a sorter with the Australian Postal Department. He was using an alias by this time, Alan Edward Brennan, and became a familiar figure in the parks and public toilets where homosexuals gathered. His killer instinct was never far away and it reasserted itself on 4 June 1961 when he befriended Alfred Greenfield in Green Park in the Sydney suburb of Darlinghurst. He succeeded in luring Greenfield to the nearby Domain Baths, a popular Sydney swimming spot, telling him he had a bag filled with booze. Drinkers hid themselves away in the many alcoves to be found at the Domain, and in one of them MacDonald and Greenfield secreted themselves. Once again, MacDonald waited until his victim was comatose through drinking before producing his knife. He stabbed him deeply in the neck and repeatedly stabbed him until he was certain he was dead. Blood from the dead man's severed arteries had spurted everywhere but MacDonald was nothing if not prepared. Prior to killing his victim he had donned a plastic raincoat.

He removed Greenfield's trousers and underpants and sliced off his genitals, throwing them into Sydney Harbour. He then wrapped his knife in the raincoat and went home.

There was a media frenzy the day after Greenfield's body was discovered. The papers described the horrific nature of the murder and the killer was immediately nicknamed 'the Mutilator'. It seemed to be a motiveless crime, however, and the police were stumped. They came up with numerous theories – a crime of passion, a murder caused by jealousy, but in spite of a reward of £1,000 for information leading to the arrest of the killer, they made no progress in their investigation.

MacDonald waited before committing his next murder. On 21 November he bought a knife with a six-inch blade and befriended forty-one-year-old Ernest Cobbin. Cobbin was already drunk and was easily lured to a nearby park with a promise of further drinking. As they sat drinking in a public toilet in the park Cobbin was puzzled when MacDonald slipped on a plastic coat. Before he could say anything, however, MacDonald's new knife was plunged into his throat. The frenzied stabbing continued as Cobbin tried to protect himself, blood spraying around the toilet cubicle and all over MacDonald's plastic coat from his severed jugular vein. Once again, as Cobbin lay dead on the ground, MacDonald pulled down his trousers and underwear and sliced off his penis and testicles, this time putting them in a plastic bag he had brought with him. Back home, he washed the severed genitals and took them to bed with him. Next day, he disposed of them off Sydney Harbour Bridge.

The police again had nothing to work on, no fingerprints, no witnesses and a victim who did not seem to have an enemy in the world. They began to patrol likely haunts of the killer but as the months passed they were no closer to catching the Mutilator.

On 31 March 1962, he felt the urge to murder again. He struck up a conversation with Frank McLean, a drunk man he met on the street, and suggested that they go into a quiet lane for a drink. As they rounded the corner of the unlit Bourke Lane, MacDonald pulled out his knife and plunged it into the neck of the six-feet tall McLean who began to struggle. MacDonald punched him in the face, knocking him to the ground before leaping on him and stabbing him again and again. As usual, he removed the clothing from the dead man's lower body and sliced off his genitals. He quickly placed them in a bag and sneaked out of the alley unseen. The next day the genitals joined the others in the murky waters of the harbour.

Sydney was now gripped by terror. Nothing like this had ever happened in the city and, worse still, the authorities were baffled, turning to clairvoyants and claiming that the killer must have had surgical experience to be able to mutilate the bodies so neatly. A special task force was assembled and, as the files on the killings grew thicker, they still came no closer to apprehending him. Even an increased reward of £5,000 failed to uncover him.

Meanwhile, MacDonald had been sacked from his job at the sorting office and decided to use his savings to open a delicatessen. He lived above the shop and was as happy as he had ever been in his life. Before long, however, he felt ready to kill again.

He met a petty thief and vagrant, James Hackett, in

a bar in the centre of Sydney and took him back to his flat where they carried on drinking. When Hackett passed out on the floor, MacDonald used a knife from his delicatessen downstairs to stab him in the neck. But Hackett woke up and in the ensuing struggle MacDonald was accidentally stabbed in the hand. He became enraged, viciously stabbing Hackett in the heart.

The room was awash with blood and he had stabbed his victim so much that the knife was bent and blunt. He tried to sever the penis but gave up, exhausted, falling asleep where he sat. The following morning he awoke in the midst of a charnel house. There was so much blood that it threatened to drip through into the shop below.

He cleaned himself up and went to the hospital to have his hand stitched and the rest of the day was spent trying to clean the room of blood and dragging the dead man's body to the space under his shop. The room was impossible to clean, however. Blood still covered the walls and the floorboards had been stained red by it. There was only one thing to do. He packed his bags and fled to Brisbane where he found a room in a boarding house, grew a moustache and died his hair black. Every day he expected to hear that Hackett's body had been discovered and that the police were looking for a man named Brennan.

The police did eventually find the body, but by the time it was discovered, it had decomposed so badly that the cause of death could not be ascertained. Presuming it to be the body of the shop-owner Brennan, they closed the case. Once again, William MacDonald had got away with murder even though he was so paranoid that he did not know it.

He might have got away with it completely if he had not made the fatal mistake of returning to Sydney. About six months after they had buried the man presumed to be Alan Brennan, one of his old workmates was astonished to see him walking down a Sydney street. MacDonald ran away as soon as the man approached him, but before long the police had been informed. The next day, one newspaper ran a legendary headline, 'Case of the Walking Corpse' describing the strange incident. Witnesses began to come forward and the police built a case that proved that Brennan was, in fact, the Mutilator.

By now, however, in spite of another disguise, he had been spotted, working in Melbourne on the railways. The police swooped and the Mutilator was at last in custody.

At his trial the jury took little time to arrive at a guilty verdict. William 'the Mutilator' MacDonald was sentenced to life in prison. After almost beating another prisoner to death in 1964, he was declared insane and sent to a psychiatric hospital for the criminally insane. In 1980 he was sane enough to be released back into a mainstream prison where he languishes to this day. However, although he is allowed out now and then on day trips, he claims to have no desire to be released on parole, ironically believing that the streets of Sydney are not safe.

RICHARD KUKLINSKI: THE ICEMAN

Born in 1935, in Jersey City, Richard Kuklinski turned out to be rather a strange child. At first he took pleasure in killing the neighbourhood cats, but, in 1949, at the age of fourteen he had graduated to bigger fish, beating to death another boy who had made the mistake of bullying him. He enjoyed this first murder; it made him feel 'empowered', as if he was 'someone' and from that point on he brooked no defiance or disrespect. The cold-blooded killer who became known as the Iceman was born.

At six-foot five, and three hundred pounds, Kuklinski was giant of a man who developed an uncanny means of detaching himself emotionally from the hundred or so people he killed. In TV documentaries made about him, he describes how when he made his first hit, using a car bomb triggered by gasoline, he walked away from the scene, feeling nothing. He reckoned it was a result of the abuse heaped upon him and his brother during their childhood by their drunken father. Aged twenty-five, his brother Joey raped and murdered a twelve year-old girl and threw her body off the roof of a building. He was sentenced to life in Trenton State Prison.

Kuklinski was a master of the art of murder and over the years, he experimented with many different ways of dispatching his hits. He tried everything – firearms, including a miniature derringer, ice picks, hand grenades, crossbows, chainsaws and even, on one occasion, a bomb attached to a remote-control toy car.

He was unafraid to try things out and it did not matter if innocent bystanders got hurt as he did it. Once, he wanted to see how effective the crossbow was as a means of killing. He put the crossbow in his car and went for a drive. Pulling over at the side of the road, he opened his car window as if to ask directions, and when a man approached, Kuklinski raised the crossbow and fired an arrow which went straight through the man's head, killing him on the spot. On another occasion, he turned to a complete stranger at a set of traffic lights and calmly shot him with the crossbow.

The Iceman's favourite dispatch method, however, was cyanide. 'Why be messy?... You do it nice and neat with cyanide,' he told Dominick Polifrone, an undercover Alcohol Tobacco and Firearms agent. He cunningly mixed the cyanide with the liquid in a nasal spray and would spray the solution in the face of his target. Cyanide attacks the cellular enzyme system that processes the body's utilisation of oxygen and the victim experiences a burning sensation in the mouth and throat, grows dizzy and disoriented and is, basically, asphyxiated. Aside from its effectiveness, however, what he liked best about cyanide was that it was hard to detect because it is rapidly metabolised by the body. The only way you know it has been ingested is a bitter almond smell that can be detected in the victim's mouth.

Nevertheless, he would happily use whichever method was appropriate to the situation and to his paymasters and would then bring into use his special talents for the disposal of the victims' bodies. On one occasion, he stuffed a body into a steel drum and left it beside a hot dog stand. Every day for weeks, Kuklinski would stop, buy a hot dog and lean on the oil drum. Then one day it just disappeared. He never found out what happened to it and its grisly contents.

His most famous disposal gave rise to his nickname, the Iceman.

Robert Prongay was known as Mr. Softee on account of the fact that he owned an ice cream van. However, he was also an army-trained demolitions expert, highly skilled in the art of destruction. As well as selling ice cream, Prongay also worked as a hitman for gang-leader, Roy DeMeo and he and Kuklinski had a lucrative sideline selling pornography.

It was from Prongay that Kuklinski learned about cyanide. To demonstrate it to Kuklinski, one day Prongay walked up to a complete stranger in the street, sprayed him and then watched the man collapse to the pavement and die within a matter of seconds. Prongay was Kuklinski's source for the deadly poison.

Prongay also liked to experiment and he and Kuklinski wondered if freezing a body could disguise the time of death. If it did, it could prove invaluable in ensuring that a killer need not worry about an alibi. They selected a small-time crook called Louis Masgay as their guinea pig. Masgay wanted to purchase a quantity of video-tapes from Kuklinski and on 1 July 1981, he left home with £95,000 in cash, never to return. His van was later found abandoned, the cash long gone.

They hung Masgay's carcass for a time in an industrial freezer in a warehouse rented by the Iceman. But he is also thought to have spent some time in the freezer in Prongay's ice cream van, lying there while Mr. Softee dispensed vanilla and pistachio ice cream cones to the children of North Bergen.

When Masgay's corpse was finally discovered, two years later, shot and wrapped in plastic bags, the medical examiner thought it strange that the clothing he was wearing was the same as on the day he had left home with the £95,000 but the body looked fresh. The giveaway was that Masgay's tissue was found to contain crystals of ice and his heart was still partially frozen. Kuklinski had been either too careful in wrapping Masgay's body in layer after layer of plastic or too impatient to let the body thaw completely. He became the cops' chief suspect and the name 'Iceman' began to stick.

As for Prongay, Kuklinski and he had a falling out during which Mr. Softee made the fatal mistake of threatening the Iceman's family. Kuklinski shot him to death in his ice cream van in 1984.

Kuklinski, meanwhile, maintained a normal, fairly affluent family life in a New Jersey suburb, his neighbours blissfully unaware of how he earned his living. He had married his wife, Barbara, in 1961, but domestically, he was violent and abusive and she lived in constant fear of his fierce temper. After he had been imprisoned she revealed that at different times he had attempted to smother her with a pillow, had threatened to shoot her, had tried to run her over with a car and had broken her nose three times.

He had drifted into crime many years previously

while working at a film lab. On the side he was selling porn videos to the Gambinos but he wanted to be a hitman. At first they were suspicious of his enthusiasm for killing and they limited his activities to smaller crimes. But Kuklinski told Roy DeMeo that he would do anything for money and to find out if he had what it took, DeMeo took him for a walk. They passed a man, a total stranger, who was out walking his dog. DeMeo ordered Kuklinski to kill the man. Without a moment's hesitation Kuklinski walked past him before turning and shooting him dead. From that point on, they decided to exploit his love of killing. He would kill men he could lure into deals that involved large amounts of cash being handed over for non-existent goods or he would dispatch fellow criminals who knew too much. He carried out contract killings for the Mafia and snuffed out people who, quite simply, just annoyed him.

Gary Smith, an associate of Kuklinski, fell into the category of a man who knew too much. He would steal cars for Kuklinski who would re-sell them. However, the police were on to him and, just before Christmas 1982, a warrant was issued for his arrest. The last thing Kuklinski needed was for Smith to start talking. So, he shielded him, moving him from one New Jersey motel to another, helped by another car thief, Danny Deppner. Smith was hard to control, however, and it was just a matter of time before he would be picked up. There was only one way to deal with the situation.

Smith was holed up with Deppner in the York Motel off Route 3, close to the Lincoln Tunnel. One evening, when Kuklinski had brought hamburgers for him and Deppner, Smith grabbed the bag of food, not realising that Kuklinski had rustled up a special recipe of his own for the ketchup, adding just a dash of cyanide. Smith hungrily wolfed down the burger. At first nothing happened but then, the poison began to work and Smith began to choke. It was taking time, however, so Deppner hurried it along, placing a chord from one of the lamps around his throat and tightening it until Smith was no longer breathing.

The plan had been for Deppner's wife to show up with a car to remove the body but when she failed to show the two men decided to hide the body beneath the mattress and box springs of the bed. It took four days for the stench in the room to be reported and the mattress to be removed to reveal the bloated body of Gary Smith. Incredibly, in that time, three couples had used the bed.

Deppner, of course, now knew too much and his body was discovered in January 1983, only a few miles from a ranch at which Kuklinski's family were known to go riding. Although the cause of death was stated as 'undetermined', pinkish spots – a sure sign of cyanide poisoning – were noted on the body. The Iceman became the chief suspect and the net began to tighten.

It was decided that Special Agent Dominick Polifrone would lure Kuklinski into a deal so that he could be caught on tape admitting something or be caught in the act of planning a murder.

When Polifrone eventually hooked up with Kuklinski in 1986, pretending to offer an arms and cocaine deal, Kuklinski began to brag about his methods, especially his use of cyanide. Kuklinski asked if he could get him some cyanide making it obvious to Polifrone that the Iceman was planning another hit.

To expedite matters, Polifrone asked Kuklinski to help him take care of a 'rich Jewish kid' who wanted to buy coke from them and would be carrying a lot of cash. They decided to put cyanide in an egg sandwich. However, the 'cyanide' Polifrone brought was actually just quinine. On the day, however, Kuklinski took the sandwiches and left, feeling that something was not right. He failed to return and the task force that had been formed to manage the case, realised their undercover agent was in mortal danger. They moved in and Kuklinski was arrested.

At his trial, he was found guilty of five murders, but,

fortunately for him, the lack of eyewitness testimony meant he escaped the death penalty. He was given two sentences of life imprisonment, for each of which he would serve a minimum of thirty years. That would make him one hundred and eleven years old before he would be eligible for parole.

He didn't make it, though. He died of a heart attack in Trenton State prison in March 2006, the same one in which his brother had been incarcerated. He was seventy years old.

In an interview in prison before he died, he smiled and said, 'I'm not the Iceman. I'm the nice man.'

HENRY LEE LUCAS
AND OTTIS TOOLE

The Montague County Courtroom in Texas sat in stunned silence. It was 21 June 1983 and they were present at the arraignment of a forty-six-year-old drifter called Henry Lee Lucas who had been arrested for illegal possession of a firearm. The authorities suspected him of involvement in the disappearances of two women, Kate Rich and Frieda 'Becky' Powell and had charged him with their murders – Lucas surprised everyone present by confessing that he had indeed stabbed Kate Rich to death. When his attorney tried to intervene, he waived his right and added that he had had sex with the girl's body before cutting it into pieces small enough to burn in a wood stove behind his cabin. Furthermore, he had also killed Kate Rich, he added, before announcing to the stunned courtroom, 'and at least a hundred more.' By the following day, Henry Lee Lucas was front-page news across America and US police departments were dusting off their unsolved murders files in anticipation of at last pinning them on someone. He claimed victims in Florida, Louisiana, Oklahoma, and West Virginia but officers even had to field telephone calls from police officers in Great Britain and France wondering whether Lucas had ever visited Europe.

Lucas was born in desperate poverty in a one-room shack in rural Virginia in 1936. His father had lost both his legs in a train accident and his mother, Viola, fed her family through prostitution and making moonshine whiskey. She apparently had no problem with entertaining a client at home and it mattered little to her if it was in full view of her husband and any of her eight children.

Viola was abusive, especially when drunk. When he was five, Viola struck Henry on the head with a wooden board, knocking him unconscious for three days. After this incident, he suffered from headaches and blackouts. She also wounded him with a knife around his left eye which was replaced with a glass eye after it had been further damaged in an incident at school. It is hardly surprising that people found the young Henry Lee Lucas sullen and antisocial.

His future career was guided by one of his mother's lovers who taught him to have sex with the carcasses of dead dogs and sheep and he first murdered someone aged just fourteen in 1951. It was claimed that he wanted to know what it was like to have sex with a person, but she had to be dead first.

The law caught up with him for the first time in 1952. He robbed a shop and was sentenced to two years in a reformatory. Released, he was in trouble almost immediately and was sentenced to four years in the Virginia State Penitentiary. This boy did not learn lessons, however; he escaped, stole a car and was arrested in Michigan. He served the remainder of his time, with some added on for the escape, and emerged from prison to go and live with his half-sister in Tecumseh in Michigan.

On 11 January 1960, while Lucas's mother, now aged seventy-four was visiting her daughter, she and her son drank too much and had a huge argument over a woman he was going to marry. Henry became violent and years of anger at his mother boiled up resulting in him stabbing her in the neck, killing her. He was arrested and convicted of second-degree murder. Sent to prison, he tried to kill himself and was sent to a psychiatric hospital. He was released after serving half of his twenty-year sentence but was back inside again shortly after, sentenced to three and a half years for attempting to abduct two young girls. On the outside again, he moved to Pennsylvania where he married but was soon separated from his wife when she caught him interfering with her two young daughters.

Lucas took to the road, travelling to Florida where he hooked up with a like-minded soul – twenty-nine-year-old arsonist and serial killer, Ottis Elwood Toole, a school dropout of low intelligence who had first had sex at the age of ten thanks to his older sister and a homosexual neighbour. He had been abandoned by an alcoholic father and was brought up by his mother, a religious zealot who liked to dress Ottis like a girl. It has been written that Toole's grandmother was a devil-worshipper whom he would watch in cemeteries digging up the body parts she needed for her rituals. Toole also first killed at fourteen, driving a car over a man who had picked him up for sex. When he met Lucas in 1976 in a rescue mission in Jacksonville, he was already wanted in connection with four murders.

It was around this time, Lucas later claimed, that he killed hundreds of people, Toole assisting him in 108 of the murders. 'I had no feelings for anybody; I came in contact with them, they had to die,' he later said. He described how he killed in many different ways in order to avoid creating a pattern that police would recognise. 'I killed them in every way there is except poison – there's been strangulations, there's been knifings, shootings and hit-and-runs.'

In 1982, however, Lucas first had sex with Becky Powell, Toole's twelve-year-old niece who was on the run from a juvenile detention centre. When she then ran off with Lucas, Toole was filled with a jealous rage that he vented by killing nine people in six different states in just over a year. He also set forty fires and it was as he was setting fire to a building in Florida that he was finally caught. He went to jail for twenty years.

Lucas wandered around Texas with Becky before the pair moved into a Pentecostal commune, the House of Prayer, near Stoneburg, Lucas earning money through doing odd jobs. Becky soon decided, however, that she wanted to go back home and although Lucas was initially reluctant, they set off, hitch-hiking in the direction of Florida. On the road, Lucas tried to dissuade the girl once again from going home. The discussion became an argument and he stabbed her to death with a carving knife before having sex with her body. He decapitated her and cut her corpse up into nine pieces, scattering them in a nearby field. He then returned to the House of Prayer, telling everyone that she had jumped into a truck, leaving him behind. A few weeks later he went back to the field and took her remains back to his house where he burned them in a stove.

Three weeks after Becky's murder, he decided to kill a woman he had been doing some work for, eighty-two-year-old Kate Rich. Going to her house to drive the elderly lady to church, instead, he drove her down a dirt road and stabbed her in the heart. Again, he had sex with her corpse before hiding it in a drainage pipe.

He left the House of Prayer the next day, drifted around California for a month before returning to the drainage pipe in which he had hidden Kate's body. But he was a suspect in her disappearance and was soon pulled in for questioning. He even took a polygraph – lie detector – test which, amazingly, he passed. Afterwards, he returned to the drainage pipe, extricated her body and burned it in his stove at the House of Prayer.

When Lucas was arrested, he claimed to have been mistreated, stripped naked and held in a cell for four days without cigarettes and bedding. He had not been allowed to call a lawyer, he said. His confessions, he claimed, were an attempt to obtain better treatment. Although a bone fragment in his stove belonged to Kate Rich and an almost complete human skeleton found near his house was the same age and size as Becky Powell, the coroner did not positively identify either set of remains. Lucas, for his part, confessed to these murders, but recanted later, as he did with most of his confessions.

He began to be flown to all the states where he claimed he had killed, meeting with investigators and answering their questions about unsolved murders.

Police claimed that they had been able to clear 213 unsolved murders off their books as a result of his confessions.

Lucas was having a ball, being treated better than a murderer should be. He was rarely handcuffed and seems to have been able to wander around prisons and police stations perfectly freely. He was even taken to dine in restaurants outside prison.

Some remained unsure, however. Texas Ranger Phil Ryan was sure that Lucas had killed but was very unsure about many of the murders he claimed to have committed. To test this, he invented a couple of murders to which Lucas readily confessed. Nonetheless, by December 1983, investigators were confident that he was clearly associated with at least thirty-five murders. On occasion he would give details that had not been in the press. A conference involving one hundred and seven officers from eighteen states took place in January the following year and it was announced that seventy-two cases of murder could be ascribed to Lucas and Toole and that they were suspects in another seventy-one.

There remained suspicions but there were also instances, according to some investigators, where he provided undeniable evidence that he undoubtedly committed a murder that had been presented to him. In 1984, Jim Lawson, an investigator from the sheriff's department in Scotts Bluff County, Nebraska, was looking into whether Lucas was involved in the 1978 murder of a schoolteacher, Stella McLean. Lawson was initially sceptical, throwing in a few questions to test Lucas, but he said that Lucas dealt with his questions correctly and offered testimony that made him believe that he had killed the woman.

He provided details of clothing in many cases, and even did drawings of many of his victims. He had detailed information about the locations of the murders, being described by one investigator as 'like a walking Rand-McNally', referring to the series of US road maps.

Although Lucas would ultimately be convicted of eleven murders, the case that brought him the death penalty was the killing dubbed the Orange Socks Murder. An unidentified woman was discovered in Williamson County, Texas in late October 1979 and the only items of clothing she was wearing were a pair of orange socks. Lucas had confessed to the murder on both audio tape and on video, but there were suspicions about the amount of editing that seemed to have been carried out on the tapes, leading some to speculate that the gaps were the times in which police officers were coaching him in the details of the girl's death. Furthermore, work records and cheque-cashing details showed that at the time of

Orange Socks' death, Lucas was actually somewhere else. The Texas Attorney General was certain that the guilty verdict would be overturned in the appeals court and consequently did not intervene in the case. He was wrong.

Lucas later claimed his confession in this case was no more than an attempt to commit 'legal suicide'. He wanted to die.

Ottis Toole got there before him, dying of cirrhosis of the liver in September 1996 while serving six life sentences in a Florida prison. Henry Lee Lucas, too, would escape the death penalty that he received for the Orange Socks murder in 1979. Then-Governor George W. Bush, later President of the United States, did not believe Lucas had committed all the murders he claimed and commuted his death sentence to one of life imprisonment. He died in prison of heart failure on 13 March 2001, aged sixty-four.

Before he died, he estimated that he had confessed to as many as three thousand murders.

ANDREI CHIKATILO: CITIZEN X

Why did he kill so many people and in such a horrific way? Perhaps it was because of his terrible childhood; his father was a prisoner of war during the Second World War and there was desperate famine in Russia, a famine so bad that there were reported instances of cannibalism. Human flesh was bought and sold and Chikatilo was told by his mother that his ten-year-old brother had been kidnapped, killed and eaten.

He was examined and found to be sane before being brought to a court in Rostov where he was kept in a large iron cage. The court was full, some two hundred and fifty people screaming and snarling at him when he was brought in. The trial was a fiasco and there was little doubt from day one that Chikatilo would be found guilty. His efforts at pretending to be mad – drooling and rolling his eyes, singing, speaking nonsense and claiming that he was being 'radiated' – were to no avail.

They found him guilty on fifty-two counts of murder and five of molestation. The people in the courtroom cried out for him to be handed over to them so that they could do to him what he did to his victims and it is reported that the Japanese offered a million dollars for his brain so that they could study it.

On 14 February 1994, however, Andrei Chikatilo was taken to a soundproofed room, told to face the wall and not turn round. He was then executed with a shot behind the right ear.

Chikatilo killed his first victim on 22 December 1978. He lured nine-year-old Lena Zakotnova into an abandoned shed, where he attempted to rape her. Lena wasn't going to give in without a fight, and while trying to control the struggling child, Chikatilo slashed her with a knife, ejaculating whilst doing so. This confirmed his psychological connection between violent death and sexual gratification; a common denominator in all his future attacks.

Someone had seen Chikatilo with the victim shortly before she disappeared, but his wife provided him with a cast-iron alibi which meant he received no further police attention. Instead, twenty-five-year-old Alexsandr Kravchenko – a man with a previous rape conviction – was taken in for questioning. He cracked under pressure and confessed to the crime, possibly as a result of brutal and extensive interrogation. Kravchenko was found guilty of the murder at his trial and was executed in 1984.

The police were convinced they had got their man and this seemed to be confirmed when there were no more documented victims for the next three years. Chikatilo had probably been scared off by his brush with the law, which had left his reputation heavily scarred. Having been made redundant from his teaching job at a mining school, Chikatilo was finding it impossible to obtain another position due to the old claims of child abuse. He decided to take a job as a clerk at a factory in Rostov, which involved quite a lot of commuting. This travel gave him unlimited access to a range of young victims over the next nine years.

His second documented victim was seventeen-year-old Larisa Tkachenko, on 3 September 1981. She was strangled, stabbed and gagged with earth and leaves to try and stop her from crying out. Using brutal force afforded Chikatilo sexual release, and a pattern started to emerge. He seemed to focus his attention on young runaways of both sexes, talking to them as they waited for a train or a bus. Once he had gained their confidence he lured them into forested areas, where he would brutally attack them using his knife as a substitute penis. He even resorted to eating the sexual organs of some of his victims, or biting off the tips of their noses or tongues. With each attack it appears that his perversions increased. In his early victims, Chikatilo slashed them across the eye area, and in some cases actually removed the eye from the socket. He later explained to a psychiatrist that he believed his victims kept an imprint of his face in their eyes, even after they were dead.

Now the authorities were aware that there was a serial killer on the loose – a virtually unknown phenomenon in the Soviet Union. Despite the fact that the press were still being censored, rumours gradually started spreading and public fear grew. As the body count mounted there were whispers of werewolf attacks and alien intervention, but whatever it was the people were starting to get scared.

Major Mikhail Fetisov, was the Moscow detective with the unenviable task of heading the investigation. Aware that there was a pattern to the attacks, he assigned a specialist forensic analyst, Victor Burakov, to assist him in the case. They concentrated on any known sex offenders, and the mentally ill, but the latter were prone to false confessions which kept leading the investigating team up a dead-end street. Progress was painfully slow, especially as, at this stage, not all the bodies had been discovered, so the true body count was not known to the police.

As each new body was discovered, the forensic evidence mounted. The police were convinced that their killer had the blood type AB, evidence obtained from the semen samples collected from the crime scenes. They also found identical grey hairs on several of the bodies.

In the year 1984, a further fifteen victims were added to the police list. They decided to mount a series of massive surveillance operations concentrating on bus and train stations. Chikatilo was hanging about the bus station waiting for an appropriate victim when the police approached him. He behaved strangely when they asked him what he was doing, and they decided to take him in for questioning. However, his blood type did not match those on the police forensic records, so his name was crossed off the suspect list for a second time.

What the forensic team didn't realise at the time was that Chikatilo's blood type (A), was not the same as that found in his other bodily fluids (type AB). He was a member of a minority group of people known as 'non-secretors'. About twenty per cent of the population are non-secretors which, in layman's terms, means that this person puts none of their blood type into other bodily fluids, such as saliva or semen. As the police only had a sample of Chikatilo's semen and not his blood, once again the killer was able to escape police suspicion. Modern DNA techniques would not allow the same mistake to be made.

After his second brush with the law, Chikatilo found work as a travelling salesman for a train company based in Novocherkassk. He kept his head down until 1985, when his lust got the better of him and he murdered two women.

Burakov, now extremely frustrated at the lack of progress being made in the case, enlisted the help of a psychiatrist by the name of Alexandr Bukhanovsky. He studied the case notes and made his report, describing the killer as a 'necro-sadist', or someone who achieves sexual satisfaction from the suffering of others. He placed the killer's age somewhere between forty-five and fifty, significantly older than the police had originally suspected. Desperate to catch their killer, Burakov decided to interview a known serial killer, Anatoly Slivko, just before his execution, in an effort to gain an insight into the mind of a mass murderer. Just as they felt they were getting close to understanding the person behind the killings, the attacks seemed to dry up. The police believed that the man had either been put in prison for some other crime or perhaps he had died. Whatever the reason, there were no more attacks until early in 1998.

In his next bout of attacks, Chikatilo changed his modus operandi, not taking his victims from bus or train stations, possibly because the police had continued their surveillance of these areas. Over the next two years Chikatilo claimed another nineteen victims. As the number increased, so the killer started taking more and more risks, this time focusing primarily on young boys. Instead of luring them into forested or quiet areas, he killed them in public places where the risk of detection was far higher. There was a victim discovered with a hammer blow to the head, a mother and daughter who had been killed at the same time, and yet another with his eyes stabbed and part of his upper lip missing.

The police were now under enormous pressure to catch the serial killer, and more and more patrols were put out in the hope of luring the prey into their net. They targeted areas where they thought Chikatilo might search for victims and even used undercover policemen and women in the hope of flushing him out. Chikatilo, however, managed to evade capture, although on one occasion he came very close to being found out. On 6 November 1990, fresh from killing one of his victims, Sveta Korostik, a patrolling policeman noticed a man behaving suspiciously. He stopped to speak to Chikatilo and took down his details. Back at the police station they realised his name was linked to a previous arrest in 1984, and they decided to put him under surveillance.

The police followed Chikatilo wherever he went and when he continued to act suspiciously, accosting women and even being seen receiving oral sex from a prostitute in the street, they decided to pick him up. He was carrying a briefcase and when the police asked him to open it up, inside they found a jar of Vaseline, a long knife, a length of rope and a rather filthy looking towel – not items that a man would normally carry to work!

Chikatilo was arrested on 20 November 1990, but he still refused to confess to any of the killings. Burakov asked the psychiatrist, Bukhanovski, who had prepared the original profile, to interview him on the pretext that he was trying to understand the mind of a killer for a paper he was writing. Chikatilo was flattered that he should be asked and opened up to the psychiatrist, providing extensive details of all his killings. He explained that his prime object was to clear the world of all undesirables – vagrants, runaways and prostitutes. He told the psychiatrist that he had difficulty in obtaining an erection, and that he used a knife as a substitute penis. He also told him the story about the eyes, but that he had stopped believing it which explains why he stopped damaging the eyes at a certain point in his killing spree. He went on to say that he could only get gratification if he committed violence – 'I had to see blood and wound the victims'. He talked about placing his semen inside a uterus that he had just removed and as he walked back through the woods, he would chew on it – 'the truffle of sexual murder' – as he described it. Not only would he tear at the victim's mouth with his teeth, but he also got a sort of 'animal satisfaction' from chewing or eating the nipples or testicles.

Chikatilo eventually told the psychiatrist where the police could find the bodies that had not been discovered and told him that it was quite a relief to have actually been caught. Chikatilo bragged and claimed he had taken the lives of fifty-six victims, although only fifty-three could actually be verified. The figure was, however, far in excess of the cases that the police had originally attributed to their serial killer.

Chikatilo decided to play at being 'mad' in the hope that they would be more lenient at his trial. His ploy did not work, though, and he was declared sane and fit to stand trial on 14 April 1992. Due to the serious nature of his crimes and also to keep him apart from the relatives of his victims who were after his blood, Chikatilo had to stand in an iron cage throughout the trial. The media referred to him as 'the maniac', as behaviour became more and more strange as the proceedings progressed. He would either stand in the cage looking extremely bored staring up at the ceiling, or start manic singing and talking gibberish. At one point he even dropped his trousers and waved his genitals at the courtroom.

The Judge was not convinced by his manic behaviour and on several occasions overruled Chikatilo's defence lawyer. It was clear from the start that Chikatilo was going to be found guilty. Despite this foregone conclusion, the trial dragged on well into August and given the judge's bias, surprisingly the verdict was not announced until almost two months later on 15 October 1990. He was found guilty on fifty-two of the fifty-three murder charges, and sentenced to death for each individual murder.

Chikatilo felt he had a good case for appeal and centred his claim on the original psychiatric evaluation. He still maintained that he was not mentally sane and had not been aware of what he was doing at the time of the killings, but his pleas fell on stony ground. He was executed sixteen months later by a shot to the back of the head.

The psychiatrist who had been a big part of his capture, Aleksandr Bukhanovski, became somewhat of a celebrity and went on to become an expert on both sexual disorders and the minds of serial killers.

PEDRO ALONZO
LOPEZ

It was a sweet little tea party. A man chatted away to three young girls aged between nine and twelve and poured drinks for them. The strange thing was, however, that the girls did not reply to his conversation. Neither did they pick up their cups. That was because they were all dead, killed by their host, the man who would later come to be known as the 'Monster of the Andes', Pedro Alonzo Lopez. Lopez is one of the most prolific serial killers in history, murderer of at least three hundred young girls and women across Colombia, Ecuador and Peru.

Colombia was a dangerous place to be born in 1949. Violence was a daily occurrence as civil war and lawlessness blighted the country. By the end of the next decade some 200,000 people would lose their lives in a country where the crime rate was fifty times that of any other nation. It was into such a world that Pedro Lopez was born, in Tolmia, seventh of the thirteen children of a prostitute. Life was tough and his mother was not afraid to use violence against her children. At least, however, it was a home and not the streets that Pedro feared so much. At the age of eight, however, he was cast out onto those feared streets after his mother caught him fondling a younger sister sexually.

The young boy was terrified but was relieved when a man approached him on the street where he was scavenging for food and offered him food and a roof over his head. Unfortunately, the man was lying. Pedro was taken to an abandoned building and repeatedly sodomised by the stranger. He returned to the streets even more terrified than before, sleeping wherever he could find some shelter, in doorways, alleys and abandoned buildings.

Eventually, he decided to move on, travelling to Bogota, the country's capital city. While begging on the streets, he was seen by an American couple who were horrified by his plight. They decided to take Pedro in and, although mindful of the last occasion on which someone tried to help him, he accepted their kindness. This time it was genuine and he was given a room and enrolled in a local school. It seemed that his luck had changed.

It did not last long, however. In 1963, when he was twelve years old, he was sexually molested by a male teacher at the school. He responded angrily, stealing cash from the school office and running away. He returned to the streets, begging and scavenging for food once again. He also began to steal, graduating by his mid-teens to stealing cars that he sold to crooked garages that would change number plates, give the car a new coat of paint and sell it on. He was good at it and made a good living until he was arrested, aged eighteen, and sentenced to seven years in prison.

After only two days in prison, Pedro was attacked and gang-raped by four other inmates. He swore revenge, making a knife from stolen kitchen utensils and it took him just two weeks to kill each of his four assailants. The prison authorities treated the murders as self-defence and just two years were added to his sentence.

There is little doubt that his time in prison unhinged Pedro Lopez. He had never been able to have relationships with women due to his mother's treatment of him and in prison these feelings escalated into fear and hatred of all women. On his release in 1978, aged twenty-nine, he launched his gruesome campaign to kill as many women as he could.

He travelled throughout Peru, picking his young victims from the Indian tribes in the region. He claimed that at this time, he probably killed around one hundred. He would search for potential victims in the markets of the region. He said that he always looked for a girl with a 'certain look' on her face, a look he described as one of 'innocence and beauty'. She would be a 'good girl', helping her mother and he would stalk them for three days, sometimes, waiting for a moment when the girl was left alone. Then he would approach her, offering her a necklace or a hand-mirror before leading her to the edge of whatever town or village they were in where he would already have prepared graves in which earlier victims were sometimes already lying. He would cuddle the girl until sunrise and then rape her before strangling her with his bare hands. His chilling description of the actual murder was, 'It was only good if I could see her eyes, it would have been wasted in the dark – I had to watch them by daylight. There is a divine moment when I have my hands around a young girl's throat. I look into her eyes and see a certain light, a spark, suddenly go out. The moment of death is enthralling and exciting. Only those who actually kill know what I mean.'

It usually took between five and fifteen minutes for the girls to die and he would remain with them for some time afterwards, ensuring that they were dead. If they were not, he would strangle them all over again. He liked to bury them together – 'My little friends like to have company,' he has said.

On one occasion, as he kidnapped a little girl in northern Peru, he was caught by some Ayacucho Indians. They stripped him naked and tortured him and were just about to bury him alive when an American missionary working in the area intervened, persuading them that he should be handed over to the police. The authorities, however, had little interest in the case as it had been brought to them by Indians and they simply deported him back to Ecuador.

He now spent his time in Ecuador and also made frequent stopovers in Colombia, killing all the time and probably averaging at least three murders a week. The authorities, did notice an increase in the number of disappearances of young girls, but put it down simply to the growth of sex slavery in South America.

They began to think again, however, when, in April 1980, a flash flood in the area around the town of Ambato in Ecuador unearthed the bodies of four children who had been reported missing. The bodies were badly decomposed, making it impossible to determine how they had died, but they had very obviously been murdered and then hidden.

Just a few days later, Carvina Poveda was shopping at a local market, near where the bodies had been found, when a man tried to abduct her twelve-year-old daughter, Marie. She screamed for help and the man, Marie in his arms, tried to make his escape.

However, the market traders realised very quickly what was happening and chased the abductor. They caught him and restrained him until the police arrived on the scene to arrest him.

At first he refused to talk to them, but they tricked him. They disguised a local priest as a prisoner and locked him in the same cell as Lopez. Lopez began to boast to the man about what he had done, the hundreds that he had killed. Soon, the priest could take no more and begged to be let out. However, the police had their evidence and Lopez was confronted by it.

He confessed to the murders of around 110 girls in Ecuador, 100 in Colombia and more than 100 in Peru. He added, however, that he preferred the girls in Ecuador as they were 'more gentle and trusting, more innocent.' He blamed his actions on his mother and the difficulties he had encountered while young. He had decided, he said, to make as many girls suffer the way he had, as he could.

Initially, the investigators did not believe him. It seemed too outlandish. However, he led them to one of his burial sites where they uncovered the bodies of fifty-three girls, aged from eight to twelve. A further twenty-eight burial sites were visited but no more bodies were found. It was presumed that floods and animals had removed the bodies from where he had buried them.

Back at police headquarters, he was charged with fifty-seven murders, a figure that his confessions soon increased to one hundred and ten. The director of Prison Affairs, Victor Lascano, later told reporters, however, 'I think his estimate of three hundred is very low.'

Lopez was sentenced to life in prison but was released in August 1994, only to be re-arrested an hour later by Colombian police officers in connection with a twenty-year-old murder. He was declared insane and kept in a secure wing of a Bogota psychiatric hospital. In 1998, however, he was found to be sane and was released on $50 bail. He was sought for arrest on another murder charge in 2002.

THE GREEN RIVER KILLER

Gary Leon Ridgway was sixteen years old when he stabbed his first victim, a six-year-old boy that he had lured into some woods. The boy survived but later described Ridgway walking away from him, laughing as he said, 'I always wondered what it would be like to kill someone.' Gary Ridgway would experience that feeling many, many times in the years to come. In the early 1980s he would murder forty-eight young women, mostly prostitutes, but is thought to have murdered many more. He is one of America's most prolific serial killers but because of police incompetence and negligence, it took twenty years to bring him to justice.

As is often the case with men who grow into murderers, Ridgway's childhood was a difficult one. He was born in Salt Lake City in Utah to Thomas Ridgway and Mary Steinman, the family moving to McMicken Heights in Washington State while he was still young. His mother was a domineering woman who fought constantly with her husband. It took its toll on Gary and at fourteen he was still wetting his bed. Even at that age his mother was still washing his genitalia with her bare hands, a humiliating experience for a teenage boy and one that undoubtedly impacted on his relationships with women.

He was far from bright, with an IQ of only eighty-two, and this was reflected in his performance at school where he was forced to repeat years before finally graduating. He was obsessed with pornography and found it difficult to maintain stable relationships with women. His first two marriages fell apart due to infidelity on both sides.

The first sign that a serial killer was on the loose in the area of the Green River on the outskirts of Seattle, came on 15 August 1982. Forty-one-year-old Robert Ainsworth was sailing his rubber raft downstream when to his horror he saw what he thought were a pair of eyes staring up at him out of the water. Then he made out the face and body of a young black woman. Trying to catch the body with a pole, he overturned his raft and fell into the water only to find another body, that of another, half-naked, black woman floating just beneath the surface next to the first.

When police officers arrived and began a search of the area, they discovered a third young woman's body lying on the grass thirty feet from the others. She had been strangled and a pair of blue pants were knotted around her neck. Sixteen-year-old Opal Mills had put up a fight – the bruises on her arms and legs were testament to that – and had died less than twenty-four hours before being found.

The girls in the water, identified as thirty-one-year-old Marcia Chapman and seventeen-year-old Cynthia Hinds, had also been strangled. Police also found rocks inserted in their vaginas. Chapman had been dead for more than a week and Hinds had only been dead for a few days. Whoever had killed them had murdered three times in just a couple of weeks.

It was worse than that, however. Deborah Bonner's body had been found a few days earlier lying across a log in the river and the previous month Wendy Lee Coffield had been found floating in it. Going back six months produced the body of Leanne Wilcox who had turned up in an empty patch of ground a few miles from the river. All had been strangled. The police knew they were dealing with a serial killer.

A special task force was assembled, led by Major Richard Kraske and Detective Dave Rechert. The FBI provided help in the form of serial killer profiler, John Douglas, and Bob Keppel who had worked on the case of another serial killer of women, Ted Bundy, eight years before.

Often in the days before computers made data management simple, officers investigating murder cases were inundated with information that proved difficult to marshal. Investigators were swamped and much information and evidence was lost or overlooked. Civilian volunteers were enlisted just to help to control the flood of tip-offs and information from the public.

The murdered girls had all been prostitutes working in Seattle's main red-light area, a strip that stretched from South 139th Street to South 272nd Street. The many girls working there were interviewed and a number provided evidence of suspicious characters. Still more, however, distrusted the police and clammed up when approached for information.

They had soon pulled in their first suspect following information from a prostitute, but the man was released soon after due to lack of evidence connecting him to the killings.

They then began to focus on a man driving a blue and white truck. Two of the women reported that he had abducted them and tried to kill them. He had picked them up and as soon as they were in the truck pulled a gun on them. They were both viciously raped but one managed to escape from the truck and the other he let go.

They pulled in a man named Charles Clinton

Clark, a butcher who drove a blue and white truck and who also owned a couple of handguns. Clark confessed to attacking the two women but his modus operandi did not fit the Green River Killer's and he had alibis for the time when the murdered girls had disappeared. He was charged with rape and the search resumed for the killer.

He was busy again. Two sixteen-year-olds – Kase Ann Lee and Terri Rene Milligan – had disappeared in the middle of August and on 15 September, nineteen-year-old Mary Bridgett Meehan, eight months pregnant, disappeared while she was taking a walk.

Detective Reichert began to suspect an unemployed taxi-driver who was working as a volunteer on the case. He fitted the profile of the killer that John Douglas had put together – a confident, but impulsive middle-aged man who would probably get a thrill out of returning to the scenes of the murders. He was undoubtedly local, knew the area, and had strong religious convictions. He would also have a deep interest in the ongoing investigation. The taxi driver was questioned and was put under surveillance throughout the winter of 1982. He was the main suspect, even though he denied having anything to do with the killings and there was no evidence to link him to them. They made his life hell, even arresting him for unpaid parking tickets.

The girls continued to disappear and bodies continued to turn up at an alarming rate. On 26 September, seventeen-year-old prostitute, Gisele Lovvorn, who had been missing for two months, was found near Sea-Tac International Airport. Between then and the following April, fourteen girls, aged from fifteen to twenty-three, vanished. They were mostly prostitutes who worked the strip.

On 30 April 1983, Marie Mulvar, working on the strip, was seen talking to a potential customer by her boyfriend. She climbed into his dark-coloured truck and they drove off. The boyfriend had thought something was not quite right, however, and jumped in his car and followed them. He lost them when he was stopped at a traffic light. He never saw Marie again.

However, he did see the truck again, about a week later. He followed it to a house on South 348th Street and informed the police. The owner of the truck was none other than Gary Ridgway, a truck painter. Ridgway was visited by investigating officers but denied ever having met Marie Mulvar. The detectives believed him and, incredibly, the matter was dropped, even though a similar truck to Ridgway's was involved in the disappearance of another prostitute, Kimi Kai Pitsor. This piece of information was never linked to the Marie Mulvar disappearance and the

Green River Killer was free to carry on relentlessly cleaning up, as he saw it, the streets of Seattle.

By the spring of 1983, there was a great deal of criticism of the investigation. The taxi-driver remained a suspect but it was becoming evident that he was unlikely to be revealed as the killer. The millions of dollars being spent on the case did not prevent more murders. On 8 May, the body of Carol Ann Christenson was found by a family gathering mushrooms in woods near Maple Valley. The killer had taken a great deal of care with the corpse's presentation. Her head was covered by a brown paper bag and a fish had been positioned carefully on her neck. Another fish decorated her left breast and between her legs he had placed a bottle. He had crossed her hands over her stomach and on her left hand he had bizarrely placed some ground meat. She had been in water at some point and had been strangled. Her death was undoubtedly the work of the Green River Killer.

As the weather warmed up, so did the killer. Nine more young women disappeared during the summer and more bodies were found. In June, the remains of an unidentified seventeen- to nineteen-year-old woman were found on Southwest Tualatin Road; in August Shawnda Summers and another unidentified woman were found near the airport. Before

Christmas 1983 another nine disappeared while more bodies were discovered, those of seventeen-year-old Delores Williams, twenty-three-year-old Gail Matthews, Yvonne Antosh and Constance Naon. A thorough search of the area around the airport in late October uncovered the skeleton of twenty-two-year-old Kelly Ware.

Mary Meehan was found on 13 November, surrounded by a bizarre array of items including a piece of clear plastic tube, three small bones, two yellow pencils, two small pieces of plastic and, near her pubic hair, a large clump of hair.

A month later, a new dumping area was discovered when they found the skull of Kimi Kai Pitsor in Auburn, in the vicinity of Mountain View Cemetery. It was the fifth such dumping-ground used by the killer. Profiler, John Douglas, noted that most of the victims had been found near areas where waste was illegally dumped; the killer dumped the women's bodies in such places, he reasoned, because he considered them to be no more than 'human garbage'.

Ten bodies were found in the first few months of 1984 but by May it seemed as if the momentum was going out of the killings. The number seemed to be slowing down. They enlisted the help of serial killer, Ted Bundy, in trying to work out the killer's rationale and although they learned much about the mind of a serial killer, they found little to help them nail their man.

Bodies continued to turn up but not as frequently as before. Two were found in October and December and then another on 10 March 1985. Three months later a man working on a patch of land in Tigard, Oregon, turned up two bodies with his bulldozer. Three more were found the following winter and a further three during the summer of 1986.

Suspects continued to be brought in, only to be released shortly after. Eventually, however, Ridgway re-emerged as a suspect. He had been brought in after trying to solicit an undercover police officer posing as a prostitute in May 1984. He agreed to undergo a lie detector test which he passed and was released. However, they looked into his past and learned a number of things of great interest. Firstly, he had been accused of trying to choke a prostitute near the airport in 1980. When he had claimed that she had bitten him, he had been released. They also found that he had been stopped in 1982 with a prostitute in his truck. She had been Keli McGinness who was now listed as missing. He had then been questioned about the disappearance of Marie Mulvar and was known to frequent the dumpsites where many of the bodies were found. Critically, he was found to have been off work or absent whenever a girl had disappeared. They got a warrant to search his house and brought him in for questioning. But, there was still not enough evidence to charge him and he was released from custody.

Bodies of girls who had been missing for a number of years continued to be found but by 1991 the task force, once the largest in American police history, had been reduced to just one man.

In April 2001, Dave Reichert, now the Sheriff of King County, reopened the investigation, hoping that new methods and technology might shed some fresh light on the Green River Killer's identity. They tested DNA from semen found on some of the bodies and discovered to their delight that it matched Gary Ridgway's DNA. On 30 November, Ridgway was arrested on his way home from work and charged with four counts of murder.

To the outrage of many people, Gary Ridgway avoided the death penalty, making a plea bargain in return for admitting to forty-eight murders and leading police to the dumping sites for many more bodies. He was sentenced to forty-eight life sentences without parole and a further 480 years for tampering with evidence at the scene of a crime.

He has since claimed to have actually killed ninety women.

HERMAN MUDGETT
A.K.A. H. H. HOLMES

If you are looking for a mass killer, then Herman Mudgett would surely be high up on the list. It is estimated that he may have murdered as many as two hundred victims, mainly young ladies, for the sheer pleasure of cutting up their bodies. The name in itself, Herman Webster Mudgett, sounds like it should have been made up by a writer of comedy. He was born in a small town, Gilmanton in New Hampshire, but there was certainly nothing humorous about his characer. In fact he was America's first identified serial killer.

Mudgett was the son of Levi Horton Mudgett and Theodate Page Price, a family who had descended from the first settlers to the area. His father was a strict disciplinarian, and as a young boy Mudgett had to put up with bullying and taunts from older boys. He claimed that, as a child, he had been forced by other students to view and touch a human skeleton after they found out about his fear of going to the doctor's surgery. The bullies had initially brought him there to scare him, but instead he was utterly fascinated.

In fact Mudgett was so fascinated with death, that he started to research the subject at the Ann Arbor medical school where he was a student. He became an expert in acid burns and boosted his student allowance by body snatching. He would steal the corpses, render their bodies unidentifiable and then collect on the life insurance policies that he had previously taken out under a fictitious name. This became quite a lucrative business until a nightwatch-man caught him red-handed, removing a female corpse. His hopes of a medical career were dashed when he was dismissed from the school. However, he would go on to successfully defraud insurance com-panies, swindle people out of their money, commit bigamy, sell phoney elixirs, but most of all commit many, many murders.

His accumulated knowledge of medicine allowed Mudgett to launch a criminal career. In 1886, he moved to Chicago and changed his name to a far more distinguished Henry Howard Holmes. Seeing an advertisement for a pharmacist in the local paper, Holmes applied for the post. Before speaking to the woman behind the counter, Holmes took a few minutes to study the chemist shop. After deciding that the job would suit him nicely, he introduced himself to the owner's wife, Mrs Holton. She told Holmes that her husband was terminally ill, which left the burden of running the business to her. The couple lived in an apartment above the chemist shop, and Holmes watched as Mrs Holton struggled to fill out a prescription form as per husband's instructions. Holmes seized the opportunity, took the pen from Mrs Holton and deftly filled in the form. Needless to say Mrs Holton hired him on the spot.

After Mr Holton died, Holmes arranged to buy the chemist, but it wasn't long before he started to default on the payments. Mrs Holton threatened to take him to court, but before any action could be taken she mysteriously disappeared. Holmes explained to the regulars that she had moved to California to get over the death of her husband, but no one ever saw or heard from her again.

Using the respectable chemist business as a cover, Holmes set about to pursue a more sordid line of business. The chemist shop had been so profitable that it had given Holmes enough funds to buy a vacant plot of land, on which he planned to build a luxurious house. But this was going to be no ordinary house, it was specially designed by Holmes himself. As each stage of the three-storey building progressed, Holmes would hire a new set of builders so that no one would get suspicious about the maze of secret passages, trapdoors, chutes, dungeons and shafts. By the time the house had been completed, Holmes had employed over five hundred workers, which strangely enough, no one ever questioned until many years later when the press described the house as 'Murder Castle'.

Holmes was determined to make sure that no one could figure out why his building was such a strange design. It contained a strange assortment of rooms, some secret, some lined with lead and others without any windows at all. Some of the windowless rooms were fitted with gas jets, while others had walls that slid across making the room either bigger or smaller. From some of the rooms there were large chutes that ran into zinc-lined bathtubs in the basement. A huge kiln, a lime vat and, what has been described as an autopsy table, also occupied the basement.

It was from here that Holmes began his new career – a career of murder. The house was finished just in time for the great Chicago Exposition of 1893. Holmes knew that the city would be full of visitors, many of whom were to be his prey. He lured the girls and young ladies to his 'castle' where he attempted to seduce them before plying them with drugs. The girls would then be put into one of the empty shafts that ran throughout the building. When the girls came round from their drugged sleep, they found themselves trapped behind a glass panel in an airtight death chamber, into which Holmes would pump lethal gas. The bodies were then sent down a chute to the basement where large vats containing acid and lime waited ominously for the body parts that were to come. The body was first placed on the dissecting table, where Holmes would cut up the corpses, removing any particular body organs that took his fancy. Anything he didn't want, he simply disposed of in the acid tanks.

Holmes later admitted that he murdered as many as two hundred girls during the Chicago Exposition alone. He would have continued with his gruesome trade had not the creditors started to move in on him. By the time the Exposition ended, Holmes' finances were in a bad way. Holmes decided the best way out of his predicament was to leave Chicago altogether, but before he left he had one final piece of business to complete. He had murdered two visiting Texan sisters and, rather than dispose of their remains, Holmes decided to make some money out of the insurance company policy he had taken out on the house. He set fire to 'Murder Castle', but his plans were foiled when the insurance company refused to pay out. The insurance had alerted the police of their suspicions regarding the fire and they started an investigation.

Strangely, the police work was not very thorough and didn't produce enough evidence to convict Mudgett, but of course he was not aware of this and decided to flee.

This time Holmes turned up in Texas, where he managed to trace the relatives of the sisters he had murdered. Having befriended them, Holmes then tried to swindle them out of their $60,000 savings. However, luckily they were suspicious of Holmes and alerted the police, so once again he took to the road, this time on a stolen horse.

The police caught up with Holmes in Missouri, this time using the name H. M. Howard. They charged him with a fraud attempt, but with the help of a 'not so straight' lawyer, Holmes was granted bail and was once again on the run.

Despite the vast numbers of people that Holmes had killed, it was not this depraved business that finally brought him to justive. It was yet another insurance fraud scheme. Stupidly, Holmes double-crossed a fellow criminal, an infamous bank robber called Marion Hedgepeth. He had met Hedgepeth when they were both serving time in a Philadelphia jail while Holmes was being held during a fraud investigation. Holmes was released but not before telling Hedgepeth about his plans to defraud an insurance company out of $10,000. The plan was:

Holmes' loyal follower Benjamin F. Pritezel was to take out an insurance policy on himself and then disappear. Holmes would secure a cadaver, disfigure it, and then later help identify it as Pritezel's body. Holmes would also arrange for a lawyer to act on behalf of Pritezel's family to make sure that they collected the insurance money. This was where he needed to be careful, he needed to find a crooked lawyer to make the scheme work. And this was where Hedgepath came into the equation. For a fee of $500, Hedgepath put Holmes in touch with a shady lawyer.

The scheme worked like a dream, but Holmes made one big mistake, he did not give Hedgepath his share of the money. Hedgepath immediately went to the police and told them the whole story.

What Hedgepath and the police didn't know was that Holmes had actually murdered Pritezel. He had tricked Mrs Pritezel into helping him perpetrate the fraud by using three of her five children, Howard Nellie, and Alice. They helped to identify the body of their father, even though they believed it was just a cadaver that Holmes had 'sculpted' so that it had physical similarities. After the children helped Holmes identify the body, he murdered them in cold blood and then moved on to the next stage of his plan – to get rid of Mrs Pritezel and her remaining two children. This plan was foiled though because Hedgepath had already been to the police and informed them of Holmes' activities. The police hired Pinkerton Detective Agency to assist them in their enquiries, aware that they had long had suspicions about the man called Holmes. He was finally arrested in Boston in November 1894, but it was only when they searched 'Murder Castle' back in Chicago that the true evil of his past was revealed. Not only were there a number of intact skeletons, but also countless fragments of human bone.

Throughout his questioning by the agency, Holmes refused to reveal any details about what had happened to Mrs Pritezel's three children. Fearing the worst, Detective Geyer set out to try and discover their fate. In Chicago, Geyer discovered that all of Holmes' mail had been forwarded to Gilmanton, New York, then to Detroit, Toronto, Cincinnati, Indianapolis and then on from there. Geyer followed the trail relentlessly for eight months. He searched each address that Holmes had stayed at along the way until he eventually came to 16 Vincent Street in Toronto. The house had indeed been rented to a man that fitted Holmes' description. The man had been travelling with two little girls. The neighbour said that the man had asked if he could borrow a spade, claiming that he wanted to dig a hole to store potatoes in for the winter. Geyer borrowed the same spade and started to dig in exactly the same location. To his dismay he found the bodies of Nellie and Alice Pritezel hidden several feet under the earth. When he searched the house, Geyer found a large trunk in one of the bedrooms, from which a piece of rubber tubing protruded which was attached to a gas pipe. Apparently, Holmes had told the girls he wanted to play hide and seek and tricked them into climbing into the trunk. The fate of the third child was never discovered.

When the story appeared in the *Chicago Tribune*, they offered their readers a look inside the 'Murder Castle'. There were lurid illustrations and even a map showing the entire layout of the building. The bottom floor of the house had been used as a drug store, a sweetshop, a restaurant and a jewellery store by Holmes himself. The third floor had been divided into small apartments and guest rooms which apparently had never even been used.

It was the second floor that had all the bizarre additons and also thirty-five guest rooms. Many of them were fitted out as ordinary bedrooms, but many had no windows and were lined with sheet iron and asbestos. These were fitted with trapdoors that led to smaller rooms beneath, equipped with lethal gas jets. However, it was the basement that revealed the true 'chamber of horrors'. This underground chamber was located seven feet below the rest of the building, and it was here that they found Holmes' blood-spattered dissecting table, his surgical implements, his macabre laboratory of torture devices, various jars containing poison and a wooden box that still contained a number of women's skeletons. Built into one of the thick walls was a crematorium, still containing ash and portions of bone. The more the workers excavated the site, the more atrocities they uncovered. The police gradually managed to build up a dossier of Holmes' potential victims, but no one who worked on the house would ever forget what they had seen.

The house sat empty for several months after the investigators had left, but not surprisingly it attracted curiosity-seekers from all over the city. Then on 19 August, Murder Castle burned to the ground. Three explosions woke the neighbourhood just after midnight, followed by a blaze that caused what was left of the building to collapse. A gas can was later discovered in the house, but the mystery as to who had place it there was never solved. Maybe it was an accomplice of Holmes who was trying to hide his role in the house of horrors, or possibly a neighbour who was outraged by what had taken place there.

For a long time the site where Murder Castle had been located remained vacant. Then in 1938 a Post Office was built on the site. Even after the Post Office was constructed, the site still continued to mystify as strange occurrences were often reported. People who walked their dogs past the site claimed their animals would pull away from the site, barking and whining at something they could see or sense.

The trial of Herman Mudgett, aka Holmes, began in Philadelphia just before Halloween 1895. It only lasted for six days but it was one of the most sensational of the century. He became the first murderer in the United States to defend himself at the trial and he created many exciting scenes in the courtroom. He was described as being outstanding, clever and shrewd as an attorney, but his efforts were to no avail. On November 30, the judge passed a sentence of death. Holmes was scheduled to die on 7 May 1896, just nine days before his thirty-sixth birthday.

Even at the end he remained unrepentant. He was led from his cell to the gallows and a black hood was placed over his head. After he dropped through the trap door his heart continued to beat for nearly fifteen minutes, leading to speculation that his spirit was still carrying on his gruesome work from beyond the grave!

PEE WEE GASKINS JR.

Donald Gaskins was never going to amount to much more than trouble. His upbringing saw to that. Born in 1933 in rural South Carolina, he never knew who his father was, being called Junior Parrott – Parrott being his mother's maiden name until he was thirteen years of age. He was small, so they also called him 'Pee Wee'.

Until she married in 1943, Pee Wee's mother enjoyed a series of liaisons with men who either paid no attention to her son or who paid too much attention by beating him. Within a few years, Pee Wee found himself with four half-siblings but one thing had not changed – his new stepfather beat him like many of the others. For Pee Wee, it was just life, however.

He was an angry boy, especially towards girls who brought out the worst in him, resulting in frightening temper tantrums, irrational violence and criminality.

He did not hang around school for long; it offered little to a kid like him who was good with his hands and just wanted to be working with machinery. He found work at a local garage and teamed up with two boys, Danny and Marsh, forming a gang they called 'The Trouble Trio'. And they certainly were trouble, stealing from petrol stations and breaking into houses. They made so much money from their thefts that they were able to buy a car that enabled them to break into houses further afield and to visit brothels in Charleston and Columbia. They were not fussy, however, and they practised their new found sexuality on younger boys as well.

One day they raped Marsh's sister, promising her cash if she would keep quiet about it, but she ran to her father who strung Pee Wee and Marsh up in a barn by their wrists and whipped them with a leather strap.

Pee Wee was left alone now but soon had a partner and was back in business as a burglar. One night in 1946, he was surprised in the middle of a break-in by a girl he knew. She chased him with a hatchet, but he grabbed it from her and hit her on the scalp and on her arms. He was arrested and jailed for assault with a deadly weapon with intent to kill. He was sent to the South Carolina Industrial School for Boys until he reached the age of eighteen. When they called him

Gaskins in court, it was the first time he had ever heard his real name.

Reformatory was a terrifying place to be and on only his second night Pee Wee learned just how terrifying it was when he was jumped in the shower, beaten and raped by a gang of twenty boys. The only way he was able to avoid such attacks was to accept protection from his dorm's Boss-Boy. He paid for his protection with daily sex and the Boss-Boy also loaned Pee Wee to his friends.

Pee Wee wanted out and succeeded in escaping after thirteen months with four other boys. They were all recaptured the following day but on the way back to the reformatory, Pee Wee jumped off the back of the truck, running to a hideout he used to have when he was in The Troublesome Trio. He was found by a local police officer who persuaded the fourteen-year-old to give himself up. He was punished with thirty lashes and thirty days' hard labour isolation, digging ditches under the hot sun and being beaten at night for the slightest violation of the rules.

He escaped again, managing to stay at large for six days before he was tracked down by bloodhounds. This time it was fifty lashes.

Escaping a third time, he made his way to an aunt's house in Williamsburg County. He was persuaded to return when the warden promised him leniency, but, of course, it was a trick and he returned to the same old horrific routine of beatings, whippings and gang rapes. He could not take it and punched a guard after a week, following which he was taken unconscious after a beating to the state mental hospital. In 1950, aged seventeen, he was sent back to the reformatory but he escaped again, this time joining a travelling carnival where he fell in love with and married a thirteen-year-old girl, the first of the six wives he would have. She persuaded him to give himself up in order to serve the last three months of his sentence; he spent them in solitary confinement.

Freedom proved difficult and he worked at four different jobs in his first six months out of reformatory. It was not long, however, before he was getting into trouble again. With a fellow former reformatory inmate he burned and looted tobacco barns, often collaborating with landowners on insurance frauds. Meanwhile, he was working by day on a tobacco farm. Rumours spread about who was responsible for the fires, however, and one day when his boss's daughter tormented him with the accusations, he picked up a hammer and smashed her skull, almost killing her. He pleaded guilty and thought he had got away with an eighteen-month sentence but had neglected to get his plea bargain in writing and was sentenced to five years. When Pee Wee swore at the judge he added on another year for contempt of court. He was sent to South Carolina State Prison in the autumn of 1952.

At first it was alright – no Boss-Boys, but he was approached one day and told, 'You belong to Arthur'. For the next six months he shared a cell with a brutal rapist.

The only way to escape from this hell was to prove yourself, to become one of the men who ruled the prison, known as Power men. To do that he would have to murder. His target was a vicious convict, Hazel Brazell. Gaskins ingratiated himself with Hazel, buying him food and becoming one of his hangers-on. One day, however, he found Hazel on the toilet and slit his throat with a stolen knife.

He told the authorities that he killed Hazel in a fight and the charge was changed from murder to manslaughter, resulting in an extra three years in prison. He endured six months in solitary and emerged a Power man. No one would touch him now.

A couple of years later, in 1955, he learned that his wife was filing for divorce and decided to break out. He hid in a rubbish barrel and jumped from the truck that took it out of the prison. He stole a car and drove to Florida, rejoining the carnival. Soon, he was married again, to a nineteen-year-old but the marriage ended after just two weeks.

He fell in love next with a contortionist but she gave him up to the police and he was arrested, jailed for three months in Tennessee for various infractions and six more for slashing another inmate during a fight before being sent back to South Carolina. Things were going from bad to worse. Back in South Carolina, he was put into solitary and then FBI agents came to arrest him for driving a stolen car across a state line while he had been with the contortionist. That earned him three years in prison in Atlanta, Georgia.

He shared a cell in Georgia with three bodyguards for the mafia boss, Frank Costello, head of the Luciano Family who was doing time for tax evasion. Costello nicknamed him 'the little hatchet man' and Pee Wee learned a lot from him and his men.

In August 1961, he was finally eligible for parole and walked out of prison after nine years with a new suit, in the pocket of which were $20 and a ticket home to Florence, South Carolina.

Pretty soon, however, he was back breaking into houses and frequenting bars looking for cheap sex.

He found work as a general assistant and driver to a travelling preacher, George Todd, but as they travelled the country, Pee Wee was taking every opportunity to break into houses. He also married again, a seventeen-year-old this time. It did not stop his roving eye, however, and he was arrested for the rape of a twelve-year-old girl in Florence County. He managed to escape, however, and fled to Greensboro where he could not resist marrying another seventeen-year-old. That one lasted three months, quite long by Pee Wee Gaskins' standards.

He bounced around a few ex-wives until one gave the police his whereabouts and he was arrested again. He got six years this time for the rape and a further two for his escape.

His reputation went before him and his time in prison was easy. He was paroled in November 1968, aged thirty-five, determined never to return to prison. However, as he later said that did not mean not doing anything wrong; it meant not being caught. And that meant leaving no witnesses to his criminal activity.

He found a place to live in Sumter, South Carolina working in construction. Women were still a huge problem for him and when one rejected him, he still became enraged.

Everything changed in September 1968 when he picked up a young, blonde hitchhiker and asked her for sex. When she laughed at his proposition, he turned on her, beating her unconscious and then raping and sodomising her on an old logging road. She was still alive when he dumped her in a swamp. It made him feel terrific. He had found what he wanted to do now and travelled the coastal highways at weekends looking for likely victims. He had found and killed two more by Christmas 1969.

Soon, he was killing on average one girl every six weeks. He would torture them in different ways, trying to keep them alive and suffering for as long as he could. He killed eleven girls that year and even succeeded in kidnapping and killing two girls at once. One girl he kept alive for four days. He hit her with a hammer and cut her throat when he had done with her.

Soon he had also moved on to killing boys, mistaking two long-haired boys for girls one day, but killing them and sodomising them anyway. He cut off their genitals while they were still alive and cooked them and ate them before putting them out of their hellish misery.

Between 1969 and 1975 Pee Wee Gaskins killed dozens of people, eighty or ninety by his own estimation.

In 1970, he had begun to carry out more difficult murders, what he called his 'serious murders' of personal friends, family and acquaintances. His fifteen-year-old niece Janice Kirby and her friend seventeen-year-old Patricia Alsobrook were the first. He had often thought about raping Janice and one night when the girls needed a lift home, he seized the opportunity. He raped them both before drowning them and burying them in separate spots. The police spoke to him about their disappearance but they had nothing much to go on and he got away with it.

He married again in January 1971, his new wife pregnant with his child, and they moved to Charleston. The killing continued, however. He killed Eddie Brown, a twenty-four-year-old gun-runner and his wife, Bertie, before he moved on with his wife to Prospect, South Carolina in July 1973. Three more were dead at his hands before the end of the year – fourteen-year-old runaway, Jackie Freeman was first, spending three days being tortured and raped by Gaskins. Then a few months later, he offered to drive twenty-three-year-old Doreen Dempsey and her two-year-old daughter Robin Michelle to the local bus station in the old hearse he had bought, driving her instead into some woods and demanding sex. When she refused, Gaskins killed her with a hammer before raping and sodomising the little girl. He strangled her as well and buried them both together in the woods.

In 1974, he shot a man who owed him money before stabbing to death his girlfriend. Another man was killed after making a play for Pee Wee's wife. He claimed not to have killed him for trying but for the way he did it. 'I mean if he had come straight to me like a man and asked to make a deal with me for my wife, I would probably have given her to him, for a night or a week, or to keep, if the offer was good enough,' he said, matter-of-factly.

A grandfather by 1975, he kept on killing. He drowned three hippies in January but made the fatal mistake of recruiting ex-convict Walter Neely to help him get rid of their van. By the end of the year he would regret that decision.

He next was contracted to kill a wealthy Florence County farmer but a woman involved in the plot, Diane Neely, Walter's ex-wife, told another ex-convict Avery Howard, about Gaskins' part in the killing and they demanded $5,000 from him. He killed them.

It all ended with the killing of thirteen-year-old Kim Ghelkins who, as usual, had rejected his advances. He raped, tortured and strangled her, burying her in the woods. Then he killed a couple of boys who broke into his workshop. For some unaccountable reason he again recruited Walter Neely to help him dispose of their bodies, pointing out the graves of countless others of his victims as he did so.

However, Kim Ghelkins' parents suspected Gaskins of killing their daughter and when a Sumter deputy sheriff searched his house, he discovered items of Kim's clothing. They were unable to pin murder on him just yet, but they charged him with contributing to the delinquency of a minor. He tried to flee but was arrested at the local bus station.

Shortly after his arrest, Walter Neely told the police everything he knew. He took the police officers to Pee Wee's graveyard and they began to dig up bodies.

On 28 May 1976, he was sentenced to death but a few months later, the US Supreme Court invalidated South Carolina's death penalty statute and his sentence was commuted to eight life sentences. He would confess to many more, of course, becoming easily South Carolina's most prolific serial killer to date.

He was not done with killing yet, however.

In prison, in 1982, he became involved in a plot to kill another inmate Rudolph Tyner, on behalf of the son of one of his victims. Tyner was on Death Row, the state having been able to reintroduce the death penalty. Pee Wee tried to poison him, feeding him all kinds of drugs, but the man would not die. He merely suffered from bad stomach pains. That having failed, he constructed a bomb, using a plastic explosive that was smuggled in past the guards. Tyner allowed Gaskins to connect a homemade intercom between their cells and Gaskins provided him with a receiver made from a plastic cup filled with explosive. On the night of 12 September 1982, Tyner placed the cup against his ear, and Gaskins sent a charge along the wire. As Pee Wee laughed his head off, Tyner had his blown off.

They got him for this one. This time he was sentenced to die.

Hours before the time for his execution Pee Wee tried to stage his own exit, slashing his arms and wrists with a razor blade that he had swallowed days earlier and which he had now regurgitated. They caught him, however, stitching him up in time for him to go to the electric chair at 1.10 am on 6 September 1991. His final words were, 'I'll let my lawyers talk for me. I'm ready to go.'

GERALD EUGENE STANO

He was never right. Born Paul Zeininger in Schenectady, New York, in 1951, he followed the path taken by three of the other four children his mother had given birth to and was put up for adoption. He was given a home by Eugene Stano, a manager for a large corporation and his wife Norma, a social worker. It had taken some time to place Paul. He was a difficult child and had even been declared unadoptable by a number of doctors, social workers and psychologists who had examined him. He had been a victim of serious neglect, was suffering from malnutrition and was described as functioning at an animalistic level. For example, he had acquired the habit of removing his nappy and playing with and even eating his own faeces. Nonetheless, the Stanos believed they could provide him with a good home. They changed his name to Gerald Eugene Stano.

His early upbringing stayed with him, however, and he had numerous problems as a child. He was emotionally distant and wet the bed until he was ten years old. Above all, however, he was unable to relate to other children and found it difficult to make friends. He became a loner and a target for bullies. Girls laughed at him and he withdrew even further into himself.

He responded by becoming anti-social and no stranger to the police. In the late 1960s, he was arrested for setting off a fire alarm and was again in trouble a short while later for throwing rocks from a motorway bridge at cars passing underneath. To prevent him being sent to a juvenile detention centre, his parents enrolled him in a military school. It was to no avail, however – he was caught stealing money from other students.

The Stanos decided to make a fresh start, moving to Norristown, Pennsylvania, but it made no difference to their wayward son's behaviour. He was skipping school and still stealing from his schoolmates as well as from his parents. So desperate was he for recognition and attention that he took money from his father's wallet on one occasion to bribe other members of the school athletics team to let him win a race. Needless to say, he continually failed academically and did not graduate from high school until he was twenty-one, having been forced to repeat three years.

After school, he enrolled at a computer school, leaving home and moving into a motel. Amazingly, he did well, graduating and finding a job at a local hospital. It seemed for the first time as if his life was on track. It was short-lived, however. Within weeks, he was fired for stealing money from his colleagues. He moved back in with his parents.

In the early 1970s he moved to New Jersey where he began seeing a young girl with mental problems. She was soon pregnant and her father was after Gerald with a gun. He agreed to pay for an abortion for the girl.

His life was in freefall and he began drinking heavily and experimented with drugs, moving all the while from job to job. He moved to Florida at his parents' insistence to look after his elderly grandmother. Again, he moved from job to job and the reasons for moving on were always the same – he was late or failed to turn up at all for work or was discovered to be stealing.

It was 1975 and he tried to sort his life out. He stopped drinking and gave up drugs. He dated and fell in love with a hair stylist and in June of that year, he married her. Her father gave him a job at the service station he owned and finally it appeared that Gerald was settled. It lasted no more than a few months. Soon, he had returned to his old habits. He was drinking again and beating up his wife. Just six months into the marriage, she filed for divorce.

But all the while Gerald had been busy and his other life soon began to become known.

On 17 February 1980, the decomposed body of a young woman was found in wasteland near Daytona airport. The body had been concealed with branches, lying on her back with her arms at her side and her head turned upwards. She had not been sexually abused. However, she had lain there a long time and the decomposition rendered it difficult initially to discover exactly how she had died. When she was turned over, however, the investigating officers saw that she had been stabbed repeatedly in the back, indicating that the killer had lost his temper and become enraged.

She was identified as Mary Carol Maher, a twenty-year-old student at a local college. An autopsy reported that she had been the victim of a frenzied knife attack and that she had been stabbed repeatedly in the back, chest and legs.

Just over a month later, a woman walked into a police station in Daytona Beach. She was a prostitute and wanted to report an attack on her by a man who had picked her up. She had been looking for business on Atlantic Avenue when the man, driving a red Gremlin with tinted windows, pulled up. She had agreed on a price with him and they had gone to a motel room. Once there, however, the man had refused to pay her upfront and an argument had ensued during which he had produced a knife, cutting her on the right thigh. He screamed at her, insulting her for being a prostitute and then ran off.

The woman was determined that he be caught and said that she would be able to identify her assailant. He was of average height, a little plump, wore glasses and had a moustache. Furthermore, she was certain she had spotted his car parked outside an apartment building not far away. When they ran the number plate through the computer, it turned out that it belonged to twenty-nine-year-old Gerald Eugene Stano, a man who had been arrested on several occasions but had never been convicted of anything.

When they looked closely at Stano, they began to realise that he was a perfect match for the man they were looking for in connection with the murder of Mary Carol Maher, a month previously. They had been looking for a white male, aged late thirties or early forties, living locally and driving an ordinary car. Their suspect would have a hot temper and would hate women. He would be driven crazy by rejection and he had killed before and would undoubtedly kill again.

Stano was brought in for questioning on the

aggravated assault and battery of the prostitute. Detective Sergeant Paul Crow was in charge. Crow was a Vietnam veteran and had been a student at the FBI's Homicide Investigation School where he had learned about criminal psychology and profiling.

Crow began to push Stano, learning that whenever the suspect lied, he leaned back in his chair and when he told the truth, he leaned forward. Eventually, Stano told him that he had merely given Mary Carol Maher a lift from a hotel to Atlantic Avenue where he said he had left her. But then he changed his story. What had actually happened was that twenty-year-old Mary had decided to hitchhike home from a bar. Stano had picked her up and it was not long before she realised she was in trouble. As they idled at a traffic light, he placed his hand on her leg and said 'I want some right here.' She had laughed at him and rejected his advances. Furious at her rejection of him, he pulled out a knife and stabbed her as hard as he could several times in the chest. She had tried to get the car door open but he slashed at her leg and dragged her back in, closing the door. She then fell forward, hitting her head on the dashboard. By now she was dying and making gurgling sounds.He stabbed her a couple of more times in the back but began to worry that she was making a mess of his car and took her somewhere to dispose of the body.

The police now began to suspect that Stano had been responsible for other murders and re-opened other cases of missing women. They presented him with a photograph of Toni Van Haddocks, a twenty-six-year-old prostitute who had gone missing on 15 February. He denied ever seeing her, but they were certain he was lying. Meanwhile, they charged him with the first-degree murder of Mary Carol Maher.

The body of Toni Van Haddocks was discovered in the middle of April when a man discovered a human skull in his garden. Nearby they found more remains and clothing. She had been killed by multiple stab wounds to the head.

They questioned Stano again, but this time, he broke down and confessed. They began to dig back into the missing person files and came up with a number of likely cases. Sixteen-year-old Linda Hamilton had disappeared on Atlantic Avenue and had been found dead near an old Indian burial ground in July 1975; Nancy Heard was found just north of Ormond Beach in January 1976. Her body was concealed by a covering of branches and she had been posed just like Mary Carol Maher. Eighteen-year-old Ramona Neal was found in Tomoka State Park in May 1976. She had also been concealed by a layer of branches.

They checked in other areas. Another young

woman's body had been found 100 miles west of Daytona Beach, lying in a swamp, but again covered by branches. In Titusville, fifty miles to the south, another young woman had been murdered; she had been seen walking along Atlantic Avenue shortly before her disappearance and was found naked and covered by branches.

Similar unsolved murders were found in Stuart, Florida, where Stano had lived in the early 1970s and in New Jersey where he had also lived, they found at least two murders that seemed similar – young women posed and covered in branches.

Confronted by all this, Stano decided to enter a plea bargain, pleading guilty to the murders of Toni Van Haddocks, Mary Carol Maher and Nancy Heard for which he received three consecutive life sentences, each with a mandatory minimum of twenty-five years behind bars. Stano went to Florida State Prison.

Before long, however, he began to miss the attention he had been getting during the court proceedings and while he was being held in the county jail. He wrote to Detective Sergeant Crow, offering to confess to many more murders. He was returned to the county jail and began to reel off the killings. He confessed to killing seventeen-year-old Cathy Lee Scharf of Port Orange, Florida, whose decomposed body had been found in a ditch near Titusville in January 1974; twenty-four-year-old Daytona Beach inhabitant, Susan Bickrest, who was found in Spruce Spring Creek in December 1975 and twenty-three-year-old Mary Muldoon of Ormond Beach who was discovered in a ditch in November 1977. Nineteen-year-old Janine Ligotino was added to the catalogue of killings and seventeen-year-old Ann Arceneaux, both found near Gainesville in 1973. Seventeen-year-old Barbara Ann Bauer had been found in 1974 near Starke and the body of an unidentified woman was located in Altamonte Springs in 1974. Thirty-four-year-old Bonnie Hughes, eighteen-year-old Diana Valleck, twenty-one-year-old Emily Branch, seventeen-year-old Christina Goodson, twenty-three-year-old Phoebe Winston, eighteen-year-old Joan Foster and twelve-year-old Susan Basile – he confessed to the killing of all of them. For good measure, just as the interview was drawing to a close, he remembered a couple of others – thirty-five-year-old Sandra DuBose, found dead in 1978 and seventeen-year-old Dorothy Williams, killed in 1979 and found near Atlantic Avenue.

Needless to say, Gerald Stano was sentenced to death but his confessions continued for several more years. His deathly tally was eventually estimated to be forty-one.

On 23 March 1998, after numerous appeals and several stays of execution – one of them just three hours before he was due to be executed – Gerald Stano walked to the death chamber after a last meal of a Delmonico steak, bacon bits, baked potato with sour cream, French bread with butter and a tossed salad topped with blue cheese dressing. For dessert, he had mint chocolate chip ice cream and two litres of Dr Pepper.

JOHN WAYNE GACY

On St Patrick's Day in 1942, John Wayne Gacy Jr was born to Marie and John Gacy. He had an older sister named Joanne and in 1944 Karen was born. The Gacys lived on the northern side of Chicago, where they attended a Catholic school. John Jr was a hard-working child. He sought employment after school and had good working relationships with his colleagues. Although he wasn't one of the popular crowd at school, John he was well liked by his teachers. At home he doted on his mother and sisters, but his relationship with his father was always a little strained. John Sr was an alcoholic and would often beat his mother in full view of his children. Despite the verbal abuse hurled at him and his sisters, John Jr loved his father and constantly craved his attention and devotion.

As Gacy approached his teenage years his health suffered two blows, the first being was when he was just eleven years old. Gacy was playing with a swing set when part of the apparatus struck him on the head. For the following five years Gacy suffered from blackouts. It wasn't until he was sixteen that this was investigated by doctors and a blood clot was discovered. He was put on medication which controlled these episodes. At seventeen he began complaining of severe heart pains and was diagnosed with having a non-specific heart ailment. These heart pains occurred frequently, but as doctors could not find an exact cause, he had to put up with them.

Gacy did not pass his last year of high school and so dropped out and moved to Las Vegas. Failing to establish himself or a career there, he moved back to Chicago and enrolled in business college, finally graduating with a diploma. Things were starting to look up, he excelled in various retail outlets, racing up the management tracks and moving out of town to Springfield, Illinois. However, during this time his health took another turn for the worse. He'd put on a huge amount of weight and started suffering from his heart problem again. Shortly after a spell in hospital for his heart, Gacy was admitted for a spinal injury.

Despite being quite an unwell man, Gacy threw himself into various organisations that worked to improve the local community, even earning himself the title of 'Man of the Year' for his work at the Jaycees. His reputation grew and he a well respected member of the community – little did they know there was another side to Gacy Jr.

In 1964, twenty-six-year-old Gacy married Marlynn Myers. The couple moved to Iowa where Gacy worked for his father-in-law at a branch of KFC, one of a few franchises the Myers' family owned. Gacy again proved to be a valuable employee, continuing his volunteer work on the side. He established himself at the Iowa chapter of the Jaycees. Gacy and Marlynn had two children during this time, a son followed by a daughter. Everything was looking great for Gacy, but beneath this hard-working and charitable exterior lived a cold-blooded sadist, and the truth was finding its way out.

The rumours had been circulating for years. Gacy had started a club in the basement at Jaycees for young boys, and it was known that alcohol was available to them. There were whispers that Gacy made sexual advances towards the club members, whispers that were confirmed to be fact when Gacy was arrested following allegations from a minor named Mark Miller. He claimed Gacy had tricked him into being tied up and had then violently sodomised him. Gacy denied this, claiming he had paid Miller for sex and as such it had been fully consensual. Four months later Gacy hatched a revenge plot and bribed a local man to beat up Miller.

This backfired and when the police got involved Gacy was revealed as being behind the ludicrous plan. Finally, Gacy was indicted for sodomy and was sentenced to ten years at Iowa State Penitentiary. However, by the summer of 1970 he was paroled and back out in the real world.

While he'd been in prison his wife had divorced him and his father had died. Gacy decided he needed a fresh start in a new place and moved to 8213 West Summerdale Avenue in Norwood Park Township, Cook County. He quickly became a hit with the neighbours, throwing themed parties which hundreds are said to have attended. Gacy was popular and admired and he loved the attention. However, he was unable to tame his perverse urges. Within a few months of his 'fresh start' he was back to his old tricks, firstly forcing a young boy at a bus terminal to commit sexual acts on him. When this went to trial the boy failed to arrive in court and without his testimony Gacy was free to walk.

In the summer of 1972, Gacy married for a second time, Carole Hoff, a divorcee with two daughters. Carole was aware of Gacy's past but moved her family into his house regardless. It wasn't long before his step-daughters and neighbours started to question a rancid stench that seemed to permeate the property. Gacy always had an excuse, claiming there was a build-up of moisture in the crawl space beneath the house. Of course only he knew there was something far more disturbing down there.

In 1974, Gacy started his own construction company, PDM Contractors. He employed mainly teenage boys, apparently to keep his costs low, but really to indulge in his predatory urges, something his wife was beginning to become suspicious of. His relationship with Carole began to fall apart and when she discovered gay pornography in the house and he admitted he enjoyed sex with men more than her, she was horrified and filed for divorce. His second marriage was over.

Around this time Gacy decided to get into politics, and tried to capture the attention of the local Democratic Party by offering to use his team to clean their offices free of charge. He got back into volunteering work to try and impress the party members. As a sideline he would dress up, somewhat sinisterly, as his alter ego, 'Pogo the Clown', to entertain the children's wards in local hospitals. Later that year Gacy's efforts were acknowledged and he became secretary treasurer. However, his career in politics was over before it started. Rumours of Gacy's predilection for young men were starting to spread after an incident with Tony Antonucci, an employee at PDM Contractors. According to Antonucci, Gacy inappropriately propositioned him and had to threaten to hit him with a chair to get him to back down. A month later Gacy tried again to assault Antonucci, trying to trick him into being handcuffed. Antonucci played along but made sure he was not properly cuffed, and when he saw his chance he overpowered Gacy and handcuffed him instead. Gacy promised never to do this again and Antonucci believed him, incredibly working for him for another year.

From 1975, young men employed by Gacy started to disappear with alarming regularity. The first to go was Johnny Butkovich. Gacy decided to withhold two weeks of Butkovich's pay to save himself some cash. Butkovich was outraged and went to Gacy's house to demand the money, taking a couple of friends for back-up. Gacy refused to pay Butkovich and they began shouting at each other, eventually Butkovich realised Gacy wasn't going to pay up so the posse stormed off. He dropped his friends off at their houses and was never seen again. In June 1976, seventeen-year-old Michael Bonnin disappeared on his way to catch a train. On 13 June 1976, Billy Carroll Jr, a local troublemaker known for arranging sexual rendezvous between teenage boys and adult males for profit, simply vanished. On 12 December 1976, seventeen-year-old Gregory Godzik dropped his girlfriend home after a date. The next day the police found his car but no trace of Godzik. On 20 January 1977, John Szyc was out driving and never seen again. Szyc's car, however, became an interest to the police when it was spotted trying to flee a petrol station without paying for gas. The driver was an employee of Gacy's and the police questioned why he was now in possession of it, Gacy claimed Szyc had sold him the car before he'd left town.

On 15 September 1977, eighteen-year-old Robert Gilroy failed to meet friends at the bus stop. His father, a police sergeant, ordered a huge search party but could find no trace of Robert. In December 1977, Gacy struck again, this time not killing his victim. The man reported that Gacy had kidnapped him at gunpoint and raped him but, for unknown reasons, this never led to an arrest.

In March 1978, Jeffrey Rignall was lured into Gacy's car. He was then chloroformed and taken back to Summerdale Avenue unconscious. Once there Gacy raped and tortured Rignall and then drove him to Lincoln Park where he dumped him beneath a statue. Rignall had been in and out of consciousness throughout the ordeal due to the chloroform, and had remembered parts of the journey in the car. One night he successfully pieced together the route and arrived at the house on Summerdale Avenue. He reported this to the police and they arrested Gacy in July 1978.

However, he was not kept in custody at this point.

In December 1978, another young man went missing, fifteen-year-old Robert Piest. Robert had been working at a pharmacy and his mother had come to pick him up at the end of his shift. He told her he was meeting a contractor who had offered him a job. Robert seemed to be taking a long time and Mrs Piest was getting concerned, she searched the local area but couldn't find him. After three hours had passed she called the Des Plaines Police Department. Lieutenant Joseph Kozenczak headed the investigation into Robert's disappearance. As soon as he learned that Robert had been to meet Gacy he went to Gacy's house and asked him to go to the station. Gacy, unbelievably, said he couldn't go as there had been a death in the family and he had some phone calls to make. He was questioned a few hours later at the police station but claimed to know nothing about the boy's disappearance. Gacy was released without further questioning. The next day Lieutenant Kozencazk looked into Gacy's past and found his conviction for sodomy years earlier, he was convinced Gacy was guilty.

On 13 December 1978, having obtained a search warrant, the police went to Gacy's house and searched it in his absence. An inventory was taken and a catalogue of disturbing articles were recovered including weapons, drugs, pornography and an eighteen-inch rubber dildo. Some more random items, trophies perhaps, that were found included several rings, a roll of film and some clothing that would be far too small for the obese Gacy. They decided to search the crawl space and were repulsed by the same revolting smell that had shocked Carole's daughters years earlier. They decided it must be a sewage problem and left. Back at the station Gacy was questioned about the items they'd confiscated, however, at this time they had no proof linking him to Piest, so he was released but kept under twenty-four-hour surveillance.

At the laboratory they'd examined one of the rings they found, which turned out to belong to John Szyc. They dug a little deeper and found that three of Gacy's employee's had disappeared without a trace. Deeper still, they discovered that the roll of film had been in Piest's possession on the day of his disappearance. The police had enough evidence to return to Summerdale Avenue to look for more. Gacy must have realised it was over, and confessed to one murder. He directed the police to a burial site at the property but they decided to take another look at the crawl space first. They began digging and soon started unearthing human remains, the scale of Gacy's murderous career was frightening.

On 22 December 1978, Gacy confessed that he had killed at least thirty people. He detailed how he would make them wear handcuffs and then sexually assault them. To silence their screams he would shove socks or underwear down their throats and then rape them. Some of his victims were discovered naked but with an item of clothing still lodged in their throat. In total twenty-seven bodies were found buried in the crawl space, some had been stored almost on top of each other as Gacy was concerned he was running out of room. He had thrown five other victims into the Des Plaines River. The last body to be found was the missing boy that had led to Gacy's arrest, Robert Piest. The young boy's body eventually washed up on the shore on 9 April 1979. Piest's family filed a lawsuit against the Iowa Board of Parole, the Department of Corrections and the Chicago Police Department for negligence; if Gacy had been kept in custody for the Rignall rape case he would never have killed Robert.

On 6 February 1980, the trial began in Cook County. Gacy pleaded not guilty by reason of insanity, claiming the only thing he was guilty of was 'running a cemetery without a licence'. Despite his clever attempt at dodging the death penalty, the evidence was too damning. He was found guilty and eventually executed on 10 May 1994, aged fifty-two.

TED BUNDY

No wonder Ted Bundy turned out the way he did, one of America's worst serial killers, murderer of around thirty young women, a killer who, even in death, was unable to leave his victims alone, visiting their bodies long after he had hidden them in the mountains, grotesquely applying make-up to them, lying with them and even having sex with them.

He had been born at a home for unmarried mothers in 1946 in Burlington, Vermont. He was possibly a result of incest between his young mother and his violent and abusive grandfather, Samuel Cowell. Various other men have been posited as his father, however. To avoid the social stigma that an unmarried mother and her family had to contend with in those days, Samuel Cowell, and his wife Eleanor took him in, however, passing him off as their own son and Bundy grew up thinking that his mother was his sister. It would not be until university that he would learn the truth of his birth.

He grew up a loner, found it hard to build relationships and had no real friends. His fellow students thought he was socially inept. He withdrew further into himself and lived in a world of pornography – especially the violent kind – and became a petty crook. He was a compulsive thief and was arrested twice as a teenager for theft.

In 1951, his mother met and married a man named Johnny Bundy and the boy was adopted by his stepfather, legally changing his name to Bundy. In spite of all his stepfather's efforts to involve young Ted in family life, the boy remained emotionally distant.

He was not a bad student, however, and won a scholarship to the University of Puget Sound, studying psychology and Oriental Studies. After two semesters, however, he transferred to the University of Washington in Seattle. He started going out with a woman he met at university but she found his lack of maturity difficult to handle and dumped him when she graduated in 1968.

Around this time, he discovered the truth about his parentage and it changed him. He became more focused and less retiring, managing the Seattle office of Nelson Rockefeller's 1968 presidential campaign. Meanwhile he was doing well at university and had begun another relationship, with Elizabeth Kloepfer, a divorced secretary with a daughter. They would be together for six years until his imprisonment for kidnapping in 1976.

He graduated with a degree in psychology in 1972 and in 1973 enrolled at the law school at the University of Puget Sound. He dropped out in 1974, just around the time that young women began to disappear in the northwest.

It is not certain when Ted Bundy murdered for the first time. Some experts believe it may have been while he was still a teenager. The earliest killings that can definitely be attributed to him, however, took place in 1974 when he was twenty-seven.

His modus operandi was cunning. He would pretend that he was injured and incapacitated in some way. He would wear a plaster cast on an arm or use crutches. Then he would seek someone's help to carry something, such as books, to his car. At the car, he would bludgeon them with a crowbar and drag them into the vehicle. He was sometimes seen and almost caught on a number of occasions. Once, eight different witnesses came forward to tell police about a man called Ted, his left arm in a sling, who had been approaching people looking for help unloading his sailing boat from the back of his car. One woman went with him, but became suspicious when she found that he did not have a boat attached to his car. His victims were often students, perhaps more gullible than older people and tragically the remains of a number of them were never found. He was nothing if not vicious. Sometimes he decapitated his victims with a hacksaw and he often kept several of the heads in his room or apartment. He got rid of some of his victims on Taylor Mountain in Utah but, unable to leave them alone, even in death, he confessed to visiting the bodies long after he had put them there, gruesomely applying make-up, lying with them and even having sex with them. This would continue until putrefaction had set in.

Young female students began disappearing with frightening regularity. On 12 March 1974 he kidnapped nineteen-year-old Donna Gail Mason and murdered her. Susan Rancourt vanished a month later from the campus of Central Washington College in Ellensburg. Kathy Parks disappeared from Oregon State University at the beginning of May and Brenda Ball left the Flame Tavern on 1 June and was never seen again. Ten days later, Georgeann Hawkins vanished as she returned to her sorority house from her boyfriend's dorm. On 14 July, two girls, Janice Ott and Denise Naslund, disappeared in Lake Sammamish State Park in Issaquah.

In almost all these cases, witnesses reported a man with a leg or an arm in a cast, calling himself 'Ted' and looking for help to carry something to his car which was a Beetle. As the bodies of some of the missing girls began to turn up, the police launched a manhunt.

Several people, having seen a description of the killer, reported Bundy to them, but they quickly dismissed the clean-cut young student from their enquiries.

In the autumn of 1974 he enrolled at the University of Utah Law School where he resumed his killing that October. Nancy Wilcox was last seen in a VW Beetle on 2 October and sixteen days later, he raped, sodomised and killed Melissa Smith, the seventeen-year-old daughter of the Police Chief of Midvale. Laura Aime left a Halloween party in Lehi, Utah and disappeared only to be found by hikers a month later in American Fork Canyon.

At a shopping mall in Murray in Utah, he persuaded Carol DaRonch that he was a police officer and that someone had been seen trying to break into her car. She went with him back to the car where he asked her to accompany him to the police station. En route, he suddenly tried to put handcuffs on her but she fought him, only just stopping him from bringing the crowbar down on her head. She managed to escape from the car and he drove off, kidnapping and killing seventeen-year-old Debbie Kent at a nearby high school within an hour of leaving DaRonch.

In 1975, he began to kill in Colorado. On 12 January, Caryl Campbell disappeared from a tavern in Snowmass where she had been on holiday with her partner and his children. She was found a month later.

A Vail ski instructor, Julie Cunningham, vanished in the middle of March and Denise Oliverson in Grand Junction in April. He carried on, killing Lynette Culver in Pocatello, Idaho in May 1975.

He was finally arrested on 16 August 1975 in Granger, Utah, for the innocuous misdemeanour of failing to stop for a police officer. However, they discovered a ski mask in his car as well as the implements of his trade – a crowbar, handcuffs, rubbish bags, an icepick. At first they thought they were merely the tools of a burglar but they began to link him to the murders and when he was identified by Carol DaRonch in an identity parade, he was charged with kidnapping. He was sentenced to fifteen years.

However, the Colorado authorities were also pursuing him for murder and he was extradited to the jailhouse at Pitkin County Court in Aspen.

Unbelievably, on 7 June 1977, Bundy escaped during a recess in which he was allowed to visit the courthouse library. He jumped out of a courthouse window a couple of floors up and made his escape into the unsuspecting holiday crowds. He was not wearing leg-irons or handcuffs and so blended in perfectly.

Roadblocks were established on all exits from Aspen, bloodhounds were brought in and police leave was cancelled as the authorities were seriously embarrassed by his escape. Bundy stayed where he was but after six days he stole a Cadillac. Arousing suspicions with reckless driving at a roadblock, he was arrested by a couple of alert deputies.

Nonetheless, Bundy was well aware that a death sentence awaited him and, incredibly, this would not be the last time he would break free. The date for his next trial was set for 9 January 1978 and it would take place in Colorado Springs. Therefore, he had to get away before he was moved.

Somehow, he managed to amass a sum of $500 while being held in a prison at Glenwood Springs, Colorado and on 30 December escaped through the roof space above his cell. In town, he stole an MG that broke down in a blizzard in the mountains. He succeeded in stopping another car and sweet-talked his way into a lift to Vail. He made his way by bus, train and plane to Tallahassee in Florida, renting a room in a boarding house under the name of Chris Hagen.

Shoplifting and stealing purses and credit cards kept him in funds and he created a whole new identity for himself, obtaining a false birth certificate and social security card.

A free man again, his old urges returned and death was once more on his mind. He had taken a room close to Tallahassee University which was convenient for him, but disastrous for a number of women students. On 14 January, he killed two women students sleeping at the Chi Omega sorority house. Lisa Levy and Margaret Bowman were bludgeoned and strangled and he also sexually assaulted Levy. Another two students were hit on the head and seriously injured.

Nita Neary was just returning from a night out. She found the door to the building open which was very unusual and became suspicious when she heard someone running down the stairs. She hid in an alcove as the footsteps approached. Bundy, clad in a woollen hat pulled down over his face and clasping a piece of wood wrapped in cloth, ran past her out of the door. Upstairs, she found a charnel house. One of the girls Bundy had failed to kill was staggering along a corridor, blood dripping from a horrendous head wound. The other survivor was found in a similarly bad condition. The police were called and the dead girls were discovered.

Bundy had battered Lisa Levy with the piece of wood and had then strangled her, biting her on the buttocks and the nipples. He had used a bottle of hairspray to sexually assault her.

His work was not over for the night, however. He broke into a nearby house in which student Cheryl Thomas was sleeping. Police found her alive, sitting on her bed, blood pouring from her head. There was a mask at the foot of the bed. Unfortunately, although there were hairs on the mask and bite marks on Lisa Levy, forensic science was far from the sophisticated art that it is today and this was exacerbated by the fact that Ted Bundy was completely unknown to the Florida authorities.

A few weeks later, a twelve-year-old girl from Lake City was reported missing, having been seen getting into a car. Her body was found eight weeks later in a state park in Suwannee County. She had not been the first he had tried to abduct. A fourteen-year-old had a narrow escape a few days earlier when a man, claiming to be from the Fire Department had approached her. At that moment, as she was about to climb into his car and drive off, the girl's brother turned up. The man left the scene but the brother was immediately suspicious of the man's story and took down the registration of the van he was driving. The girl's father was a policeman and when he had the number checked, he found it belonged to a man called Randall Regan who told him that his licence plates had recently been stolen. He then discovered that the vehicle had also been stolen. He took his children to the police station and showed them mug-shots of various villains, amongst which was a picture of Ted Bundy. They instantly recognised him as the man who had approached her.

It was getting too hot for Bundy. He moved to Pensacola, having stolen an orange Volkswagen Beetle. This was probably a mistake as it was a car that was hard to forget. Officer David Lee was curious when it drove past him at ten in the morning of 15 February. A check of the car's licence number found it to be stolen. Officer Lee turned on his blue lights and set off in hot pursuit.

Bundy stopped at a petrol station and Lee pulled up behind using his loudspeaker to order Bundy out of the car and to lie on the ground. Bundy did as he was ordered at first, but then began to struggle as the officer tried to handcuff him. He pushed Lee away and took off. The policeman pulled his gun, shouted the mandatory warning and fired. Bundy was not hit, but he fell to the ground pretending to be wounded. When the officer approached, he sprang up and started to struggle with him once more. This time, however, Officer Lee was too strong for him and succeeded in cuffing him. Ted Bundy was in custody for the final time.

They linked him immediately to the murder of Kimberley Leach. The van he had driven that day was full of incriminating evidence, including fibres of her clothing, blood matching her blood type and Bundy's semen and blood was also matched to samples found on the dead girl's underwear. They charged him with her murder and added the deaths of the two Chi Omega girls and his various other assaults to his charge sheet.

On 24 January 1989, after countless appeals, Ted Bundy was executed in the electric chair at the State Prison at Starke in Florida.

RICHARD TRENTON CHASE

When Richard Trenton Chase walked into a hospital looking for the person who had stolen his pulmonary artery, perhaps something should have been done. Or perhaps they should have acted when he told them that his bones were coming out of the back of his head or that his heart kept stopping. His worst fear, however, was that his blood was turning to powder and that he needed blood from other people and creatures to refresh it. They did put a stop to that, but not before the 'Vampire of Sacramento' had killed six people in just one month.

He was born in 1950 and by the age of ten was a bedwetter, a pyromaniac and liked to torment and kill animals. His father was a disciplinarian and he claimed that he was abused by his mother. He was smoking dope and drinking at an early age.

He would later claim that his problems arose from the fact that he was unable to have sex, being unable to maintain an erection. He saw a psychiatrist about the problem when he was eighteen and was told that it might be caused by repressed anger, possibly at his parents. How right he was.

He left home and took a room in a house, frightening his flatmates with his bizarre behaviour. By this time, he was taking a lot of drugs – marijuana and LSD – and was drinking heavily. One day he boarded up his bedroom door, creating an 'escape hatch' through the back wall of a cupboard. He had no compunction about walking around the apartment naked, even when there were visitors. He was asked to leave. When he refused, his flatmates moved out instead.

It was the worst thing that could have happened because now he was free to indulge his weirdest fantasies. He was admitted to hospital with blood poisoning, but when they discovered that he was ill because he had injected himself with the blood of a rabbit, he was committed to a mental hospital. It transpired that he had been capturing and killing various animals that he would then eat, sometimes raw and sometimes blended with Coca-Cola into a ghoulish drink. He believed that this concoction would prevent his heart from shrinking.

There was debate as to whether he was actually suffering from paranoid schizophrenia as one psychiatrist diagnosed or whether he was a victim of drug psychosis, having taken so many drugs – especially LSD – during the preceding years. He eventually walked out of the hospital after seventy-two hours, even though they recommended that he stay to undergo further treatment.

He was a mess, five feet eleven in height but weighing just over ten stones. He returned to live with his mother, now divorced from his father, and retreated once more into a drug haze. Soon, he had moved out again and had his own apartment.

He was now regularly eating animals raw, still putting their innards into a blender and making them into a drink. Eventually he was committed again, deemed to be a schizophrenic suffering from somatic delusions. He was given anti-psychotic medication but it seemed to have little effect. In 1976, he escaped and went to his mother's house. Returned eventually to the hospital, staff entered his room one day to find him with blood smeared all round his mouth and face, claiming that he had cut himself shaving. When they looked outside his window, they found the bodies of a number of dead birds whose blood he had drunk. It is little wonder that they began to call him Dracula.

Released eventually into the care of his mother, he was thought no longer to be a danger to the public but his mother weaned him off his medication, believing it was turning him into a zombie. She found him an apartment and he resumed his old habits, catching cats, dogs and rabbits and eating them. He once telephoned a family to explain to them that he had eaten their family pet and had drunk its blood.

Worse still, however, he began buying guns and practising with them.

On 3 August 1977, he was found by police officers in the Nevada desert, wandering around in the nude, his body smeared with blood. In his car were two rifles and a blood-filled plastic bucket containing what appeared to be a liver. He claimed that the blood was his, that it had seeped out of him. When they analysed the liver it was found to have come from a cow.

He was beginning to think about killing to obtain the blood he believed he needed to keep him alive. At the time, in Los Angeles, the serial killer, the Hillside Strangler, was on the rampage. Chase became obsessed and followed every development in the case in the media.

On 29 December 1977, he claimed his first victim.

Ambrose Griffin was a fifty-one-year-old engineer from a neighbourhood in East Sacramento who had just returned from a shopping trip with his wife. They were carrying groceries into the house from the car and Ambrose was just walking back to the vehicle to bring in another bag. Suddenly he fell to the ground as if he had been poleaxed. Mrs. Griffin immediately presumed he had suffered a heart attack and he was, indeed, dead by the time the ambulance arrived. It was no heart attack, however. Doctors found two bullet holes in him; he had been shot dead.

The next day they found shell casings not far away and a twelve-year-old boy reported that a man, probably in his mid-twenties, with brown hair, had shot at him from a brown Pontiac TransAm as he rode past him on his bike. Nothing came of the report, however.

A woman reported that she believed that a bullet had been fired into her kitchen a couple of days before Ambrose Griffin was killed. They found a .22 bullet there, the same calibre bullet that killed Griffin.

On 11 January 1978, Jeanne Layton spied a tall young man with long unkempt hair walking towards her house. He tried her patio door which was, fortunately, locked, before trying her windows which were also bolted shut. Returning to the door, she met him there, not unlocking it. He stood there, expressionless, staring at her. He turned, lit a cigarette and walked off through her back yard.

That same day, Robert and Barbara Edwards were bringing in their groceries from their car when they heard noises coming from inside their house. They ran in just as someone jumped out a back window. The house had been turned upside down and they were horrified to find that the burglar had urinated in a drawer that contained baby clothes and had defecated on the bed of one of their children.

Chase later told investigators that he would walk along a street, trying doors until he found one that was unlocked. Sadly, Teresa Wallin's door was not locked. She was twenty-two years old and three months pregnant. Before he entered, Chase enigmatically left a .22 bullet in her mailbox. She was carrying a bag of rubbish when he bumped into her in the house and it fell to the floor as he raised the handgun he was carrying and fired one bullet that hit her palm and travelled up through her arm and a second that went into her head. Just to be sure, as she lay on the ground, he pumped another bullet into her skull.

He dragged the body into the kitchen and went to work. When Teresa's husband came home that evening he screamed at the sight he found in the couple's bedroom. She lay on her back, her breasts exposed and her trousers and underwear down around her ankles. Her left nipple had been sliced off and her body cut open below the sternum. Her spleen and intestines had been ripped out and other organs had been sliced and stabbed. Her kidneys had been cut out and then replaced. A yoghurt carton near her body was ringed with drying blood. He had used it to drink Teresa's blood.

On 27 January, thirty-eight-year-old Evelyn Miroth was babysitting her twenty-month-old nephew about a mile from where Chase had so brutally murdered Teresa Wallin. Her friend Daniel Meredith paid her a visit. Evelyn's son, Jason, was supposed to go to play with the daughter of a friend, but failed to turn up. So, the woman sent her daughter round to find out what had happened. There was no reply when the girl rang the doorbell but she was certain she heard movement from within the house. The woman grew worried and she and other neighbours went to the house where they found a scene of utter carnage. Daniel Meredith had been shot in the head and lay in a pool of blood in the hallway. Evelyn was lying naked in her bedroom, her legs wide open. She, too, had been shot in the head and as with Teresa Wallin, her stomach had been sliced open and her intestines ripped out. She had been sodomised, stabbed through her anus into her uterus and he had cut her neck and attempted to cut out an eye. He had, it seemed, collected her blood in some kind of container. Beside her on the bed lay her son, Jason, with two bullet holes in his head, the bullets fired from point-blank range.

Bloody footprints had been found at the Wallin house and they were in evidence once again here. A description provided by a girl of a man seen near Evelyn Miroth's house matched that of a man who had apparently been walking round the area asking people for magazines.

There was one thing missing at the murder scene, however – the baby that Evelyn had been babysitting. All that was left was a bullet hole in a pillow in the baby's crib and a lot of blood.

After drinking Evelyn's blood at the murder scene, Chase had mutilated the baby's body in the bathtub where pieces of brain were found. He then took the child home with him and cut off its head. He ate several of its internal organs.

Meanwhile, a desperate manhunt was launched.

They estimated him to be a very disorganised killer who, in all likelihood, was mentally ill in some way, possibly paranoid, and probably a user of drugs. He was a loner, white and very thin. These crimes were opportunistic and not planned in any way. He left footprints and fingerprints and was walking around in broad daylight wearing blood-stained clothing. He just did not care. He did not have a car as the murders were carried out in the same vicinity. With chilling certainty, they knew that he would kill again many more times, if he was not apprehended.

It was a lucky break that led to his capture. Nancy Holden was stopped by Chase in a shopping centre and, although she had known him years ago, she did not recognise the skeletal thin, unkempt man with an odd look on his face. She was going to walk past him but he asked her, 'Were you on the motorcycle when Kurt was killed?' He had surprised her because ten years earlier, her boyfriend Kurt had been killed in an motorcycle accident. She thought suddenly that he looked familiar and asked him who he was. He replied 'Rick Chase'. His whole manner made her nervous and she tried to get away from him, hurrying to her car, but he followed her. She managed to get in, lock the doors and drive off, very shaken.

Shortly after she saw a police sketch of the man the police were looking for in connection with the murders and realised it was Chase. She informed the police and they began to look into his background. They found out about his mental illness, that he had registered a .22 handgun and had been busted for drugs a number of times. They set off for his house.

There was no reply and they pretended to leave the vicinity of the house but shortly after he emerged carrying a box. They rushed him and after a struggle, he was read his rights and taken into custody. It seemed beyond doubt at that moment that he was their man. His orange parka and his shoes were bloodstained and the box contained bloody rags and paper. He claimed to have been killing dogs but when they went to his apartment they learned the truth.

It was a charnel house. Everything was blood-stained including the crockery, food and drinking glasses. In the kitchen they found human brain tissue and an electric blender was bloody and smelled of rotting flesh. Ads selling dogs were highlighted in newspapers and, chillingly, alongside circled dates on a calendar marking the dates of the murders of Teresa Wallin and Evelyn Miroth, were another forty-four dates throughout the remainder of the year that were similarly annotated.

On 24 March, the baby's body was found in a box near a church. Its head was under its torso and there was a bullet-hole in the forehead.

Richard Trenton Chase was found guilty of six counts of murder in the first degree in spite of his defence that he was insane. He was sentenced to die in the gas chamber at San Quentin.

On Boxing Day, 1980, three years after he had been sentenced to death, a guard checking on Chase in his prison cell, noticed that he was lying awkwardly. On entering the cell he discovered that he was dead. He had been taking a daily dose of Sinequan for the delusions and hallucinations from which he suffered, but had hoarded them until he had enough and then swallowed them. The 'Vampire of Sacramento's' heart had really stopped beating for good.

ANATOLY
ONOPRIENKO

'I'm not a maniac,' he said. 'If I were, I would have thrown myself onto you and killed you right here. No, it's not that simple. I have been taken over by a higher force, something telepathic or cosmic, which drove me. I am like a rabbit in a laboratory. A part of an experiment to prove that man is capable of murdering and learning to live with his crimes. To show that I can cope, that I can stand anything, forget everything.'

Anatoly Onoprienko, murderer of at least fifty-two people in the Ukraine, believed that he was controlled by a higher force, ordered to kill by voices in his head. He felt no remorse, he stated, for the victims of his extraordinary bloodlust, describing himself as 'a beast of Satan'. Furthermore, he added, if he was ever to be released from prison, he would kill again. 'After what I have learnt out there, I have no competitors in my field. And if I am not killed I will escape from this jail and the first thing I'll do is find Kuchma (the

Ukrainian president) and hang him from a tree by his testicles.'

Onoprienko's killings followed a striking pattern. Usually, he would find an isolated house – not difficult in the largely agricultural Ukraine. He would shoot everyone in the house, including children, steal any valuables and then set it on fire. Anyone who got in his way as he made his escape would also be dispatched. The country was seized by a kind of hysteria and troops patrolled the streets of one village where Onoprienko had struck several times.

At one stage, the authorities believed they had their man. Twenty-six-year-old Yuri Mozola was arrested in March 1996, suspected of being the killer. For three days he was brutally tortured by six officers of the Ukrainian Security Service. They used electric shocks, beat him and burned him, but he would not confess. Eventually, he died and his torturers were tried and sent to prison.

Meanwhile, Onoprienko roamed the countryside, selecting his next victims.

He had been born in the town of Laski in the Zhitomirskaya Oblast but his mother had died when he was still very young and his father had put him into a Russian orphanage. The fact that his older brother had remained with his father angered Onoprienko throughout his life and may have been a contributing factor to the rage that he took out on entire families.

Although he may have started killing earlier, according to his confession, he killed for the first time in 1989. He had started out with a friend, Sergei Rogozin, stealing items from houses. One night, however, they were disturbed as they went about their business at an isolated house outside of town. To cover up their tracks and dispose of any witnesses, they murdered the whole family of two adults and eight children.

The two men eventually went their separate ways, but Onoprienko carried on with his new career. A few months after his first killings, he shot and killed five people, an eleven-year-old boy amongst them, who were sleeping in a car. Again, he had approached the vehicle with the intention only of robbing it, unaware that there were so many people inside. In fact, he claimed, had he known they were inside he would have steered clear of it. Nonetheless, he set fire to it after shooting all of its occupants.

It was several years before he killed again. On Christmas Eve, 1995, he broke into the home of a forestry teacher in the village of Garmania in Central Ukraine, shooting the man and his wife and two children with a sawn-off, double-barrelled shotgun. He then set fire to the house and fled the scene with the couple's wedding rings, a small gold cross, a pair of earrings and a bundle of clothes. As he left, he shot dead another man who was coming along the road. 'I just shot them,' he said later. 'It's not that it gave me pleasure, but I felt this urge. From then on, it was almost like some game from outer space.'

A fortnight later, on 6 January, he again went 'hunting' – as he called it, stopping cars on the Berdyansk-Dnieprovskaya Highway and murdering their drivers. He killed four people in that one day.

Eleven days later, he drove to the town of Bratkovichi where he broke into the Pilat family home. He shot all five members of the family, including a five year-old boy. He set fire to the house just before dawn but as he was leaving, was seen by two people, a twenty-seven-year-old woman named Kondzela and a fifty-six-year-old named Zakharko. He shot and killed both.

On 30 January, he travelled to Olevsk where he broke into the house in which the Dubchak family lived. He shot the father and his son and viciously beat the mother and daughter to death with a hammer. The girl was particularly defiant, refusing to show him where the family kept its money after seeing her parents killed.

On 27 February, he was in the town of Malina in the Lvivskaya Oblast region. He shot a man and woman named Bodnarchuk in their house before brutally hacking to death with an axe their two daughters who were just seven and eight years old. An hour later, he shot a neighbour and then cut his body up with the axe. He claimed later that an inner voice was telling him to kill these people.

He killed for the final time on 22 March in the tiny village of Busk, not far from Bratkovichi. There, he killed the Novosad family and set fire to their house.

Onoprienko's killing spree was brought to an end more by luck than anything else. He had been living at the home of a cousin, Pyotr Onoprienko and Pyotr had stumbled upon a stash of weapons hidden in the house. Realising they could only belong to his cousin, Anatoly, he had ordered him to leave the house. Anatoly had become very angry and threatened to kill Pyotr's family at Easter. Understandably frightened, Pyotr telephoned the police on 7 April.

A detective named Igor Khunev took the call, reporting it to his superior, Deputy Police Chief, Sergei Kryukov. Coincidentally, Kryukov had just been reading a report on a recent killing that mentioned a Russian-made Tos-34 hunting rifle that had been stolen locally. He was curious. A report had been made about a weapons cache and this rifle had been stolen. He decided to follow it up. A task force was put together consisting of twenty officers. They went to the house to which Onoprienko had relocated on Ivana Khristitelya Street in a convoy of unmarked cars and were deployed around the apartment building. Onoprienko had moved in with a woman who had a couple of kids and they were all out at church while he remained at home. When the officers rang the doorbell, he thought it must be them coming home. Instead, they pounced upon him when he opened the door, quickly handcuffing him. Immediately, Kryukov noticed an Akai stereo in the living room. He recalled that just such a stereo had been stolen from the Novosad family that had been murdered in Busk.

They asked Onoprienko for identification and he indicated a closet in which they would find it. However, he had already concealed a pistol in the closet and made a dive for it as soon as the door was opened. They overcame him and took him back to the police station while a search of the house was undertaken. They found 122 stolen items, all related to unsolved murders. They also found the sawn-off Tos-34 rifle.

At the police station, Onoprienko initially remained silent. Bogdan Teslya, considered to be the best interrogator in the area, was brought in, but Onoprienko said that he would only speak to a General. Gradually, however, the killer began to talk, firstly about his childhood and then about the killings and what made him do it.

They began calling him 'Citizen O' in the media and it took several years for the case to come to court. The trial began on 12 February 1999, in the city of Zhytomir. It was a sensation. Like the notorious Russian mass murderer, Andrei Chikatilo, Onoprienko sat in an iron cage. Members of the huge audience spat at him and he had to be guarded because the police were afraid that the crowd would take matters into their own hands and kill him, especially as many feared that he would receive a sentence of only fifteen years in prison, the maximum sentence in the Ukraine, if the death sentence was not applied.

He said very little, refusing to make a statement and replying, 'None,' when asked what his nationality was.

The verdict was never really in doubt. The judge sentenced him to death by shooting. However, at the time, Ukraine, as a Council of Europe member, was committed to the abolition of capital punishment and Onoprienko's sentence was, accordingly, commuted to life imprisonment.

Dr Harold
Shipman

Hyde undertaker, Alan Massey had noticed something strange about patients of Dr Harold Shipman who had passed away. Certainly, there was an unusually high number of them for one doctor, but, additionally, they all had some things in common. They were mostly female, living on their own and they were almost always fully clothed. They might be seated on a chair or lying on a bed, but always – or at least in ninety per cent of cases – with their clothes on. And there was never any sign that the person had been ill. They had just died where they were.

Dr Harold Frederick 'Fred' Shipman is the most prolific serial killer the world has ever known. The number of murders he committed probably exceeded that of the next in line for that dubious honour – the Colombian serial killer, Pedro Lopez who killed 300 girls and women in the 1970s. In fact, although the official figure for Shipman's murders is put at 215, The Shipman Enquiry held subsequent to his trial examined the cases of 500 patients and accepted that the toll may be higher. It reported that there was a real suspicion that he had killed another forty-five people but that the evidence was insufficient for certainty. 'In a further thirty-eight cases,' it said, 'there was too little information to form any opinion on the cause of death.' Other sources suggest that the death toll at Shipman's hands may even be as high as 1000.

Many theories have been put forward as to why this Yorkshire man born into a working class family in 1946 turned out the way he did. Some have suggested that he was merely exhibiting the normal character-istics of the psychopath – the need for control and the desire to manipulate. Others say that he was fascinated by drugs and that his position as a doctor gave him the opportunity not only to obtain them in large quantities, but also to experiment with them, trying out different dosages and seeing how far he could push a patient before the drugs would prove too much for her body to cope with. Another theory put forward is that he had a fascination with death and the process of dying and derived some kind of perverse pleasure from being in its presence. Many, however, have suggested that his targeting of elderly women and the method he used, usually an injection of morphine or diamorphine – heroin – merely reflected the death of his mother, that he was somehow trying to recreate it every time he killed someone.

His mother, Vera, was a snob. Neighbours who knew the family describe her as having a superior air and being extremely fussy about who her children – Harold, Clive his younger brother and Pauline his older sister – played with. Of her three children, however, there was little doubt who her favourite was. She considered her middle child, Freddy, to be the one with most potential to do well and she pushed him to ensure that he did.

Freddy, like his mother, had something of a superior air about him. He did not mix well with the other children, even though he played sports, usually the ideal way to make enduring friendships.

When Vera was diagnosed with terminal lung cancer, Freddy played a leading role in looking after her, running home from school to make her a cup of tea and sit at her bedside chatting about his day. It is probably too glib to say that it was from this time that he developed the bedside manner that he would use to great effect later as a doctor. He must have undoubtedly been fascinated by the arrival of the doctor to administer injections of morphine to his mother to alleviate the severe pain she was suffering as the cancer reached its last stages and she entered her final months. One day, he may have thought, I would like to have that kind of power over people.

If Vera had seen potential in her son, he certainly had to fight to fulfill it. He had been a bit of a plodder at school and it was a struggle to get into Leeds University Medical School. Then he only passed his exams at the second time of asking. Nevertheless, he was a doctor and he served the normal hospital internship to launch his career.

He is remembered from those days as a loner, someone who did not fit in and who was unable to engage socially with his colleagues. That meant, of course, that he never had a girlfriend, but he surprised everyone by marrying early. Primrose came from a similar background to his own, with a controlling mother, and was just seventeen – three years younger than him – and pregnant when they walked down the aisle.

By the age of twenty-eight, in 1974, he had two children and a job in a medical practice in Todmorden in Yorkshire. The awkward loner seemed to have gone and he was now an outgoing and respected member of the local community. But he was still irritatingly aloof, and was often rude to the people with whom he worked. He was stubborn and confrontational with colleagues and often seriously embarrassed people. Nonetheless, he worked hard, was enthusiastic and brought new ideas to the practice which his colleagues appreciated. Trouble was brewing, however.

He began to suffer from blackouts, explaining them away when asked about them as epilepsy, but the receptionist at the practice discovered that there were anomalies in the amount of pethidine – a morphine-like analgesic – Shipman had been prescribing to a number of patients. The practice immediately launched an investigation, unknown to Shipman. It emerged that many of the patients to whom Shipman had claimed to prescribe it had neither needed nor been administered the drug.

Shipman was confronted on the issue during a staff meeting and he threw a tantrum and stormed out, threatening to resign. His behaviour seemed irrational and uncharacteristic to his stunned colleagues. This was exacerbated shortly after when Primrose Shipman, his wife, burst into a meeting at the practice about what they should do with Shipman. She shouted at them that he would never resign and that they would have to force him out.

They obliged and he went into a drug rehabilitation centre in 1975. He was convicted of drug offences, prescription fraud and forgery but was fined only £600 and allowed to continue to practise medicine.

Of course, there have been suggestions that perhaps the pethidine was not actually for his own personal use. Perhaps, they say, he was already killing patients back then.

Remarkably, within two years, he was back working as a medical practitioner, having been given a job at the Donneybrook Medical Centre in Hyde in Greater Manchester. He had persuaded his employers that he was contrite for his earlier problem but was now clean and trustworthy. They believed him and he threw himself back into his work with the same enthusiasm and commitment that had initially impressed his colleagues at his previous place of work. He was still sarcastic and superior on occasion but never with those on whom he was trying to make an impression.

He gained respect and the trust of his patients but in the next twenty-four years, he would callously murder at least 236 of them.

It was, however, one particular case that would finally uncover the horror for which Shipman was responsible.

Kathleen Grundy had been mayor of Hyde and was a wealthy, energetic and very active eighty-one-year-old who still worked tirelessly for local charities. On 24 June 1998, she uncharacteristically failed to turn up as arranged at the local Age Concern Club where she would help to serve meals to pensioners less able than herself. When anxious friends drove to her home and found her lying on a sofa, dead, they immediately called her GP, Dr Shipman.

Shipman had already made a call at the house earlier that day and was, in fact, the last person to see her alive. He later told police that he had visited in order to take blood samples for some research into aging. He arrived, pronounced her dead and the sad news was given to Mrs Grundy's daughter, Angela Woodruff. Shipman informed her that a post mortem would not be needed as he had seen the dead woman so recently.

After her mother's funeral, however, Mrs Woodruff received some disturbing news from a firm of solicitors who claimed that they were in possession of a copy of her mother's will. Mrs Woodruff was very surprised as she was herself a solicitor and had handled all her mother's affairs. She was even more surprised when she learned that her mother had left her doctor, Harold Shipman, £386,000. However, when she was able to view the document, she immediately became suspicious. Not only was it badly typed and badly worded, the signature purporting to be her mother's looked all wrong.

It would have been completely out of character for her mother, a meticulous, organised and careful person, to have produced such a document. She spoke to the people who had witnessed the will and decided there was something very wrong – she came to the grim conclusion that Dr Shipman had murdered her mother to get his hands on her money.

She took her suspicions to the police who concurred that the will was amateurish and immediately recognisable as a fake.

Mrs Grundy's body had to be exhumed so that tissue and hair samples could be taken and sent for analysis. Meanwhile, police searched Shipman's home and office. It was all done very suddenly and before Shipman could learn that a body had been exhumed so that there was no opportunity for him to dispose of any evidence. Shipman, self-confident to the point of arrogance, was calm and collected as they carried out their searches, looking on contemptuously as if they were beneath him.

When asked if he had a typewriter – they were searching for the machine that had typed Mrs Grundy's will – he produced an old Brother portable typewriter. He spun them an unlikely story that Kathleen Grundy used to borrow it from him. It was taken away and found to be the very machine on which the dead woman's will had been typed. At his house they also found a considerable amount of jewellery.

The information that really surprised them, however, was the news from the lab that Mrs Grundy's body contained a high level of morphine and that was what had killed her. Astonishingly, Shipman would later claim that she had been a morphine addict.

Many have suggested that Shipman's use of morphine instead of another drug was a sign that he actually wanted to be caught. He would have known very well that morphine is one of the few drugs that stays in body tissue for a very long time.

It became clear that they were looking not just at one murder and the scale of the potential body count was frightening. Police began to check people who had died following a visit from Shipman and who had not been cremated. Of course, the records on his computer showed that his patients had suffered from the correct symptoms that led to their death. When the hard disk of his computer was looked at, however, it showed changes being made by Shipman within hours of his patients' deaths.

His trial began in Preston, Lancashire on 5 October 1999. He was charged with fifteen murders and also faced one charge of forging Kathleen Grundy's will. The prosecution opened by stating that when Shipman killed, he was 'exercising the ultimate power of controlling life and death, and repeated the act so often he must have found the drama of taking life to his taste.'

Shipman's modus operandi soon began to become apparent. He would obtain a huge amount of drugs by false pretences and then inject it into his elderly patient. A few hours later the patient would die or be close to death. He would pretend to call an ambulance and then pretend to cancel it when he found the patient had died. Of course, there were no records of these fake phone calls.

Of the blood samples he claimed to have taken from Kathleen Grundy on the day she died there was no trace. He initially said he had sent them away for analysis but then changed his story, telling his interrogators that he had mislaid them under a pile of papers on his desk and had then thrown them away because they were of no further use.

He claimed not to carry morphine but this was exposed as a lie when it transpired that he had given a woman called Joyce Dudley a shot of morphine to ease her pain when she was supposedly dying.

His callousness was also exposed. He seemed unable to inform people that their loved ones had died without making them jump through hoops, classically manipulating the situation until they finally realised what he was not saying outright, that their mother or wife was actually dead.

The tragedy unfolding was dreadful. In one case, he dosed Jim King, who was incorrectly diagnosed as having cancer, with huge amounts of morphine. When he became worse, Shipman told him he had pneumonia and wanted to give him another injection. Jim and his wife resisted, wary of Shipman because Jim's aunt and father had both died after visits from him. They would later learn that their relatives had been murdered by Shipman and that Jim had had a narrow escape.

On 31 January 2000, the jury unanimously found Harold Shipman guilty on fifteen counts of murder and one of forgery. He received fifteen life sentences and an extra four years for the forgery charge.

Using his bedsheets, Shipman hanged himself in his prison cell at Wakefield prison on 13 January 2004. It is said that he did it so that his wife Primrose would be eligible for an NHS pension to which she would not have been entitled if her husband had reached the age of sixty. He was controlling to the bitter end.